Baseball Research Journal

Volume 52, Number 1

Spring 2023

Published by the Society for American Baseball Research

BASEBALL RESEARCH JOURNAL, Volume 52, Number 1

Editor: Cecilia M. Tan
Interior design and production: Lisa Hochstein
Copyediting assistance: Keith DeCandido, Davy Andrews
Proofreader: Norman L. Macht
Fact checker: Clifford Blau

Front cover art by Gary Cieradkowski / Studio Gary C

Published by:
Society for American Baseball Research, Inc.
Cronkite School at ASU
555 N. Central Ave. #406C
Phoenix, AZ 85004

Phone: (602) 496–1460
Web: www.sabr.org
Twitter: @sabr
Facebook: Society for American Baseball Research

Contents

From the Editor

I think one of the things that intrigues us endlessly about baseball is how it lays bare the difference between our expectations and what actually happens. The tension between what we hope for (or pessimistically expect) and what actually occurs drives our interest like a coiled spring. Everyone "knows" that when Bobby Witt Jr. gets on base there's a high likelihood he'll try to steal, and that knowledge sharpens our attention and heightens the feeling of anticipation. How you feel about whether he succeeds or not is, of course, dependent on your rooting interest, and ultimately eliciting those feelings is the purpose of spectator sports (and other entertainment). Sports make us feel stuff, and if they didn't, we literally "wouldn't care."

But to get back to the gap between expectation and reality. Sometimes we're pleased when things go as expected because it ratifies our worldview—Aaron Judge hit a home run—and at least some of sabermetrics is about building a worldview that conforms to reality, about understanding what's actually happening in the game so we can set our expectations of what to predict. That's true whether we're employed by a team to project a prospect's ceiling or a fan in the stands trying to decide whether we're emotionally "all in" on our team this year.

The paradox in baseball, though, is that although we feel satisfied when our predictions come true, the most notable, most memorable, and most delightful and/or heartbreaking things that happen on the field are often the ones where expectations were completely defied—Bucky Dent hit a home run. Or Mariano Rivera blew a save. Or a team went from worst to first. We're drawn to tales of the strange and unusual.

The first section of articles in this issue of the *BRJ* is all about the unexpected. These include unusual circumstances (players on strike, or out with COVID, leading to extraordinary measures to play games as scheduled), unusual outcomes (coming out of the bullpen and inducing a triple play on the first batter faced), or both (pitchers giving up zero hits not being credited with "no hitters" because of unusual circumstances).

But our interest in the unusual is not at odds with the desire to understand the usual: they are mutual pursuits. Only by knowing what is usual can we experience surprise. This magnetic tension also drives our interest in history, as we reflect on how different things look from a distance, on the contrast between the world we know and expect in the present and the status quo in past eras or in other lives. In that spirit I find our explorations of 19th century baseball to be fascinating, but that also leaves room for some unexpected inclusions, like this issue's special feature, an excerpt from Paula Kurman's forthcoming memoir about life as Jim Bouton's wife.

Ultimately, any issue of the *BRJ* should serve as a workout for the expectation engine in our brains. Learning new things, challenging our expectations and adapting to new data, is how our intellect remains as flexible as a shortstop and as expansive as Coors Field. Enjoy.

— Cecilia M. Tan,
April 2023

4

Paper Tigers

How a Player Strike Put a Team of "Misfits" on a Major League Field for a Day

Kevin W. Barwin

One of the most unusual baseball games in American League history took place at Shibe Park, Philadelphia, on May 18, 1912. Nominally a contest between the Philadelphia Athletics and the Detroit Tigers, the men who suited up for the Tigers that day were locally recruited ballplayers, while the real Tigers players bought tickets to sit in the stands and take in the spectacle. How did this turn of events come to pass?

The origins of the crazy contest lie in New York City's American League Park. commonly known as Hilltop Park. On May 15, 1912, the Tigers were there to play a four-game set with the New York Yankees (nee Americans). Ty Cobb, Detroit's irascible but extremely talented batsman, had received much vocal abuse in the previous game and the May 15 game was not very different; from the moment Cobb walked on the field New York fans hurled insults and vile epithets at the volatile Tigers star.[1] The hot-tempered Cobb, who often fought with opponents and even teammates whenever he felt an injustice had been done to him, seethed under the barrage of verbal abuse. One fan in particular, Claude Luecker—a Tammany Hall clerk who regularly sat behind the home dugout—routinely got on Cobb's nerves whenever the Tigers came to town.[2] On this day Luecker allegedly questioned Cobb's mother's race and morals. By the fourth inning Cobb had enough and snapped, leaping over the railing into the stands and pummeling his antagonist. A bystander yelled to Ty, "Don't kick him, he's a cripple and has no hands," to which Cobb replied "I don't care if the d---- ---- has no feet."[3] Luecker, a former pressman who had lost his left hand and three fingers of his right in a previous workplace accident, described the event to reporters. His account is lengthy, so here are some excerpts:

> When the Detroits were in the field in the third inning the boys kept it up on Cobb. Still there was no harm in what was said. I had on an alpaca coat and he seemed to single me out for he yelled back, "Oh, go back to your waiter's job."

But that did no harm. [Later] he followed this up with some vile talk. The crowd seemed to be taken back by this but then there was louder booing. I suppose I joined in the rest but there was nothing said at Cobb half as bad as he said himself and he said it first....

> In the middle of the yells, a man near me called out, "Oh, go on and play ball you half-coon."

> In other games with the Detroits I have seen Cobb who generally gets a good deal of ragging, walk on by the stands across from third base and keep up his talk with the crowd as he went along. Wednesday, after the third inning, it was different. He circled around by first base [Author's note: he had stood in the carriage lot in the outfield between innings] and then went to the bench of the Detroit players....

> Then we saw Cobb followed by a half dozen or more Detroit players each with a bat in his hand start for the section of the stand where we were. Cobb ran over to just the front of where I was and vaulted over the fence. I was sitting in the third row and he made straight for me. He let out with his fist and caught me on the forehead over the left eye. You can see the lump over there now. I was knocked over and then he jumped me. He spiked me in the left leg and kicked me in the side. Then he belted me behind the left ear.[4]

Umpire Fred Westervelt and a Pinkerton policeman separated the combatants and Westervelt ordered Cobb from the field.[5] American League President Ban Johnson happened to be at the game and witnessed the melee.[6] The game continued and Detroit won, 8–4. That evening the Tigers travelled to Philadelphia for a Thursday contest with the Athletics, but that game was rained out. On the evening of May 16, Detroit manager Hughie Jennings received word from President

Johnson that Cobb was suspended indefinitely for the Wednesday incident.[7]

Jennings had no comment, but Cobb thought he had been treated unfairly. "I should at least have had an opportunity to state my case. I feel that a great injustice has been done."[8]

On Friday, May 17, the Tigers, without Cobb, toppled the Athletics, 6–3. That day the Tigers players gathered at the Hotel Aldine and signed an agreement that they forwarded to President Johnson and also released to the press:

> Feeling that Mr. Cobb is being done an injustice by your action in suspending him we, the undersigned, refuse to play in another game after today until such action is adjusted to our satisfaction. He was fully justified in his actions, as no one could stand such personal abuse from anyone. We want him reinstated for tomorrow's game, May 18 or there will be no game. If players cannot have protection we must protect ourselves.[9]

President Johnson did not receive the telegram until he arrived at 6:40PM. in Albany, New York, where he was en route from the dedication of Fenway Park in Boston to the dedication of Crosley Field in Cincinnati. Johnson informed the press that he had wired Jennings and asked him to provide his version of the New York episode. He did not lift Cobb's suspension. Johnson responded to the players' threat to strike:

> I am amazed at the attitude of player Cobb and his teammates toward the American League, which while insistent on good order on the field and strict compliance with the rules of the game, has always extended consideration and provided protection for its players. Suspended on report of the umpire. Suspend order not to remain in force indefinitely but until investigation is completed. Any American League player who is taunted or abused by a patron has only to appeal to the umpire for protection.[10]

Johnson also informed Jennings and Detroit owner Frank Navin that if the Tigers did not put a team on the field on May 18 they would be fined $5,000. Navin immediately put it on Jennings's shoulders to field a team—any team—to avoid the fine. Jennings backed his striking players, issuing the statement: "The suspension was not warranted. I am in the hands of my players, if they refuse to play I will finish way down in the races. I expect Johnson to reconcile the matter, fine Cobb or announce definitely the length of the suspension."[11]

Connie Mack, esteemed manager and owner of the Philadelphia Athletics, met with Jennings and encouraged him to gather some local sandlot ballplayers in case the Tigers regulars carried out their threat not to take the field. Mr. Mack did not care to lose the income from a Saturday crowd, and besides, the A's likely would get an easy victory against players of lesser ability. Mack also mentioned that during the preseason the Athletics had played an exhibition game versus last year's Philadelphia scholastic champs, St. Joseph's College (and had lost the game to the collegians, 8–7).[12] Jennings possibly could convince the college team to take the field in place of the Detroit regulars? Connie put Jennings in touch with a Philadelphia sports reporter, Joe Nolan, who was familiar with the St. Joseph's team.[13]

Al Travers, an assistant student manager of the St. Joseph's team who provided team statistics to Nolan, met with him the next morning. Nolan explained why the Detroit management wanted a backup team and said the sandlotters would be paid for their efforts. Travers said he would see what he could do.[14] But the St. Joseph's team had played the day before in Carlisle, Pennsylvania, against Conway Hall and apparently declined the offer.[15] Travers then strolled to a popular Philadelphia City street corner and recruited several volunteers for the endeavor. (In several interviews in his later years Travers told the story about Nolan and going to the street corner to recruit players, but he apparently never identified any of the men he recruited).

In the meantime, Jennings pressed two of his coaches/scouts into duty, Deacon Jim McGuire and Joe Sugden.[16] Both were former major league players, but well past their baseball prime.

Cobb and his fellow players took the field before the game on May 18 but umpire Ed "Bull" Perrine waved Cobb off the grounds and the Tigers players followed.[17] The Detroit regulars left their uniforms in the locker room and proceeded to the grandstand to watch the game. The strike was on.[18] Jennings's "misfits" donned the Detroit uniforms and took to the field to warm up. Allan Travers designated himself the pitcher after Jennings told him the pitcher would get $25 while the rest would have to be satisfied with $10 each. As we will discuss, some accounts of the affair have Travers getting $50 and the others, $25.

Umpires Perrine and Dinneen yelled "Play Ball" and the unlikely contest was underway. About 15,000 fans applauded as "Colby Jack" Coombs, a veteran Athletics hurler, took the mound. Coombs had last pitched on May 14 against the Chicago White Sox after being sidelined for a groin injury he had incurred on April 20 in Washington. Mack had implied to Jennings that he would play his reserves against the Tigers' make-do team, but when the Athletics took the field, only two substitutes were in play, Harl Maggert and Amos Strunk.[19]

The play-by-play reproduced in Figure 1 is from the *Detroit Times*, but note that it is missing the details of the ninth inning.[20] The following is derived from the box scores of the day:

NINTH INNING

DETROIT: Irwin tripled. Hughie Jennings batted for Travers and struck out. McGarvey was hit by a pitch. McGarvey stole second. Leinhauser fanned. Sugden struck out to end the game. No runs, no hits, no errors.[21]

The contest lasted 1 hour and 45 minutes. Colby Jack Coombs was declared the winner.

The Tigers regulars bought tickets and watched the fiasco from the grandstand. Donie Bush, Detroit shortstop said, "It's a circus. Gosh, I'm glad I came." Jim Delahanty, one of the instigators of the strike, stated, "This is great, I wouldn't have missed it for a minute."[22] Although a second sacker of credible ability, Delahanty was released by the Tigers in August and was not offered a contract by any other club. One of five major-league brothers out of Cleveland, Ohio, Delahanty, with the exception of a two-year stint in the Federal League with Brooklyn (1914–15), would never again play major-league ball. Some say it was retribution for his role in the strike.[23]

Jennings washed his hands of the whole matter. "I put a team on the field today to save the owners of the Detroit franchise from being fined $5,000. It is now up to President Johnson of the league and President Navin of the Detroit club to settle with the 'strikers.' I do not intend to take sides one way or the other. You can say this much for me. There will be a club, professional club of some sort on the field at Shibe Park on Monday."[24]

Due to Pennsylvania Blue Laws, no professional games were played on Sundays. American League President Ban Johnson arrived at the Bellevue-Stratford Hotel in Philadelphia on Sunday May 19 and declared there would be no game on Monday and that the Tigers would not play again until the regular team was placed on the field. On Monday, Johnson, Ben

Figure 1. Play-By-Play

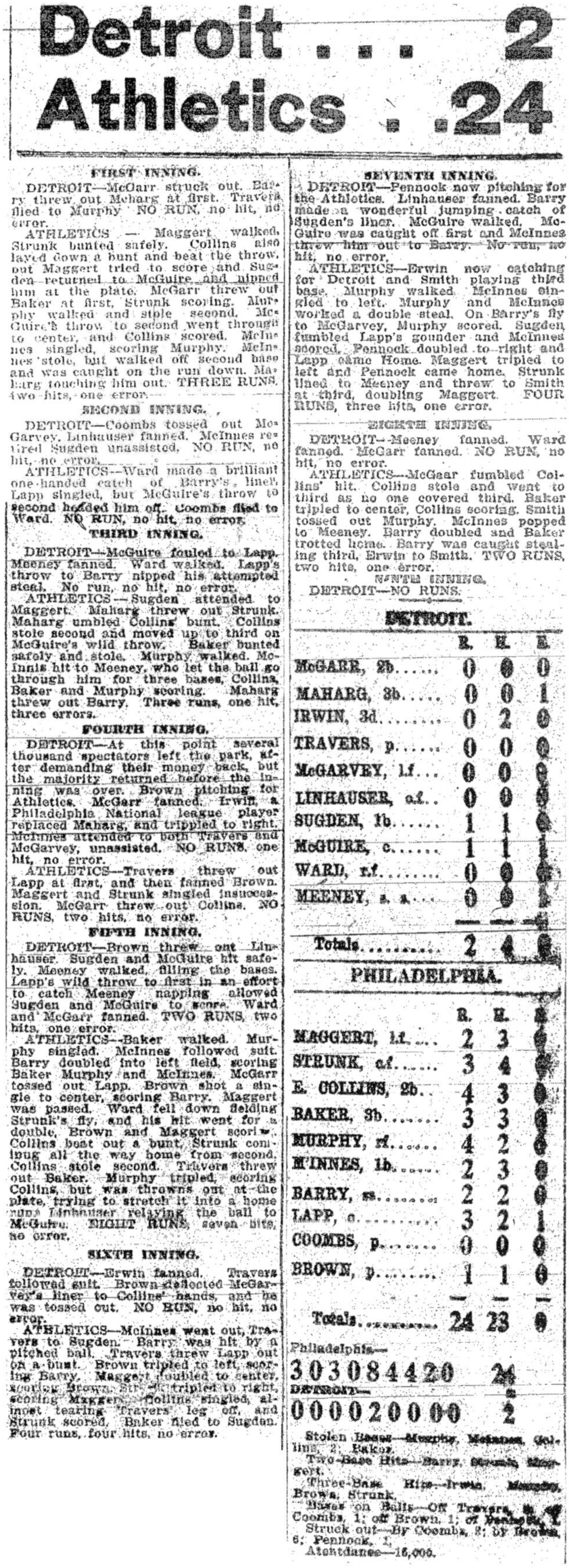

Detroit . . . 2
Athletics . .24

FIRST INNING.

DETROIT—McGarr struck out. Barry threw out Meharg at first. Travers flied to Murphy NO RUN, no hit, no error.

ATHLETICS — Maggert walked, Strunk bunted safely. Collins also layed down a bunt and beat the throw, but Maggert tried to score and Sugden returned to McGuire and nipped him at the plate. McGarr threw out Baker at first, Strunk scoring. Murphy walked and stole second. McGuire's throw to second went through to center, and Collins scored. McInnes singled, scoring Murphy. McInnes stole, but walked off second base and was caught on the run down. Maharg touching him out. THREE RUNS, two hits, one error.

SECOND INNING.

DETROIT—Coombs tossed out McGarvey. Linhauser fanned. McInnes retired Sugden unassisted. NO RUN, no hit, no error.

ATHLETICS—Ward made a brilliant one-handed catch of Barry's liner, Lapp singled, but McGuire's throw to second headed him off. Coombs flied to Ward. NO RUN, no hit, no error.

THIRD INNING.

DETROIT—McGuire fouled to Lapp. Meeney fanned. Ward walked. Lapp's throw to Barry nipped his attempted steal. No run, no hit, no error.

ATHLETICS—Sugden attended to Maggert. Maharg threw out Strunk. Maharg umbled Collins' bunt. Collins stole second and moved up to third on McGuire's wild throw. Baker bunted safely and stole. Murphy walked. McInnis hit to Meeney, who let the ball go through him for three bases, Collins, Baker and Murphy scoring. Maharg threw out Barry. Three runs, one hit, three errors.

FOURTH INNING.

DETROIT—At this point several thousand spectators left the park, after demanding their money back, but the majority returned before the inning was over. Brown pitching for Athletics. McGarr fanned. Irwin, a Philadelphia National league player replaced Maharg, and trippled to right. McInnes attended to both Travers and McGarvey, unassisted. NO RUNS, one hit, no error.

ATHLETICS—Travers threw out Lapp at first, and then fanned Brown. Maggert and Strunk singled insuccession. McGarr threw out Collins. NO RUNS, two hits, no error.

FIFTH INNING.

DETROIT—Brown threw out Linhauser. Sugden and McGuire hit safely. Meeney walked, filling the bases. Lapp's wild throw to first in an effort to catch Meeney napping allowed Sugden and McGuire to score. Ward and McGarr fanned. TWO RUNS, two hits, one error.

ATHLETICS—Baker walked. Murphy singled. McInnes followed suit. Barry doubled into left field, scoring Baker Murphy and McInnes. McGarr tossed out Lapp. Brown shot a single to center, scoring Barry. Maggert was passed. Ward fell down fielding Strunk's fly, and his hit went for a double, Brown and Maggert scoring. Collins beat out a bunt, Strunk coming all the way home from second. Collins stole second. Travers threw out Baker. Murphy tripled, scoring Collins, but was throwns out at the plate, trying to stretch it into a home run, Linhauser relaying the ball to McGuire. EIGHT RUNS, seven hits, no error.

SIXTH INNING.

DETROIT—Erwin fanned. Travers followed suit. Brown deflected McGarvey's liner to Collins' hands, and he was tossed out. NO RUN, no hit, no error.

ATHLETICS—McInnes went out, Travers to Sugden. Barry was hit by a pitched ball. Travers threw Lapp out on a bunt. Brown tripled to left, scoring Barry. Maggert doubled to center, scoring Brown. [illegible] tripled to right, scoring Maggert. Collins singled, almost tearing Travers' leg off, and Strunk scored. Baker flied to Sugden. Four runs, four hits, no error.

SEVENTH INNING.

DETROIT—Pennock now pitching for the Athletics. Linhauser fanned. Barry made a wonderful jumping catch of Sugden's liner. McGuire walked. McGuire was caught off first and McInnes threw him out to Barry. No run, no hit, no error.

ATHLETICS—Erwin now catching for Detroit and Smith playing third base. Murphy walked. McInnes singled to left. Murphy and McInnes worked a double steal. On Barry's fly to McGarvey, Murphy scored. Sugden fumbled Lapp's gounder and McInnes scored. Pennock doubled to right and Lapp came Home. Maggert tripled to left and Pennock came home. Strunk lined to Meeney and threw to Smith at third, doubling Maggert. FOUR RUNS, three hits, one error.

EIGHTH INNING.

DETROIT—Meeney fanned. Ward fanned. McGarr fanned. NO RUN, no hit, no error.

ATHLETICS—McGaar fumbled Collins' hit. Collins stole and went to third as no one covered third. Baker tripled to center, Collins scoring. Smith tossed out Murphy. McInnes popped to Meeney. Barry doubled and Baker trotted home. Barry was caught stealing third, Erwin to Smith. TWO RUNS, two hits, one error.

NINTH INNING.

DETROIT—NO RUNS.

DETROIT.

	R.	H.	E.
McGARR, 2b.	0	0	0
MAHARG, 3b.	0	0	1
IRWIN, 3d.	0	2	0
TRAVERS, p.	0	0	0
McGARVEY, l.f. . .	0	0	0
LINHAUSER, c.f. .	0	0	0
SUGDEN, 1b.	1	1	0
McGUIRE, c.	1	1	1
WARD, r.f.	0	0	0
MEENEY, s. s. . . .	0	0	1
Totals.	2	4	[illegible]

PHILADELPHIA.

	R.	H.	E.
MAGGERT, l.f. . . .	2	3	0
STRUNK, c.f.	3	4	0
E. COLLINS, 2b. .	4	3	0
BAKER, 3b.	3	3	0
MURPHY, rf.	4	2	0
M'INNES, 1b.	2	3	0
BARRY, ss.	2	2	0
LAPP, c.	3	2	1
COOMBS, p.	0	0	0
BROWN, p.	1	1	0
Totals.	24	23	[illegible]

Philadelphia—
3 0 3 0 8 4 4 2 0 — 24
Detroit—
0 0 0 0 2 0 0 0 0 — 2

Stolen Bases—Murphy, McInnes, Collins, 2, Baker.
Two-Base Hits—Barry, Strunk, Maggert.
Three-Base Hits—Irwin, Murphy, Brown, Strunk.
Bases on Balls—Off Travers, [illegible] Coombs, 1; off Brown, 1; of Pennock, 1.
Struck out—By Coombs, 8; by Brown, 6; Pennock, 1.
Attendance—15,000.

Manager Hughie Jennings had no choice but to helm a team made up of a few of his own coaches and several local recruits.

Shibe (president of the Athletics), and managers Mack and Jennings met at the hotel as they waited for Navin to arrive from Detroit. Johnson remarked that Jennings apparently forgot he was a representative of the owners and not the players.[25]

Back at the Aldine Hotel the Detroit regulars were apprehensive about their strike position but Delahanty insisted the players were still sticking together. Chairman Delahanty of the "insurgents" was busy sounding out his teammates and players of other clubs as to the formation of a players' union.[26]

At 3:35PM on May 20, Navin announced that he had reached an agreement with his striking players. Navin stated that the team would take the field in Washington without the services of Cobb, who would be suspended pending the investigation of his actions in New York, and that he, Navin, would take care of all fines inflicted upon the players for the strike.[27]

Cobb spoke to the players after Navin pleaded with them to return to the field:

> My advice to you is to stick by Mr. Navin, who is one of the best friends we all have. I can't tell you how much I appreciate the way you have backed me up and stuck by me—and I know you would go through to the finish with it—but I don't want to take the responsibility of having all you good fellows fined and blacklisted and all that. So I hope if you can see your way clear

you all will get back into the game and play for Mr. Navin—and win. I'll be with you soon, I hope.[28]

Cobb arrived in Washington on May 21 and issued the following statement to the press:

> It matters little to me when President Johnson lifts my suspension. I have made up my mind to go home tonight, no matter whether or not the suspension is lifted or not. If Johnson should decide to lay me off for a month or the remainder of the year, I will be perfectly satisfied. My action in New York was simply on a principle and the Detroit Club will be the sufferer, as my pay goes on, no matter whether I play or not. The same applies to any fine that may be assessed against me, so that if Johnson is seeking to punish me, he will find a different proposition.[29]

On that same day Ban Johnson announced that he had fined 18 of the Detroit strikers $100 each, representing $50 for each game they missed during the walk-out. Johnson further said he would deal as lightly as possible with Cobb considering the circumstances.[30] Those fined were: Sam Crawford, L.E. McCarthy (business manager), Donie Bush, Oscar Vitt, Davy Jones, Jim Delahanty, Oscar Stanage, Jean Dubuc, George Moriarty, R.E. Willet, H.H. Purnoll, Bill Burns, George Mullin, J. Onslow, B. Kocher, H. Perry, Ralph Works, and T. Covington.

In the evening hours of May 25 Johnson officially lifted Cobb's suspension and fined the Detroit star $50. Johnson stated, "Cobb did not seek redress by an appeal to the umpire, but took the law into his own hands. His language and conduct were highly censurable."[31] Johnson also promised future full protection from spectator abuse to all players and that the league had taken steps to increase police authority on all American League grounds.

Cobb was not fined for missing any games as he was under suspension during the strike.

Claude Luecker, the erstwhile victim in the affair, was described as an innocent looking gentleman "with a jovial face and merry eyes" who was determined to sue Cobb for heavy damages.[32] It is not known if Luecker ever followed through with any legal action against Cobb. However, it was later reported that Luecker had run-ins with Cobb years before the infamous incident and at that time Claude was a well-conditioned athlete who had not yet suffered the damage to his hands. Supposedly, this is why Luecker razzed Cobb and when Cobb recognized his old enemy, he went after him.[33] Little is known about Luecker's life after the episode. The time and place of his death is unknown.

We know a bit more about the men who took the field in place of the Tigers, although some mysteries about them persist.

The most interesting controversy is the shortstop position. According to *Baseball Encyclopedia* folklore, Bill Leinhauser was asked in the late 1950s to research and verify the names of his teammates of that day. Using his memory and the box score of the game, Leinhauser puts Pat Meaney at shortstop, and that is how it was noted in *The Baseball Encyclopedia* for many years. However, in the early 2000s, Bill Dougherty—a SABR member and a Batavia, New York, baseball historian—made the claim that one Edward Vincent Maney, also of Batavia, was the actual Tigers shortstop.

Dougherty's evidence included Maney's obituary of March 12, 1952, which mentions that he was a participant of that game. In a letter to his brother, Maney wrote, "I played shortstop and had more fun that day then you can imagine. Of course, it was a big defeat for us, but they paid us $15 for a couple of hours work and I was satisfied to say I played against the World Champions. I had three putouts, one error, and no hits." The player in the game *did* have three putouts and one error, however, the letter neglects to say that he walked or was hit by a pitch and that an error by the Philadelphia catcher attempting to pick him off first base resulted in the Tigers' only two runs of the game. Dougherty also provided a picture of someone in a Tigers uniform, standing next to Detroit manager Hughie Jennings on the day of the game. The grainy black and white photograph could be Maney, but due to its poor quality it is difficult to tell.

Dougherty also noted that Pat Meaney threw left-handed and that Edward Vincent Maney threw from the right side; shortstops are almost never southpaws. But many writeups of his day note that Pat Meaney was proficiently ambidextrous. Finally, there is a newspaper article in the May 23, 1912, edition of the *Batavia Daily News* stating that Batavian S. Vincent Maney played shortstop for the Detroit Tigers on May 18, 1912. The article notes that he was the office manager of the Iroquois Iron Works in Philadelphia. The Iroquois Iron Works was headquartered in Buffalo, near Batavia, and may have had an office in Philadelphia in 1912. There is a Vincent Maney in the 1912 Philadelphia City directory listed as a bookkeeper.

I believe that Pat Meaney, having been identified by Bill Leinhauser as his teammate, having been a friend of Tigers first baseman Joe Sugden, and having thrown from both the left and right side for many seasons, was the shortstop on that day in Philadelphia. Mr. Vincent Maney may have been a recruit who sat the bench, but I do not think he played shortstop that day. Ironically, in the 1880 Federal Census the Patrick Meaney family name is spelled "Maney."

To further muddy the shortstop waters, a well-known Philadelphia semi-professional shortstop by the name of Joe Harrigan is also mentioned by one newspaper of the day as having been at short, but the box score in the same paper has Meaney in the lineup and not Harrigan. Maybe Harrigan was another recruit who did not get in the game.[34]

As mentioned previously there are conflicting reports about how much each player was paid—anywhere from $10 to $50 according to newspaper accounts, Mr. Maney's letter, and Father Al Travers's interview. Would not the contracts the players signed that day state the amount of pay? Unfortunately, in 1912 major league teams only had to sign players to contracts after they had been on the club for five days. Here are the players:

James Vincent "Jim" "Red" McGarr, 23, a machinist in a locomotive factory, handled second base adequately, making only one error in four chances. "Red" possibly received his nickname from his red hair or the fact he lived on Redner Street in Philadelphia. By 1917 McGarr was employed as a Philadelphia firefighter. He served in the United States Army in WWI and was treated for shrapnel wounds and shell shock. Later in life, McGarr left the Philadelphia Fire Department and opened a café. He moved to Fort Lauderdale from Philadelphia in 1947 and died at Veterans Hospital in Miami, Florida, on July 21, 1981, the last surviving member of the "misfits" of May 18, 1912.

William Joseph "Billy" Maharg, 31, a farmhand and auto mechanic, took the field at third base. At only 5-foot-4-inches, Maharg boxed professionally and fairly successfully, 45–11 with 18 no-decisions 1900–07.[35] A featherweight pugilist, Billy was well-known for his aggressive style. Often a headliner in the Philadelphia, Lancaster, and York, Pennsylvania area, Maharg was a fan favorite whose real name was thought to be "Graham"—Maharg spelled backwards[36]—but that proved to be false.[37] Billy worked on the family farm in Fox Chase, Pennsylvania, but also hung around the Philadelphia sports scene, serving as a gofer and chauffeur for pitcher Grover Cleveland Alexander and other Phillies. Maharg was suggested to Jennings as a replacement player for the May 18, 1912, game by Detroit pitcher "Sleepy" Bill Burns, who had become an acquaintance of Maharg's while hurling for the Phillies the previous season.[38] On the last day of the 1916 major league season Maharg, then officially the Phillies assistant trainer, made his second and last major league playing appearance, pinch-hitting in the eighth inning, grounding out, and spending the ninth stanza patrolling right field without a fielding opportunity.

During WWI Billy found work as a driller for the Baldwin Locomotive Works, possibly the same place former teammate Jim McGarr worked. However, Maharg was not through with major league baseball. In 1920 Billy spilled the beans to a Philadelphia reporter that he, his friend Burns, and ex-featherweight prizefighter Abe Attell had conspired with the notorious gambler Arnold Rothstein to bribe Chicago White Sox players to fix the 1919 World Series. Maharg received immunity for his testimony.[39] Maharg eventually went to work for the Ford Motor Company in Chester, Pennsylvania, and he died in Philadelphia on November 20, 1953.

William Edwin Irwin, 34, a journeyman minor league player, was a bullpen catcher for the neighboring Phillies.[40] Ed—or Bill, as he was commonly known—would replace Maharg at third base in the fourth inning and switch to catching in the seventh. Under tragic circumstances, he was the first of the Detroit misfits to pass away. On February 5, 1916, Irwin went to a local saloon with a friend and became involved in a barroom brawl. As reported in the *Philadelphia Evening Ledger*, things went badly:

> Philly players will be shocked to learn of the death of "Bill" Irwin the young catcher who was taken south with the Phillies last spring. Irwin also helped both Doolin and Moran when they were short-handed by warming up pitchers and doing general utility work about the ball park. Irwin was thrown through the window of an uptown saloon; his jugular vein being severed. It was reported that the dead man's first name was Edward, but it was in reality the Philly recruit.[41]

At the time of his death, Irwin was working as a special officer for the Pennsylvania Railroad. In those days railroads often hired competent ballplayers to play on the company ball teams. Irwin may have

known Billy Maharg, since they both worked for the Phillies organization, and that could be how he was chosen to be a Tiger misfit.

Aloysius Stephen (Stanislaus) Travers, 20, a junior at St. Joseph's College. would take to the mound for the replacements and toss mostly slow curveballs to the Athletics.[42] Al pitched eight innings for the "paper Tigers" and gave up 24 runs on 26 hits. Aloysius was ordained a Catholic priest in 1926 and served at the Saint Andrew Novitiate in Hyde Park, New York, Saint Francis Xavier High School in Manhattan, and eventually at his alma mater, Saint Joseph's College in Philadelphia. Later he taught at Saint Joseph's Preparatory School in Philadelphia. Father Travers never cared to speak much about his day as a major league twirler. In 1955 he broke his silence and told his story in an interview with sportswriter Red Smith.[43] Reverend Travers died in Philadelphia on April 19, 1968.

Daniel John McGarvey, 24, a chauffeur, positioned himself in left field for the replacements. McGarvey served in WWI and later worked as a civilian machinist in the Philadelphia Navy Shipyard. From 1927 until 1945 he spent time on and off in United States Veterans Institutions for disabled or mentally incompetent veterans. McGarvey died on August 18, 1945, in Kecoughton, Virginia.

William Charles Leinhauser, 18, an auto machinist, patrolled center field for the substitutes. Bill became a Philadelphia policeman in 1917 and rose to the rank of lieutenant in charge of the Narcotics Bureau. Leinhauser served in the Pennsylvania National Guard for three years before serving in France in WWI. In 1953 he was briefly suspended by the Philadelphia Police Commissioner for negligent duty but was later acquitted by a police trial board.[44] He retired from the Philadelphia Police Force in 1959. It was Leinhauser who, in the mid-1950s worked with co-author S.C. Thompson of *The Official Encyclopedia of Baseball* to track down the full names and birth data of the Detroit "misfits." Leinhauser was proud to have worn Cobb's uniform during the game.[45] Bill Leinhauser died in Elkins Park, Pennsylvania, on April 14, 1978.

Joseph Sugden, age 41—Detroit Tigers coach and scout at the time of the game—came out of retirement to play first base for the misfits. Sugden was a major league catcher/first baseman for five teams between 1893 and 1905. In his youth, Sugden played sandlot baseball around the Philadelphia and Camden, New

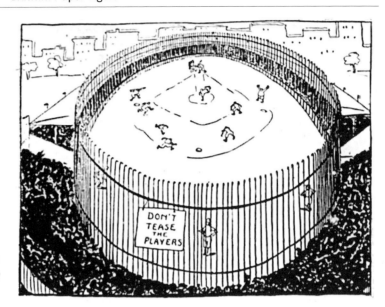

This editorial cartoon from the New York World *also ran in the* Detroit Times *with the caption: "Guaranteed to protect the noisiest fan from the hot-headest player."*

Jersey, area and began playing professionally for the Charleston Sea Gulls of the South Atlantic League in 1892. A catcher by trade and a life-long switch-hitter, Joe signed on with the Pittsburgh Pirates of the National League in 1893. Catching was a hazardous occupation in those days; protection was limited to crude face masks, thin gloves, light chest protectors and no shin guards. The Pirates carried four catchers on the roster, including the future Philadelphia Athletics owner/manager, Connie Mack.

The St. Louis Browns acquired Sugden in 1898 and then transfered him to the Cleveland Spiders the following year, in which the Spiders finished last in the National League with a 20–134 won-loss record. In 1900 Joe caught on with the American League White Stockings and the team took first place with Sugden catching most of the games. The American League was not considered a major league until 1901 and the White Stockings won the American League pennant that season, although Sugden was relegated to a backup role. Despite his increasing baseball age, Joe spent the next four years as mostly the starting backstop with the St. Louis Browns. In his last year with the Brownies, 1905, Joe met a fellow catcher Branch Rickey, a relationship that would prove fortuitous as Rickey would later hire Joe as a scout/coach. With his batting skills eroding, Joe spent 1906 and 1907 in the minor leagues with St. Paul. Not willing to give up the game he spent the next three seasons with the Vancouver Beavers of the Northwestern League.

In the spring of 1911, Jennings asked Sugden to go south with the team and coach his young pitchers. When the team went north, Sugden left to manage and play for the New Castle Nocks of the Ohio-Pennsylvania League. It would be the last time Sugden appeared in a regular season professional game until his appearance with the Detroit misfits of 1912. Sugden, although well past his prime, had kept himself in playing shape, occasionally covering first base for the Tigers as the team barnstormed its way north during the 1912 spring training season.[46] While the Tigers were in spring training at Monroe, Louisiana, Sugden's wife died suddenly back in their home in Philadelphia. When informed of her sudden illness, Joe left camp to be at his wife's side but did not make it in time. Agnes Sugden died on March 4; Sugden returned to the Tigers on March 27. During WWI Sugden applied for a passport to travel to France to work with the YMCA in aiding the American Expeditionary Force. It is not known if Sugden followed through with that endeavor. After the misfit game, Joe continued to scout and coach with the Tigers, St. Louis Cardinals, and Philadelphia Phillies until his death in Philadelphia on June 26, 1959.

James Thomas "Deacon" McGuire, 48, a 26-year veteran of the major leagues, donned the "tools of ignorance" one more time for the Tigers replacement team. Deacon had earned his sobriquet for his gentlemanly manner and sportsmanship during his lengthy baseball career. As a professional ballplayer from 1883 to 1910, Deacon had rarely been thrown out of a game or fined.[47] But on July 21, 1910, he was tossed from a game while managing Cleveland for arguing too ardently for a balk call against a Washington Nationals pitcher. The umpire who sent Deacon back to the team hotel? "Bull" Perrine, who was the infield arbiter in the "paper Tigers" game. McGuire began his big league career with the Toledo club in the American Association in 1884 and ended it 28 years later playing in the Tigers strike game. He participated behind the plate for an unfathomable 26 seasons, spending time with Toledo, Detroit (NL), Philadelphia (NL), Cleveland (AA), Rochester (AA), Washington (AA), Washington (NL), Brooklyn (NL), New York (AL), Detroit (AL), Boston (AL), and Cleveland (AL). Deacon managed the Washington Senators (1898), Boston Red Sox (1907–08), and the Cleveland Naps (1909–11). In 1912 he signed on as a Tigers coach/scout as a favor to his former Brooklyn teammate, Tigers manager Hughie Jennings. McGuire retired in 1926 to his farm in Deer Lake, Michigan, where he died of bronchopneumonia on October 31, 1936. Deacon died on Halloween, which seems appropriate since he wore a mask at work for 26 years.[48]

Patrick A. Meaney, 40, performed at shortstop for the replacement Tigers. A long-time (1892–1909) minor leaguer who started his career as a left-handed pitcher of great promise, was a friend of Joe Sugden when they played together in Camden. Sugden may have recruited Pat for the game. Meaney resided at 2231 Redner Street just a few houses from teammate Jim McGarr. Possibly Meaney recruited McGarr, or vice versa. Meaney was hurling for the Harrisburg, Pennsylvania, team when his arm went dead. Always a strong hitter, Meaney learned to throw righty, moved to right field and excelled. In 1902 he jumped to a team in San Francisco where he continued to throw from the right side. It was well-publicized that Meaney was an ambidextrous thrower, as in this newspaper account:

> An interesting story on a former coal region player comes from California. Pat Meaney who used to be the right field star for Harrisburg when the latter was in the State League went to the coast last fall and is now playing the outfield for San Francisco. Pat used to be a southpaw twirler until his arm went "dead" and he then learned to throw with his right wing and starred in the outfield. He used to perform regularly with his right hand last season....Hurt his shoulder and went back to his left.[50]

A professional and sandlot baseball player his entire life, Meaney died in Philadelphia on October 20, 1922, of a brain tumor. At the time of his death his occupation was listed as "ballplayer."

John Joseph Coffey a.k.a. Jack Smith, 18, one of the youngest of the misfits, entered the game as the Tigers third baseman in the seventh inning, with Irwin moving from third to behind the plate, relieving McGuire. Jack had worked as an office boy prior to his incarceration for larceny in the Pennsylvania Industrial Reform School in Huntingdon, Pennsylvania, on March, 16, 1912. His troubles with the law may explain the name subterfuge; maybe he was not where he should have been that day. Coffey was residing with his employer when he was arrested for larceny and receiving stolen goods. His sentence was three years at the Pennsylvania Industrial Reformatory in Huntingdon, so he was either paroled or escaped prior to joining the "paper Tigers." Two months after the game (July 13) he was alleged by Philadelphia police to have sold a large number of newspapers under false pretenses by shouting falsely that Colonel Roosevelt had been assassinated and his murderer hanged.[51] Coffey also spent time in the county jail during WWI. Later in life he worked in New York as a writer for a publishing company and as an insurance agent. He died in New York City on December 4, 1962.

Joseph Nichols Ward, 26, worked as a salesman and covered right field for the strikebreakers, making the catch of the game in the third inning. Although Ward is often given the nickname "Hap" in current biographies, there is no mention of that moniker in any write-ups of the day. A "Hap" Ward was a very popular vaudeville entertainer at that time so it is possible that is where the confusion is derived. Ward was a well-known sandlot player in the New Jersey and Philadelphia area. He worked as a salesman for Duofold Inc., an undergarment company, mostly out of Camden. Joseph claimed an exemption from the WWI draft due to being the sole provider of his mother and wife. However, in June 1918 he traveled to France and later Italy and worked for the YMCA. The YMCA supplied thousands of paid staff and volunteers to provide spiritual, mental, and physical "welfare" services to the doughboys. Ward returned from Europe in February 1919. Joseph died in Elmer, New Jersey, on September 13, 1979.

Hugh (Hughie) Ambrose Jennings, 43, the manager of both the real and "paper" Tigers, pinch-hit and struck out for Travers in the ninth inning. He began his big league career in 1891 with the Louisville Colonels and was the shortstop on the great Baltimore Orioles teams of the mid-late 1890s. In 1899 he moved on to the Brooklyn Superbas who won the National League pennant that year and the next. After a stint with the Philadelphia Phillies, he returned to Brooklyn in 1903. In 1907 Hughie was hired as manager of the Detroit Tigers and led them to the American League pennant three consecutive years (1907–09). Although he never managed another pennant-winner, he led the Tigers until 1921. In the offseason, Jennings attended Cornell Law School and eventually practiced law in the winter months. Upon leaving the Tigers he coached for the New York Giants (1921–25). After the 1925 season, Jennings retired to Scranton, Pennsylvania, where he died of tubercular meningitis on February 1, 1928. He was elected to the National Baseball Hall of Fame in Cooperstown in 1945.[52]

Other players who may have been in the dugout but not on the field were Arthur "Bugs" Baer[53] and the aforementioned Vincent Maney and Joe Harrigan.[54] Contrary to the reports of the day and subsequent ones, the substitutes were not baseball collegians; only Travers attended college at the time, and he was not on his college team. McGarvey and McGarr were reported to be former Georgetown college players, but that appears unlikely, as neither finished high school.

It is interesting to note that the game against the paper Tigers did not turn into a farce until the bottom of the fifth. After four and a half innings the score stood 6–2. The eight-run fifth inning did in the make-believe major leaguers. Their errors didn't help, but they made two spectacular plays in the outfield, hit the ball on occasion, had the game's only double play, and fielded twenty-four outs. Not bad for a pitcher who could not make his college team, a pint-sized pugilist, two baseball elder statesmen, a journeyman bullpen catcher, a former minor league star pitcher turned shortstop, a salesman, and a few mechanics, and a chauffeur. ∎

ACKNOWLEDGMENTS

Special thanks to Ancestry.com and Baseball-Reference.com.

NOTES

1. "Cobb Turns to Boxing," *New York Tribune*, May 16, 1912, 10.
2. "Ty Would Thrash Again," *The Sun* (New York, New York), May 17, 10.
3. "No Sign of Break in Baseball Strike," *The Lincoln Star*, Lincoln, Nebraska, May 19, 1912, 7.
4. "Big Baseball War May Follow Tigers' Strike to Aid Cobb," *The Evening World*, New York, NY, May 18, 1912, 1–2.
5. "Cobb Thrashes Fan," *Washington Post*, May 16, 1912, 7.
6. "Ban Johnson Sees Fight From Stands," *Washington Post*, May 16, 1912, 7.
7. "Ty Cobb Suspended," *The New York Times*, May 17, 1912, 11.
8. "Cobb Banished From Game," *New York Tribune*, May 17, 1912, 10.
9. "Tigers Ultimatum to Pres Johnson," *Boston Globe*, May 18, 1912, 1.
10. "Suspension Stands," *Boston Globe*, May 19, 1912, 9.
11. *Boston Herald*, May 18, 1912.
12. "Mackies Ease Up, St. Joseph's Win," *Philadelphia Inquirer*, April 11, 1912, 10.
13. Gary Livacari, "Allan Travers," SABR BioProject, https://sabr.org/bioproject/person.
14. "Allan Travers," SABR BioProject.
15. "St Joe Beats Conway Hall," *Philadelphia Inquirer*, May 19, 1912, 10.
16. "Detroit Players Strike; Jennings Signs Amateurs," *Pottsville Republican* (Pennsylvania), May 18, 1912, 1.
17. "Stir Up Over Ty Cobb," *Tuscaloosa News*," May 19, 1912, 1.
18. Some characterize the Tigers' walkout as the first players strike in major-league history, but five Louisville players struck during the disastrous 1889 season of the Louisville Colonels in the American Association.
19. *Commercial Tribune*, (Cincinnati), May 19, 1912, 14.
20. "Detroit Players Make Their Threat Good And Walk Off Field," *Detroit Times*, May 18, 1912.
21. The play-by-play found in the *Detroit Times* ends before the ninth inning. The preceding is derived from the box scores of the day.
22. "Detroit Team On Strike," *The New York Times*, May 19, 1912, 1.
23. "Grave Story-Jim Delahanty," RIP Baseball.com
24. "Quakertown Not Quiescent When Quasi Tigers And Champs Play," *Canton News Democrat*, May 19, 1912, 12.
25. "Baseball Strike Growing Worse," *Plainfield Daily Press*, May 20, 1912, 9.
26. "Johnson Calls Of Game With Detroit," *The New York Times*, May 20, 1912, 2.
27. "Big Baseball Strike Is Over," *Winona Republican Herald*, (Winona, MN), May 21, 1912, 2.
28. "Detroit Tigers Will Play Ball," *Bradford Era* (Bradford, PA), May 21, 1912, 7.
29. "Ty Cobb Quits Tigers; Will Depart For Home," *St. Louis Star and Times*, May 21, 1912, 13.
30. "Players Fined $100 Each," *Daily News* (Frederick, MD), May 22, 1912, 7.
31. "Tyrus Cobb Is Reinstated And Is Fined But $50," *Washington Herald* (District of Columbia), May 26, 1912, 39.
32. "Victim Will Sue Cobb," *The New York Times*, 32 May 20, 1912, 2.
33. "Sporting Briefs," Nashville Banner, March 3, 1913, 10.
34. "Suspension Stands," *Boston Herald*, May 19, 1912, 1.
35. Bill Lamb, "Billy Maharg," SABR BioProject, https://sabr.org/bioproject/person.
36. "Weekly Review of Sports," *Intelligencer Journal* (Lancaster), November 14, 1908, 8.
37. Bill Lamb, "Billy Maharg," SABR BioProject, https://sabr.org/bioproject/person.
38. "Detroit Team on Strike," *The New York Times*, May 19, 1912, 1.
39. Bill Lamb, "Billy Maharg," SABR BioProject, https://sabr.org/bioproject/person.
40. Bill Lamb, "Ed Irwin," SABR BioProject, https://sabr.org/bioproject/person.
41. "Seaton's Arm Is As Good As Ever, *Philadelphia Evening Public Ledger*, February 9, 1916, 12.
42. "Strikebreakers Have No Chance," *Omaha Bee*, May 19, 1912, 37.
43. "Allan Travers," SABR BioProject.
44. "Phil. Objects to Dope Smear," *The Plain Speaker* (Hazelton, PA), October 23, 1953, 2.
45. *The Official Encyclopedia of Baseball*, Revised Edition 1959, 522.
46. "First Game Of The Season Went To Tigers 9–2," *Hattiesburg Daily News*, March 27, 1912, 8.
47. "Is A Model Deacon," *Anaconda Standard* (Anaconda, Montana), April 24, 1910, 24.
48. Robert W. Bigelow, "Deacon McGuire," SABR BioProject, https://sabr.org/bioproject/person.
49. "A Club Without A Home," *Philadelphia Inquirer*, March 28, 1895, 6.
50. "Base Ball," *The Plain Speaker* (Hazelton, Pennsylvania), August 13, 1903, 1.
51. "Fake News Caller Fined," *Philadelphia Inquirer*, July 13, 1912, 5. Ironically, Roosevelt was shot in an assassination attempt in Milwaukee, Wisconsin on October 12, 1912.
52. C. Paul Rogers III, "Hughie Jennings," SABR BioProject, https://sabr.org/bioproject/person.
53. *Philadelphia Inquirer*, May 19, 1912, 15.
54. "Detroit Team Out on Strike," *The New York Times*, May 19, 1912, 1.

Instant Relief

First-Batter Triple Plays

James A. "Snuffy" Smith, Jr., Stephen D. Boren, Herm Krabbenhoft

R—O—L—A—I—D—S. The answer in the classic ad: "How do you spell relief?"

TRIPLE PLAY!!! The answer to the question, "What's the perfect remedy for a relief pitcher summoned into a diamond game with nobody out and two (or three) runners on base?"

Take for instance May 30, 1967, at Crosley Field in Cincinnati. In the top of the ninth the Reds were leading the Cardinals, 2–1. The Reds' starting pitcher, Jim Maloney, gave up consecutive singles to Orlando Cepeda and Tim McCarver, putting runners at first and third with nobody out. Cincy skipper Dave Bristol then brought in Don Nottebart to face the next batter, Phil Gagliano, who grounded the first pitch to shortstop Leo Cardenas, who, after "checking" Cepeda at third, threw the ball to second baseman Tommy Helms, forcing out McCarver. Helms then whipped the ball to first-sacker Deron Johnson to retire the batter, completing a 6–4–3 ground double play (GDP). However, after initially delaying at third, Cepeda unexpectedly bolted for home trying to score the game-tying run. Johnson alertly fired the ball to catcher Johnny Edwards who tagged Cepeda, simultaneously completing the triple play and getting the game-winning out.[1]

"All I wanted to do was get the batter to hit the ball on the ground and hope for a play at the plate," said Nottebart. As a dejected Red Schoendienst, the Cardinals manager, explained, "Just before Gagliano hit the ball, our third base coach, [Joe] Schultz, had reminded Cepeda to go right home on a play like that. There's only one place to go and that's home. You can't give them the double play. But Cepeda didn't start running right away." "It was my fault," said Cepeda. "I learned something. I'll never do that again."[2]

In this article we present the pertinent details of other examples of Instant Relief—triple plays in which a relief pitcher got the first batter he faced to hit into a rally-terminating triple play in the National League, American League, or the defunct major leagues of the American Association (1882–91), Union Association (1884), Players League (1890), or Federal League (1914–15). The time period covered is from the founding of the National League in 1876 through 2022. "A team's gotta be lucky to win a game like that," said Schoendienst after the game. As it turns out, Nottebart is one of 40 relief hurlers to experience Instant Relief.

RESEARCH PROCEDURE

All of the information needed to compose this article was obtained exclusively from the Smith-Boren-Krabbenhoft (SBK) Triple Play database.[3] The SBK TP database was created in 1997–98. Jim Smith began compiling a list of triple plays in 1967. Initially, Jim used the official Day-By-Day (DBD) records which recorded the teams involved in TPs beginning in 1912 for the American League and 1920 for the National League, but not the fielders, batters, or runners. The official records began including the fielders (but not batters or runners) beginning in 1928 for the NL and 1930 for the AL. Smith pored through the box scores and game accounts of every major league game (as presented in *The Sporting Life*, *The Sporting News*, *The New York Times*, and several Philadelphia newspapers) to ascertain the batters, runners, and fielders of those TPs as well as TPs not included in the official records. By the end of 1969, Smith (with some help from Seymour Siwoff of the Elias Sports Bureau) had determined the complete details for 377 TPs from 1900 through 1969. During the 1970s, he continued his search for TPs, focusing on the nineteenth century. By 1975 Smith had identified about a hundred TPs 1876–99. And, by 1990, with valuable help from a number of fellow SABR members—in particular, Art Ahrens, Bob Davids, Joe Dittmar, Paul Doherty, Leonard Gettelson, John O'Malley, Pete Palmer, William Richmond, John Schwartz, and John Tattersall—Jim had identified 131 TPs in the nineteenth century. Altogether through the 1990 season, Smith's list included 588 major league triple plays.

In 1988 Herm Krabbenhoft independently initiated a research effort to ascertain the details of each major league triple play from 1920 forward. With the dates of the triple plays given in the official DBD records, he recorded the details of each TP as described in *The*

New York Times. In 1991, at the SABR-21 Convention in New York, Herm learned of Smith's independent triple play research project. Herm wrote to Jim on July 6, 1991, asking if he would be interested in writing a series of articles on triple plays for *Baseball Quarterly Reviews* (BQR), the unifying theme being "Triple Plays at XYZ Stadium (Park, Field, Grounds, etc.)." Smith responded (July 11), stating that he'd be glad to write about triple plays for BQR. During the next six years Smith authored/co-authored some 80 articles providing the details for the 620 triple plays he and Herm had documented.[4]

In 1993, Steve Boren began his own independent effort to document major league triple plays. Employing the same brute-force approach utilized by Smith, Steve identified 622 major league triple plays from the 1876 through 1997 seasons. In 1997 Krabbenhoft, Smith, and Boren became aware of each others' efforts.[5] They then combined their databases to produce the comprehensive SBK Triple Play Database. At the conclusion of the 1998 season, the SBK TP database had 636 documented/verified triple plays (including the four triple plays pulled in 1998). Effort has continued during the ensuing years to keep the SBK TP database up to date as new TPs were accomplished and to search for more TPs from the nineteenth century.[6] For instance, in 2004 we (Steve) found the first and (so far) only TP in the 1884 Union Association. The SBK TP database now has complete details for a total of 738 documented/verified triple plays through the 2022 season.

The tables on pages 21–24 present details for the 40 "Instant Relief" triple plays included in the SBK Triple Play database.

RESULTS AND DISCUSSION

As shown in Table 1 (page 21, Appendix), the first relief pitcher to achieve instant relief was Paul Radford of the Boston Reds. In an American Association game on May 26, 1891, against Kelly's Killers of Cincinnati, played at Pendleton Park (also known as East End Grounds), going into the top of the ninth session, the host Cincinnati nine (who batted first, as was not uncustomary for the home team to do at the time) held a five-run advantage (18–13). Boston's hurler, southpaw Bill Daley, was in the box. Jim Canavan led off with an easy fly which keystoner Cub Stricker muffed. Yank Robinson got a base on balls. Dick Johnston followed with a grounder to shortstop Radford, who threw wildly to first, the error allowing Johnston to be safe and Canavan to tally. Then Jack Carney smashed a three-bagger, plating Robinson and Johnston. The next batter, Art Whitney, then worked Daley for a pass, putting runners at first and third. At this juncture, Boston manager Arthur Irwin had had enough and made wholesale changes—he derricked Daley, sending him to left field, switched Hugh Duffy from left field to shortstop, and moved Radford to the pitcher's box. Radford, a right-handed thrower, had been Boston's regular shortstop for the entire season (133 games, .259 batting average). Facing the righty-swinging Frank Dwyer, Radford pitched only two balls. The first one was fouled. The next one was hit as a little fly back of second. Stricker caught the ball and immediately whipped it home to catcher Duke Farrell in time to nab Carney trying to score. The backstop then rifled the ball back to Stricker who put Whitney out attempting to go to second—completing the rally-squelching triple play. As it turned out, that was Radford's only mound appearance of the season, a one-two-three performance—one batter, two pitches, three outs.

Other Game-Ending Instant Relief TPs

In addition to the two above-described accomplishments by Nottebart and Radford, there have been four other ninth-inning first-batter-faced triple plays achieved by a relief pitcher. (See Table 1, #5 and #6; Table 2 #15; Table 3 #30, on pages 21–23, Appendix). Two of them were game-enders like Nottebart's. The first one was achieved by Virgil Trucks on August 29, 1953, at Comiskey Park in Chicago. In a battle of the "Soxes," the White were leading the Red in the top of the ninth by a 5–1 score. But the BoSox were threatening. The ChiSox starting hurler, right-hander Connie Johnson, had given up a single to Floyd Baker and then walked Al Zarilla (pinch hitting for Ellis Kinder). After he missed the plate on his first two pitches to Karl Olson, the Pale Hose manager, Paul Richards, called on his ace right-handed starting pitcher—Virgil "Fire" Trucks—to extinguish the kindling and prevent an inferno. After taking a called strike (making the count 2–1), Olson ripped Trucks's next pitch down the first base line. First sacker Ferris Fain snared the ball inches off the ground, retiring Olson for the first out. Next, he casually stepped on the primary sack to double up Zarilla for the second out. Then, he nonchalantly tossed the ball to shortstop Chico Carrasquel who stepped on the middle station to triple up Baker, simultaneously precluding a conflagration and ending the game. Interestingly, according to the game account written by Edward Prell for the *Chicago Tribune*, "Fain could have made the triple play unassisted as Baker had already reached third."[7]

The most recent game-ending first-batter triple play game achieved by a relief pitcher occurred on September 8, 1991, in Montreal. The visiting Reds were trailing the host Expos by a 4–2 score. Mel Rojas was still on the hill for Montreal in the ninth. The Reds began their last-ditch at bats with a single by Hal Morris. This prompted Montreal manager, Tom Runnells, to call on his bullpen; he brought in port-sider Jeff Fassaro to square off with left-hand-batting Paul O'Neill. Cincy skipper Lou Piniella countered by sending up righty-swinging Eric Davis. Fassero proceeded to walk Davis on five pitches. So, it was up to the next batter, Chris Sabo, another right-handed hitter. Runnels went to his bullpen again, this time summoning righty-throwing Barry Jones. Piniella had to stick with Sabo since he had no left-handed-batting players left on the bench. Sabo made contact on a 1–0 pitch, sending a hard one-hopper right at the third base bag. Hot corner man Bret Barberie fielded the ball and stepped on third to force out Morris, then fired the ball to second baseman Delino DeShields who, after getting the force out on Davis by stepping on second, relayed the sphere to first-sacker Tom Foley to retire Sabo, thereby completing a game-ending around-the-horn triple play. Afterwards, Barberie mentioned that he had "thought about a triple play right before the pitch; but I never thought it would happen." Reliever Jones said, "It happened so fast. I threw the pitch, I looked around, and the game was done."[8]

Other Lefty-Righty Instant Relief TPs

The managerial chess exhibited by Runnells and Piniella has also occurred with many other first-batter-faced triple plays. Four others are of particular interest. In the game on July 30, 1924, between the Philadelphia Phillies and the visiting St. Louis Cardinals at the Baker Bowl, the Phillies had shelled the Cards' starting hurler, Leo Dickerman, for three singles and a double (plus a safe-on-error) to jump out to a 4–0 lead in the bottom of the first. After the Cardinals picked up one run in the top of the second, the Phillies were threatening to increase their advantage in the bottom half of the inning. Eighth-batting Jim Wilson led off with a double and opposing moundsman Jimmy Ring reached first with a base on balls. With runners on first and second and nobody out, manager Branch Rickey decided that it just wasn't Dickerman's day. So, with left-handed batting George Harper (who had singled in his first at bat) coming to bat again, the future Mahatma went to his bullpen, bringing in a southpaw, Bill Sherdel. Phillies skipper Art Fletcher countered by calling on the right-handed batter Johnny

Mokan to pinch hit. The substitution of Mokan for Harper had all of the makings of a sacrifice bunt, and the St. Louis first sacker had moved in on the grass in anticipation. But Mokan crossed up the opposition—or so he thought—stroking a drive on Sherdel's very first offering, straight to first baseman Bottomley, who snared the ball. He then heaved the ball to shortstop Jimmy Cooney, trapping Wilson off second base. Keystoner Rogers Hornsby dashed over to first base, where he clutched Cooney's relay, completing the triple killing. As it later developed, with the LB/RP — > LB/LP — > RB/LP maneuvering having backfired for Philadelphia, St. Louis went on to score enough runs to eventually win the game, 9–8.

The Phillies and the Cardinals were again involved on August 23, 1947, this time at Shibe Park. Through seven and a half innings, St. Louis had a two-run lead, 5–3. But the Phillies got their first two men on in the last of the eighth: Andy Seminick opened the frame with a single to center and Lee Handley followed with one to right, putting runners on first and second with no one down. The Philadelphia manager, Ben Chapman, called on lefty-batting Charlie Gilbert to pinch hit against the right-handed hurling Jim Hearn. The Cardinals skipper, Eddie Dyer, responded by calling on southpaw reliever Al Brazle. Chapman opted to stick with Gilbert (rather than bring in a right-handed pinch hitter, such as Jim Tabor). On Brazle's first pitch, Gilbert took a called strike. On the second pitch, he attempted to bunt, but fouled the ball off for strike two. Determined to lay down a bunt at all costs, Gilbert tried again. He lifted a short foul fly that catcher Del Rice was able to catch acrobatically. After quickly regaining his balance, Rice shot the ball to shortstop Marty Marion, doubling Seminick, who was almost at third base. Marion then relayed the ball to first baseman Stan Musial, retiring Handley, who was then almost at second base, completing the triple slaughter. So, the right-left maneuvering (this time RB/RP— > LB/RP— > LB/LP) again did not work out for Philadelphia. But it certainly did for St. Louis—another Instant-Relief TP. Plus the Cards won the game, 5–3.

While managerial chess is often played in the late innings, here's an example of righty-lefty maneuvering in the very first inning. On June 23, 1954, in the inaugural season of the relocated and renamed Baltimore Orioles, the O's were hosting the Boston Red Sox at Memorial Stadium. After having held the BoSox scoreless in their first at bats, the first four Orioles batters—right fielder Cal Abrams, first baseman Dick Kryhoski, center fielder Chuck Diering, and third baseman Vern Stephens—combined for a base on balls and three hits to produce one run and load the bases against the Red Sox starting pitcher, Frank Sullivan—Stephens on first, Diering second, and Kryhoski third. Scheduled to bat next for the O's was left fielder Gil Coan, a left-handed batter. Boston's manager, Lou Boudreau, called on southpaw Leo Kiely to relieve Sullivan. The Baltimore manager, Jimmy Dykes, countered with righty-batting pinch hitter Sam Mele. Mele grounded a Kiely pitch to the shortstop, Milt Bolling, who fielded the ball and flipped it to Billy Consolo at second base for the force out of Stephens. Consolo then fired to Harry Agganis at first to nail Mele, completing a straightforward 6–4–3 GDP. Kryhoski scurried home while the twin killing was being executed. Diering, who had advanced to third, audaciously tried to follow, but Agganis alertly shot the ball to catcher Sammy White in time to nail him, completing an unexpected Instant Relief triple play. Who knows what the game's outcome would have been if Diering had held at third and the next hitter, Clint Courtney, had had a chance to swing the bat? After nine innings the game was deadlocked, 7–7, and the tie was not broken until Baltimore tallied the game-winner in the 17th! By then the maneuvering and the TP were pretty much forgotten.

The most recent game combining righty-lefty maneuvering and a first-batter triple play took place on August 16, 1988, at Busch Stadium in St. Louis, in a game between the Cardinals and the Houston Astros. The Red Birds led by a 3–0 score going into the top of the eighth inning with John Costello on the hill. Gerald Young singled and Bill Doran walked, putting runners at first and second. With the left-handed batting Terry Puhl coming up, Whitey Herzog summoned southpaw Ken Daley from the bullpen. Astros skipper Hal Lanier went to his bench, choosing the right-handed batting Jim Pankovits to pinch hit for Puhl. It took three pitches to resolve the confrontational maneuvering—with a 1–1 count, Pankovits hit a grounder to third baseman Terry Pendleton, who fielded the smash and stepped on the hot corner to force out Young. He then fired to second baseman Jose Oquendo, who, after forcing out Doran, relayed the ball to first baseman Mike Laga to retire the batter for a nifty around-the-horn triple play—an Instant-Relief TP that fully justified the LB/RP—> LB/LP—> RB/LP maneuvering from the Cards' perspective. Daley also set the 'Stros down 1-2-3 in the ninth to secure the 3–0 victory.

Instant Relief TPs Initiated by the Reliever
As indicated in Tables 3 (#29) and 4 (#32), two of the Instant-Relief TP pitchers had a direct hand in the execution of the triple play. The first came on August 8, 1990, at the Oakland-Alameda County Stadium with the Athletics hosting the Orioles. Going into the last of the seventh, Oakland trailed, 4–1. Mark Williamson, in relief of starter Ben McDonald, was on the mound for the O's. The first two batters for the A's, Terry Steinbach and Walt Weiss, coaxed walks from Williamson, putting runners on first and second and bringing the potential tying run to the plate, the right-handed batting Willie Randolph. Baltimore manager Frank Robinson, eschewing the standard righty-lefty stratagem, brought in southpaw Jeff Ballard to replace the righty Williamson. Oakland manager Tony LaRussa called for a hit-and-run and Randolph smashed Ballard's first pitch for a low liner right into the pitcher's glove. The hurler then wheeled around and threw to shortstop Cal Ripken, who was covering second, to catch Steinbach off the base. Ripken then threw the ball to first baseman Sam Horn to catch Weiss off first—a First-Batter-First-Pitch Instant-Relief Triple Play (1–6–3).

The other (most-recent) instant-relief triple play with the pitcher taking part in the three-ply wipeout came on July 13, 1995, at the Kingdome in Seattle. In the top of the ninth, the visiting Toronto Blue Jays, leading the Mariners by a 4–1 score, were trying to add some insurance runs. Shawn Green and Alex Gonzalez had smacked consecutive singles, putting runners at second and first, respectively. Seattle manager Lou Piniella decided that his starting pitcher, right-handed throwing Tim Belcher, had gone as far as he could; Piniella brought in Jeff Nelson, another righty, to face the left-handed batting Sandy Martinez. On Nelson's very first pitch, Martinez bunted the ball in the air between the plate and the mound. Nelson let the ball drop, then threw to second. There, shortstop Luis Sojo first tagged out Green and then grazed the bag with his foot for the force-out of Gonzalez, before throwing to second baseman Joey Cora, covering first, to retire the batter, completing a nifty 1–6–4 trifecta for Instant Relief.

Another Instant Relief triple play in which the relief pitcher was intimately (but not officially) involved was the one pulled in Cincinnati at Riverfront Stadium on April 6, 1978—Opening Day! The Reds were hosting the Astros and had a 9–5 lead going to the bottom of the seventh. Houston brought in a new pitcher, Tom Dixon, but he got hammered—Pete Rose walked, Ken Griffey singled, Joe Morgan doubled, driving in the two runners. Then George Foster singled, sending Morgan to third, and Astros manager Bill Virdon yanked Dixon. Joe Sambito then faced Dan Driessen.

They battled to a full count. Just before the payoff pitch, Sparky Anderson flashed the run sign to Foster. Sambito pitched the ball and Driessen struck out swinging. Astros catcher, Joe Ferguson—who got the credit for Driessen's out—then threw down to shortstop Roger Metzger, covering second, causing Foster to stop and retreat toward first. Morgan then danced off third, daring Metzger to try. Metzger succeeded: heaving the ball to hot corner man, Enos Cabell, who tagged Morgan for the second out. While Morgan was being eradicated, Foster again reversed his direction and headed back to second, but Cabell rifled the ball back to Metzger in time to nail Foster and complete the strikeout-initiated Instant Relief triple play: K–2*–6-5*–6*.

Afterward, Morgan said, "I know Sparky too well. I know he never sends the man with none out, only one out. So, I figured there was one out, and, well, I panicked. I figured I'd missed an out and got caught off third. Then, when they tagged me and threw to second, I thought, 'What are you doing, dummy? There's already three outs.' I didn't realize it was a triple play." "Don't blame me," was all Driessen had to say. Morgan added, "I thought when Danny struck out there were two outs. So when George got trapped between first and second, I panicked...started jockeying toward home figuring I try to score if I get the chance. It was the first time as a base runner I've ever been involved in a triple play. That's why I say I had to be stupid. I've got to give credit to Metzger, though, for some real quick thinking." Sparky Anderson also commented on the triple play: "I should get a hard kick in the tail for not thinking. That was really stupid of me giving Foster the sign to run in that situation."[9]

Time-Consuming Instant Relief TPs

As mentioned above, in only two of the forty instant-relief TPs in our list did the instant-relief pitcher have a direct hand in the execution. The other 38 TPs involved only infielders—except for one, which also included an outfielder—on July 1, 2014, at Dodger Stadium in an interleague game between the host NL Los Angeles nine and the visiting AL Cleveland club. As it turned out, this triple killing was also doubly challenging. At the start of the bottom of the fourth, the Dodgers were trailing, 5–2. But LA plated one run and had men on first and third (Yasiel Puig and Dee Strange-Gordon, both singled). There was no one out when the left-handed batting Adrian Gonzalez stepped into the batter's box. Cleveland manager Terry Francona felt it would be best to bring in a fresh arm; he summoned southpaw Kyle Crockett to replace righty Justin Masterson. The Los Angeles manager,

Don Mattingly, stuck with left-handed batting Gonzalez. On Crockett's fourth pitch (on a 1–2 count), Gonzalez belted the ball into left field.

Left fielder Michael Brantley ran in fast, a little toward the line (his glove side), and caught the ball at the letters and, with the assistance of his momentum, rifled a one-hop bullet to catcher Yan Gomes. Gordon had tried to score after tagging up after the catch and was a dead duck. Meanwhile, Puig also tagged up at first and made a dash to second. Gomes fired the ball down to keystoner Jason Kipnis who tagged Puig sliding headfirst into second. At first, umpire Paul Nauert called Puig safe. Francona immediately called for a challenge of the play at second, and after a 1-minute, 29 second replay review, the play on the field was reversed. Puig was called out, which should have officially completed the Instant-Relief TP... Except at that point Mattingly left the Los Angeles dugout to challenge the play at home, contending that Gordon was actually safe. After a replay review—which consumed an additional 1 minute, 34 seconds—the play on the field was upheld, thereby—finally—officially completing the Instant-Relief TP.

Because of the two challenges, that triple play took longer than what might be typically be termed "Instant." There has been, however, one—at least seemingly—longer Instant-Relief TP. On May 11, 2000, at Pro Player Stadium in Miami, the Florida Marlins were hosting Atlanta. Going into the bottom of the fifth, Florida was in front, 5–4. It looked like the Marlins would be able to increase their advantage when their first two batters got on base—Cliff Floyd walked and moved to second when Preston Wilson singled. That brought up number five hitter Mike Lowell, a right-handed batter, to face starting pitcher Kevin Millwood, also a righty.

Bobby Cox decided to go to his bullpen, calling in reliever Greg McMichael, another righty. McMichael's first pitch was called a ball. His next pitch was a strike, which Lowell looked at. McMichael's third pitch was another called ball. Pitch number four was another strike, which Lowell again only looked at. At 2–2, Lowell took the bat "off-his-shoulders" on the next pitch—and fouled it. The same result followed pitches six and seven—foul balls—keeping the count at 2–2. Lowell did not swing at McMichael's next pitch, which umpire Brian Gorman called a ball. With the count now full, Lowell swung at the ninth, 10th, and 11th pitches, but fouled each one off. Finally, on McMichael's twelfth pitch, Lowell hit the ball in fair territory—a grounder to third baseman Chipper Jones, who fielded the ball and stepped on third to force out Floyd.

Jones then threw the ball to second baseman Quilvio Veras, who stepped on second to force out Wilson. Veras then relayed the ball to Andres Galarraga at first to retire Lowell and complete the rapid around-the-horn triple play—an Instant-Relief TP, even though six minutes and fifty-five seconds were consumed from McMichael's first pitch to Lowell until the ball reached Galarraga.[10]

One-Pitch Instant Relief TPs

In stark contrast to the 12-pitch effort of McMichael, single pitch first-batter TPs have been thrown by at least 13 firemen—Mike Prendergast (1918), Allen Russell (1922), Bill Sherdel (1924), Ken Ash (1930), Don Nottebart (1967), Daryl Patterson (1969), Jack Aker (1972), Mike Marshall (1973), Dyar Miller (1977), Jeff Ballard (1990), Jeff Nelson (1995), Juan Rincon (2006), and Keiichi Yabu (2008). All but one of these relievers accomplished the feat with a 0-balls-0-strikes count on the batter. The lone exception was the one-pitch first-batter TP induced by Mike Marshall on June 13, 1973, at Jarry Park in Montreal. In a game between the host Expos and the visiting Padres, the home team was ahead, 3–1, when the top of the seventh session commenced. San Diego proceeded to load the bases against starting pitcher Balor Moore—Dwain Anderson led off and singled, Gene Locklear followed with a base on balls, and Enzo Hernadez then singled. That brought up Jerry Morales, a right-handed hitter. Moore fell behind by missing the plate with his first two pitches. With the count 2–0, Expos manager Gene Mauch gave Moore the hook and brought in Mike Marshall, a righty. Padres manager Don Zimmer chose to stick with Morales rather than go to his bench for a left-handed batting pinch hitter, such as Leron Lee or Dave Marshall. Zimmer said (later), "I know he [Marshall] has to throw a strike." As reported by Tim Burke of the *Montreal Gazette*, "Throw a strike Marshall did and Morales hit a capricious hopper slightly to [second baseman] Ron Hunt's right '[Umpire] Harry Wendelstedt obscured my view somewhat,' said Hunt. 'First I see it hopping high, and the next time I see it, it's along the ground.' He chuckled a little and then added, 'It got under my glove a little.'"[11] The baserunners were off and running. Anderson scored while Hunt was getting the ball to shortstop Tim Foli, covering the keystone to force Hernandez for out number one. Foli then relayed the ball to first baseman Mike Jorgensen to retire Morales for out number two. Meanwhile, Locklear reached third easily and Zimmer, coaching at the hot corner, waved him to keep running to the plate. Locklear stumbled a little and was nailed at

the pentagon on a peg from Jorgensen to catcher John Boccabella.

Even though fireman Marshall succeeded in hurling an Instant Relief TP pitch, a run did score while the triple massacre was being executed. That was the second instance of a base runner scoring on an Instant Relief TP; the first one, as described previously, was the one that Kiely achieved for the Red Sox against the Orioles in 1954. The only other time that a relief pitcher accomplished a first-batter triple play yet permitted a runner to score was in 2006, on May 27 at the Hubert H. Humphrey Metrodome in Minneapolis. In the top of the eighth frame, with the Twins leading the Mariners, 8–4, Seattle proceeded to load the bases with no one out on a Richie Sexson double, Carl Everett walk, and an Adrian Beltre single. In the batter's box stood Kenji Johjima, a right-handed batter. On the mound was Jesse Crain, a right-handed pitcher. Twins manager Ron Gardenhire sacked Crain, who had thrown just 16 pitches in facing only the three batters now on the sacks, replacing him with Juan Rincon, also a righty hurler. On Rincon's first pitch, Johjima grounded slowly to second baseman Luis Castillo, who scooped up the ball and first chased down Beltre and tagged him before throwing to Justin Morneau at first base, retiring Johjima for the second out. On the 4–3 double play Sexson scored easily and Everett advanced to third. Morneau saw that Everett had taken too wide a turn at the hot corner; he fired the ball across the diamond to third sacker Tony Batista, who applied the triple-play defining tag.

CONCLUDING REMARKS

In this article we have provided the interesting aspects and details for fifteen of the forty Instant Relief TPs listed in the SBK Triple Play Database. The nuts-and-bolts details for the other 25 Instant Relief TPs are given in the Notes accompanying Tables 1–4. With regard to the frequency of instant relief triple plays, they're moderately rare—just 5.4% of the 738 TPs in the SBK TP database. For comparison, there have been 23 perfect games, making up 7.2% of the 318 no-hit games recognized officially by Major League Baseball (excluding the Negro Leagues).[12] Of the 339 cycles noted in the MLB record books (likewise excluding the Negro Leagues), only 9 (2.7%) also featured a grand slam homer.[13]

To wrap up this article we would like to mention that several eventual Hall of Famers participated in Instant Relief triple plays. Those who were batters are George Sisler, Lloyd Waner, Roy Campanella, and Roberto Clemente. Each of them (except Campanella) was the first out as the result of a flyout; Campanella was the second out of a groundout 5–2–3–2 double play, the third out being an overly-aggressive baserunner. HOFers who were retired as baserunners in an Instant Relief TP are Sam Rice, Bucky Harris, Hack Wilson, Jackie Robinson, Orlando Cepeda, Luis Aparicio, and Joe Morgan. Of these, three were the TP-defining third out—Harris, Robinson, and Cepeda. There have not yet been any Instant Relief TP pitchers elected to Baseball's shrine in Cooperstown (although one relieved pitcher did earn a bronze plaque in the gallery—Dazzy Vance, who twice gave way to Instant Relief TP hurlers in 1933, first to Jim Mooney and second to Bill Walker). ■

ACKNOWLEDGMENTS

We should like to thank Cliff Blau for his eagle-eyed fact-checking as well as the following people for their insights and guidance in composing and reviewing this manuscript—Jeff Robbins, Gary Stone, Patrick Todgham. We also gratefully thank Steve Hirdt and Keith Costas for providing the elapsed time information for TP # 33.

DEDICATION

We respectfully dedicate this article to the memory of the late James A. "Snuffy" Smith, Jr., our friend and colleague. Jim generously shared his superb triple play research in collaborating with Herm and Steve to create the SBK Triple Play Database. Jim's quest to track triple plays originated in 1952 when he was stationed in Heilbronn, Germany—while listening to Armed Forces Radio, he heard the game in which Cleveland second baseman Bobby Avila could have turned an unassisted triple play (but, after snaring a liner to retire the batter and stepping on the keystone to get the runner off second, he chose to toss the ball to the first baseman to triple up the runner off first, instead of chasing down the runner who was halfway to second). We, and all baseball fans, are indebted to Jim for his devoted and meticulous efforts to research triple plays. Thanks so much, Jim. It was an honor for us to collaborate with you.

NOTES

1. James A. "Snuffy" Smith, Jr., deceased, 2010. See the Dedication.
2. Lou Smith, "Triple Play, Near-Perfect Pitching—Reds Win, 2–1," *Cincinnati Enquirer*, May 31, 1967 (33); see also: (a) Earl Lawson, *Cincinnati Post*, May 31, 1967 (31); (b) Neal Russo, "Triple Play, 7 Perfect Innings," *St. Louis Post-Dispatch*, May 31, 1967 (1G).
3. We have relied exclusively on the SBK TP database, rather than other online TP databases, such as the SABR TP Database, because we feel that the SBK TP database is more comprehensive—738 documented/verified TPs in the SBK TP database compared to 733 in the SABR TP database (i.e., excluding the TP included for the rained-out game on August 7, 1878)—and because we have hard-copy documentation from multiple newspaper accounts to support the details for each of the 738 TPs in the SBK TP database.
4. James Smith, "Memorial Stadium Triple Plays," *Baseball Quarterly Reviews*, Volume 6 (Number 3, Fall 1991), 142–51. See also: Herman Krabbenhoft and James A. Smith, Jr., "American League Triple Plays—The Facts and Records," *Baseball Quarterly Reviews*, Volume 9 (Number 2) 93–101 (Summer 1995); James A. Smith, Jr. and Herman Krabbenhoft, "Federal League Triple Plays," *Baseball Quarterly Reviews*, Volume 9 (Number 3) 171–75 (Fall 1995); Herman Krabbenhoft and James A. Smith, Jr., "19th Century NL Triple Plays—The Facts and Records," *Baseball Quarterly Reviews*, Volume 9 (Number 4) 237–42 (Winter 1995); James A. Smith, Jr. and Herman Krabbenhoft, "Players League Triple Plays," *Baseball Quarterly Reviews*, Volume 10 (Number 1, Spring 1996), 60–64; Herman Krabbenhoft and James A. Smith, Jr., "20th Century NL Triple Plays—The Facts and Records," *Baseball Quarterly Reviews*, Volume 10 (Number 2), 74–82; (f) Herman Krabbenhoft and James A. Smith, Jr., "American Association Triple Plays—The Facts and Records," *Baseball Quarterly Reviews*, Volume 10 (Number 3, Winter 1996), 143–47; (g) James A. Smith, Jr. and Herm Krabbenhoft, "Triple Play," *Baseball America*, April 14–27, 1997, 63.
5. James A. Smith, Jr. and Herm Krabbenhoft, "A Doubly Appealing Triple Play," *Baseball America*, November 10–23, 1997, 39.
6. Stephen D. Boren, James A. Smith, Jr., and Herm Krabbenhoft, "Who Made the Most Triple Plays?," *Baseball Research Journal*, Volume 32 (2004), 107–9.
7. Edward Prell, "Triple Play Helps Sox Beat Boston, 5–1…Fain Snares Liner for 2, Chico gets 3d…Trucks' 2d Pitch Ends Game," *Chicago Tribune*, August 30, 1953 (Part 2, page 1).
8. Jeff Blair, "Triple play gives Expos series sweep," *The* (Montreal) *Gazette*, September 9, 1991 (C3); see also: (a) Rob Parker, "Triple play snuffs out Reds' rally in 9th," *Cincinnati Enquirer*, September 9, 1991 (C1); (b) Jerry Crasnick, "Reds' new way to lose: hitting into triple play," *Cincinnati Post*, September 9, 1991 (1C).
9. Bob Hertzel, "Rain, Runs, Ridiculous: Reds Win Opener," *Cincinnati Enquirer*, April 7, 1978 (Section B 1). See also: Earl Lawson, *Cincinnati Post*, April 7, 1978; Hal McCoy, "Sparky fined for triple kill…Charges himself $25," *Dayton* (Ohio) *Daily News*, April 7, 1978 (36); Kenny Hand, "Astro debut fizzles 11–9 in Cincy rain," *Houston Post*, April 7, 1978 (1C).
10. This time information was obtained courtesy of Keith Costas of MLB Network. Timing the TP itself via looking at the YouTube video, the time of the TP from the last pitch to the ball reaching the first baseman's glove was about 4.7 seconds. The authors gratefully thank Steve Hirdt for his superb help and cooperation in acquiring this information.
11. Tim Burke, "The Jarry Juggernaut rolls right along," *The* (Montreal) *Gazette*, June 14, 1973 (33); see also: Chrys Goyens. "Triple play helps …Expos gaining on Cubs," *Ottawa Citizen*, June 14, 1973 (27).
12. "Official No-Hitters," Baseball-Almanac, https://www.baseball-almanac.com/pitching/official-no-hitters.shtml (accessed January 8, 2023).
13. "Hitting for the Cycle Records," Baseball-Almanac, https://www.baseball-almanac.com/feats/feats16d.shtml (accessed January 8, 2023).

APPENDIX. Details for the 40 Instant Relief Triple Plays (1876–2022)

Explanatory Notes for Tables 1–4

(A) The "I" column gives the inning.

(B) The "FT" column gives the Fielding Team; the "BT" column gives the Batting Team; an asterisk (*) indicates which team was the home team.

(C) In the "Batter" column, "PHa" indicates that the batter was a pinch hitter who was announced into the game before the relief pitcher was announced into the game; "PHb" indicates that the batter was a pinch hitter who was announced into the game after the relief pitcher was announced into the game.

(D) For the "Bases" column, a number (1, 2, or 3) indicates that the corresponding base was occupied; an "x" indicates that the base was not occupied.

(E) For the "Count" column, entries bracketed with asterisks indicate that the triple play ensued on the pitcher's first pitch; a cell with the "?–?" entry indicates that the count or pitch number has not yet been ascertained.

(F) For the "TP Sequence" column, "F" indicates that the triple play started with a flyout; "G" indicates that the triple play began with a groundout; "K" indicates that the triple play commenced with a strikeout; the numbers indicate the fielders who took part in the triple play; asterisks indicate which fielders made the putouts.

(G) The notes given beneath the Table provide the reference for the pertinent articles written or co-written by Smith as well as the identities of the base runners and fielders involved in the triple play.

Table 1. Instant Relief Triple Play Pitchers (1–10)

#	Year	Date	I	FT	Pitcher	BT	Batter	Bases	Count	TP Sequence
1	1891	5-26	9	BSN	Paul Radford	CIN *	Frank Dwyer	1-x-3	0-1	F-4*-2*-4*
2	1914	4-29	6	WAS	Doc Ayers	PHA *	Jack Barry	x-2-3	2-0	F-3*-5*-6*
3	1918	5-26	8	PHP	Mike Prendergast	CIN *	Lee Magee	1-2-x	* 0-0 *	F-6*/6*-3*
4	1922	8-05	1	PHA	Charlie Eckert	SLB *	George Sisler	1-2-x	0-2	F-6*-4*-3*
5	1922	8-11	9	BOS *	Allen Russell	WAS	Clyde Milan	1-2-x	* 0-0 *	G-2-5*-3*-5*
6	1923	7-19	9	PIT	Ray Steineder	BSN *	Stuffy McInnis	1-2-x	3-2	F-5*-4*-3*
7	1924	7-30	2	SLC	Bill Sherdel	PHP *	Johnny Mokan (PHb)	1-2-x	* 0-0 *	F-3*-6*-4*
8	1927	5-29 (2)	7	SLB *	Chet Falk	CLE	Dutch Levsen	1-2-3	?-?	G-5-2*-3*-2*
9	1930	7-27	6	CIN *	Ken Ash	CHC	Charlie Grimm	1-x-3	* 0-0 *	G-4-5-2*-3*-5*
10	1933	4-23 (1)	2	SLC *	Jim Mooney	PIT	Lloyd Waner	1-x-3	2nd	F-4*-5*-3*

1. Tom Davis, Dixie Tourangeau, Jim Smith, and Herm Krabbenhoft, "American Association Triple Plays in Cincinnati," *Baseball Quarterly Reviews*, Volume 10 (Number 2) 107–13 (Summer 1996): With Art Whitney on first and Jack Carney on third—OUT-1, Dwyer [Cub Stricker (4)]; OUT-2, Carney [Stricker (4) to Duke Farrell (2)]; OUT-3, Whitney [Farrell (2) to Stricker (4)].

2. James Smith and Herman Krabbenhoft, "Shibe Park Triple Plays," *Baseball Quarterly Reviews*, Volume 7 (Number 3) 159–69 (Fall 1992): With Amos Strunk on second and Stuffy McInnis on third— OUT 1, Barry [Chick Gandil (3)]; OUT-2, McInnis [Gandil (3) to Eddie Foster (5)]; OUT-3, Strunk [Foster (5) to George McBride (6)].

3. Thomas R. Davis and James Smith, "Triple Plays at Crosley-Redland Field," *Baseball Quarterly Reviews*, Volume 7 (Number 3) 149–58 (Fall 1992): With Heinie Groh on first and Rube Bressler on second— OUT-1, Lee Magee [Dave Bancroft (6)]; OUT-2, Bressler [Bancroft (6)]; OUT-3, Groh [Bancroft (6) to Fred Luderus (3)].

4. Keith Carlson, James A. Smith, Jr., and Herman Krabbenhoft, Sportsman's Park Triple Plays," *Baseball Quarterly Reviews*, Volume 8 (Number 3) 152–67 (Fall 1994): With Jack Tobin on first and Wally Gerber on second—OUT-1, Sisler [Chick Galloway (6)]; OUT-2, Gerber [Galloway (6) to Ralph Young (4)]; OUT-3, Tobin [Young (4) to Joe Hauser (3)].

5. James A. Smith, Jr., and Herman Krabbenhoft, "Fenway Park Triple Plays," *Baseball Quarterly Reviews*, Volume 8 (Number 2) 34–50 (Summer 1994): With Bucky Harris on first and Sam Rice on second— OUT-1, Rice [Muddy Ruel (2) to Pinky Pittinger (5)]; OUT-2, Milan [Pittinger (5) to George Burns (3)]; OUT-3, Harris [Burns (3) to Pittinger (5)].

6. Richard B. Tourangeau and James Smith, "Braves Field Triple Plays," *Baseball Quarterly Reviews*, Volume 7 (Number 3) 103–9 (Summer 1992): With Billy Southworth on first and Ray Powell on second—OUT-1, McInnis [Pie Traynor (5)]; OUT-2, Powell [Traynor (5) to Spencer Adams (4)]; OUT-3, Southworth [Adams (4) to Charlie Grimm (3)].

7. James A. Smith, Jr. and Herman Krabbenhoft, "Baker Bowl Triple Plays," *Baseball Quarterly Reviews*, Volume 8 (Number 4) 222–31 (Winter 1994): With George Harper on first and Jimmie Ring on second—OUT-1, Mokan (batting for George Harper) [Jim Bottomley (3)]; OUT-2, Ring [Bottomley (3) to Jimmy Cooney (6)]; OUT-3, Harper [Cooney (6) to Rogers Hornsby (4)].

8. Keith Carlson, James A. Smith, Jr., and Herman Krabbenhoft, "Sportsman's Park Triple Plays," *Baseball Quarterly Reviews*, Volume 8 (Number 3) 152–67 (Fall 1994): With Johnny Hodapp on first, Bernie Neis on second, and Glenn Myatt on third—OUT-1, Myatt [Otto Miller (5) to Leo Dixon (2)]; OUT-2, Levsen [Dixon (2) to George Sister (3)]; OUT-3, Neis [Sister (3) to Dixon (2)].

9. Thomas R. Davis and James Smith, "Triple Plays at Crosley-Redland Field," *Baseball Quarterly Reviews*, Volume 7 (Number 3) 149–58 (Fall 1992): With Danny Taylor on first and Hack Wilson on third—OUT-1, Wilson [Hod Ford (4) to Tony Cuccinello (5) to Clyde Sukeforth (2)]; OUT-2, Grimm [Sukeforth (2) to Joe Stripp (3)]; OUT-3, Taylor [Stripp (3) to Cuccinello (5)].

10. Keith Carlson, James A. Smith, Jr., and Herman Krabbenhoft, "Sportsman's Park Triple Plays," *Baseball Quarterly Reviews*, Volume 8 (Number 3) 152–67 (Fall 1994): With Heinie Meine on first and Earl Grace on third—OUT-1, Waner [Frankie Frisch (4)]; OUT-2, Grace [Frisch (4) to Pepper Martin (5)]; OUT-3, Meine [Martin (5) to Ripper Collins (3)].

Table 2. Instant Relief Triple Play Pitchers (11–20)

#	Year	Date	I	FT	Relief Pitcher	BT	Batter	Bases	Count	TP Sequence
11	1933	8-20 (1)	5	SLC	Bill Walker	BRK *	Joe Hutcheson	1-2-x	3-2	F-4*-3*-6*
12	1944	6-03	7	PIT	Ray Starr	NYG *	Johnny Rucker	1-2-x	1-2	F-4*-6*-3*
13	1947	8-23	8	SLC	Al Brazle	PHP *	Charlie Gilbert (PHa)	1-2-x	0-2	F-2*-6*-3*
14	1951	8-14	8	BOS	Walt Masterson	PHA *	Hank Majeski	1-2-3	1-1	F-4*/4*-3*
15	1953	8-29	9	CWS *	Virgil Trucks	BOS	Karl Olson	1-2-x	2-1	F-3*/3*-6*
16	1954	6-23	1	BOS	Leo Kiely	BAL *	Sam Mele (PHb)	1-2-3	?-?	G-6-4*-3*-2*
17	1955	6-12 (2)	7	CHC	John Andre	BRK *	Roy Campanella	1-2-3	2-1	G-5-2*-3*-2*
18	1963	7-21 (2)	3	CHC	Glen Hobbie	PIT *	Roberto Clemente	1-2-x	3-2	F-3*/3*-6*
19	1967	5-30	9	CIN *	Don Nottebart	SLC	Phil Gagliano	1-x-3	* 0-0 *	G-6-4*-3*-2*
20	1967	7-15	1	BOS *	Jose Santiago	BAL	Paul Blair	1-2-x	3-2	F-5*-4*-3*

11. James Smith, "Ebbets Field Triple Plays," *Baseball Quarterly Reviews*, Volume 6 (Number 4) 230–34 (Winter 1991): With Johnny Frederick on first and Jake Flowers on second—OUT-1, Hutcheson [Frankie Frisch (4)]; OUT-2, Frederick [Frisch (4) to Ripper Collins (3)]; OUT-3, Flowers [Collins (3) to Leo Durocher (6)].

12. James A. Smith, Jr. and Herman Krabbenhoft, "Triple Plays at the Polo Grounds," *Baseball Quarterly Reviews*, Volume 8 (Number 1) 34–50 (Spring 1994): With Charlie Mead on first and Buddy Kerr on second—OUT-1, Rucker [Frankie Gustine (4)]; OUT-2, Kerr [Gustine (4) to Frankie Zak (6)]; OUT-3, Mead [Zak (6) to Babe Dahlgren (3)].

13. James Smith and Herman Krabbenhoft, "Shibe Park Triple Plays," *Baseball Quarterly Reviews*, Volume 7 (Number 3) 159–69 (Fall 1992): With Lee Handley on first and Andy Seminick on second—OUT-1, Gilbert (batting for Al Lakeman) [Del Rice (2)]; OUT-2, Seminick [Rice (2) to Marty Marion (6)]; OUT-3, Handley [Marion (6) to Stan Musial (3)].

14. James Smith and Herman Krabbenhoft, "Shibe Park Triple Plays," *Baseball Quarterly Reviews*, Volume 7 (Number 3) 159–69 (Fall 1992): With Gus Zernial on first, Allie Clark on second, and Elmer Valo on third—OUT-1, Majeski [Billy Goodman (4)]; OUT-2, Clark [Goodman (4)]; OUT-3, Zernial [Goodman (4) to Walt Dropo (3)].

15. James Smith, "Comiskey Park Triple Plays," *Baseball Quarterly Reviews*, Volume 6 (Number 4) 219–29 (Winter 1991): With Al Zarilla on first and Floyd Baker on second—OUT-1, Olson [Ferris Fain (3)]; OUT-2, Zarilla [Fain (3)]; OUT-3, Baker [Fain (3) to Chico Carrasquel (6)].

16. James Smith, "Memorial Stadium Triple Plays," *Baseball Quarterly Reviews*, Volume 6 (Number 3) 142–51 (Fall 1991): With Vern Stephens on first, Chuck Diering on second, and Whitey Kurowski on third—OUT-1, Stephens [Milt Bolling (6) to Billy Console (4)]; OUT-3, Mele (batting for Gil Coan) [Consolo (4) to Harry Agganis (3)]; OUT-3, Diering [Agganis (3) to Sammy White (2)].

17. James Smith, "Ebbets Field Triple Plays," *Baseball Quarterly Reviews*, Volume 6 (Number 4) 230-234 (Winter 1991): With Carl Furillo on first, Jackie Robinson on second, and Sandy Amoros on third—OUT-1, Amoros [Randy Jackson (5) to Harry Chiti (2)]; OUT-2, Campanella [Chiti (2) to Dee Fondy (3)]; OUT-3, Robinson [Fondy (3) to Chiti (2)].

18. James Smith and Herman Krabbenhoft, "Forbes Field Triple Plays," *Baseball Quarterly Reviews*, Volume 7 (Number 1) 22–30 (Spring 1992): With Manny Mota on first and Dick Schofield on second—OUT-1, Clemente [Merritt Ranew (3)]; OUT-2, Mota [Ranew (3)]; OUT-3, Schofield [Ranew (3) to Andre Rodgers (6)].

19. Thomas R. Davis and James Smith, "Triple Plays at Crosley-Redland Field," *Baseball Quarterly Reviews*, Volume 7 (Number 3) 149–58 (Fall 1992): With Tim McCarver on first and Orlando Cepeda on third—OUT-1, McCarver [Leo Cardenas (6) to Tommy Helms (4)]; OUT-2, Gagliano [Helms (4) to Deron Johnson (3)]; OUT-3, Cepeda [Johnson (3) to Johnny Edwards (2)].

20. James A. Smith, Jr., and Herman Krabbenhoft, "Fenway Park Triple Plays," *Baseball Quarterly Reviews*, Volume 8 (Number 2) 34–50 (Summer 1994): With Russ Snyder on first and Luis Aparicio on second—OUT-1, Blair [Joe Foy (5)]; OUT-2, Aparicio [Foy (5) to Mike Andrews (4)]; OUT-3, Snyder [Andrews (4) to George Scott (3)].

Table 3. Instant Relief Triple Play Pitchers (21–30)

#	Year	Date	I	FT	Relief Pitcher	BT	Batter	Bases	Count	TP Sequence
21	1968	9-10	5	MIN *	Bob Miller	CLE	Tony Horton	1-2-x	1-0	G-5*-4*-3*
22	1969	7-15	5	DET	Daryl Patterson	WAS *	Ed Brinkman	1-2-x	* 0-0 *	G- 5*-4*-3*
23	1970	6-26	5	CAL	Steve Kealey	KCR *	Amos Otis	1-2-x	2-2	G-5*-4*-3*
24	1972	7-02	7	CHC	Jack Aker	PIT *	Manny Sanguillen	1-2-x	* 0-0 *	G-5*-4*-3*
25	1973	6-13	7	MON *	Mike Marshall	SDP	Jerry Morales	1-2-3	* 2-0 *	G-4-6*-3*-2*
26	1977	7-14	5	CAL *	Dyar Miller	SEA	Lee Stanton	1-2-x	* 0-0 *	G-5*-4*-3*
27	1978	4-06	7	HOU	Joe Sambito	CIN *	Dan Driessen	1-x-3	3-2	K-2*-6-5*-6*
28	1988	8-16	8	SLC *	Ken Dayley	HOU	Jim Pankovits (PHb)	1-2-x	1-1	G-5*-4*-3*
29	1990	8-08	7	BAL	Jeff Ballard	OAK *	Willie Randolph	1-2-x	* 0-0 *	F-1*-6*-3*
30	1991	9-08	9	MON *	Barry Jones	CIN	Chris Sabo	1-2-x	1-0	G-5*-4*-3*

21. James A. Smith, Jr. and Herman Krabbenhoft, "Major League Triple Plays in Minnesota," *Baseball Quarterly Reviews*, Volume 9 (Number 2) 68–71 (Summer 1995): With Joe Azcue on first and Richie Scheinblum on second—OUT-1, Scheinblum [Rich Rollins (5)]; OUT-2, Azcue [Rollins (5) to Rod Carew (4)]; Horton [Carew (4) to Bob Allison (3)].

22. James A. Smith, Jr. and Herman Krabbenhoft, "Triple Plays at Washington's Robert F. Kennedy Stadium," *Baseball Quarterly Reviews*, Volume 9 (Number 2) 6–67: With Barry Moore on first and Paul Casanova on second—OUT-1, Casanova [Don Wert (5)]; OUT-2, Moore [Wert (5) to Ike Brown (4)]; OUT-3, Brinkman [Brown (4) to Bill Freehan (3)].

23. James Smith and Herman Krabbenhoft, "Municipal Stadium Triple Plays," *Baseball Quarterly Reviews*, Volume 7 (Number 4) 227–28 (Winter 1992): With Cookie Rojas on first and Paul Schaal on second—OUT-1, Schaal [Chico Ruiz (5)]; OUT-2, Rojas [Ruiz (5) to Sandy Alomar (4)]; OUT-3, Otis [Alomar (4) to Billy Cowan (3)].

24. James A. Smith, Jr. and Herman Krabbenhoft, "National League Triple Plays at Pittsburgh's Three Rivers Stadium," *Baseball Quarterly Reviews*, Volume 10 (Number 1) 22–25 (Spring 1996): With Al Oliver on first and Jackie Hernandez on second—OUT-1, Hernandez [Ron Santo (5)]; OUT-2, Oliver [Santo (5) to Glenn Beckert (4)]; OUT-3, Sanguillen [Beckert (4) to Jim Hickman (3)].

25. James A. Smith, Jr. and Herman Krabbenhoft, "NL Triple Plays in Montreal," *Baseball Quarterly Reviews*, Volume 10 (Number 1) 9–12 (Spring 1996): With Enzo Hernandez on first, Gene Locklear on second, and Dwain Anderson on third—OUT-1, Hernandez [Ron Hunt (4) to Tim Foli (6)]; OUT-2, Morales [Foli (6) to Mike Jorgensen (3)]; Locklear [Jorgensen (3) to John Boccabella (2)].

26. James A. Smith and Herman Krabbenhoft, "Triple Plays at Anaheim Stadium—Home of the California Angels," *Baseball Quarterly Reviews*, Volume 9 (Number 2) 85–87 (Summer 1995): With Bill Stein on first and Dave Collins on second—OUT-1, Collins [Ron Jackson (5)]; OUT-2, Stein [Jackson (5) to Jerry Remy (4)]; OUT-3, Stanton [Remy (4) to Tony Solaita (3)].

27. James A. Smith, Jr. and Herman Krabbenhoft, "National League Triple Plays at Cincinnati's Riverfront Stadium," *Baseball Quarterly Reviews*, Volume 10 (Number 2) 70–72 (Summer 1996): With George Foster on first and Joe Morgan on third—OUT-1, Driessen [Joe Ferguson (2)]; OUT-2, Morgan [Ferguson (2) to Roger Metzger (6) to Enos Cabell (5)]; Foster [Cabell (5) to Metzger (6)].

28. James A. Smith, Jr. and Herman Krabbenhoft, "National League Triple Plays at Busch Stadium in St. Louis," *Baseball Quarterly Reviews*, Volume 10 (Number 2) 65–69 (Summer 1996): With Bill Doran on first and Gerald Young on second—OUT-1, Young [Terry Pendleton (5)]; OUT-2, Doran [Pendleton (5) to Jose Oquendo (4)]; OUT-3, Pankovits [Oquendo (4) to Mike Laga (3)].

29. James A. Smith, Jr. and Herman Krabbenhoft, "Triple Plays in Oakland's Coliseum," *Baseball Quarterly Reviews*, Volume 9 (Number 2) 72–75 (Summer 1995): With Walt Weiss on first and Terry Steinbach on second—OUT-1, Randolph [Ballard (1)]; OUT-2, Steinbach [Ballard (1) to Cal Ripken, Jr. (6)]; OUT-3 Ripken (6) to Sam Horn (3)].

30. James A. Smith, Jr. and Herman Krabbenhoft, "NL Triple Plays in Montreal," *Baseball Quarterly Reviews*, Volume 10 (Number 1) 9–12 (Spring 1996): With Eric Davis on first and Hal Morris on second—OUT-1, Morris [Bret Barberie (5)]; OUT-3, Davis [Barberie (5) to Delino DeShields (4)]; OUT-3, Sabo [DeShields (4) to Andres Galarraga (3)].

Table 4. Instant Relief Triple Play Pitchers (31–40)

#	Year	Date	I	FT	Relief Pitcher	BT	Batter	Bases	Count	TP Sequence
31	1992	7-03	5	DET *	Walt Terrell	SEA	Omar Vizquel	1-x-3	1-0	F-5*/5*-3*
32	1995	7-13	5	SEA *	Jeff Nelson	TOR	Sandy Martinez	1-2-x	* 0-0 *	G-1-6*/6*-4*
33	2000	5-11	5	ATL	Greg McMichael	FLA *	Mike Lowell	1-2-x	3-2	G-5*-4*-3*
34	2006	5-27	8	MIN *	Juan Rincon	SEA	Kenji Johjima	1-2-3	* 0-0 *	G-4*-3*-5*
35	2007	8-27	7	CLE *	Rafael Perez	MIN	Mike Redmond	1-2-x	0-2	G-5*-4*-3*
36	2008	5-30	8	SFG *	Keiichi Yabu	SDP	Kevin Kouzmanoff	1-2-x	* 0-0 *	G-5*-4*-3*
37	2014	7-01	4	CLE	Kyle Crockett	LAD *	Adrian Gonzalez	1-x-3	1-2	F-7*-2*-4*
38	2016	7-29	8	WSN	Sammy Solis	SFG *	Brandon Crawford	1-2-3	0-1	F-3*/3*-5*
39	2017	9-08	6	DET	Drew VerHagen	TOR *	Kevin Pillar	1-2-x	1-0	G-5*-4*-3*
40	2020	7-29	7	CHC	Duane Underwood	CIN *	Shogo Akiyama	1-2-3	0-2	F-5*/5*-3*

31. Ronald Kabacinski and James Smith, "Triple Plays at Navin Field, Briggs Stadium, and Tiger Stadium," *Baseball Quarterly Reviews*, Volume 7 (Number 1) 12–21 (Spring 1992) and (Number 4) 253 (Winter 1992): With Harold Reynolds on first and Dave Valle on third—OUT-1, Vizquel [Skeeter Barnes (5)]; OUT-2, Valle [Barnes (5)]; OUT-3, Reynolds [Barnes (5) to Cecil Fielder (3)].

32. "1995 American League Triple Plays," *The 1996 BQR Yearbook*, 74: With Alex Gonzalez on first and Shawn Green on second—OUT-1, Green [Nelson (1) to Luis Sojo (6)]; OUT-2, Gonzalez [Sojo (6)]; OUT-3, Martinez [Sojo (6) to Joey Cora (4)].

33. SBK Triple Play Database: With Preston Wilson on first and Cliff Floyd on second—OUT-1, Floyd [Chipper Jones (5)]; OUT-2, Wilson [Jones (5) to Quilvio Veras (4)]; OUT-3, Lowell [Veras (4) to Andres Galarraga (3)].

34. SBK Triple Play Database: With Adrian Beltre on first, Carl Everett on second, and Richie Sexson on third—OUT-1, Beltre [Luis Castillo (4)]; OUT-2, Johjima [Castillo (4) to Justin Morneau (3)]; OUT-3, Everett [Morneau (3) to Tony Batista (5)].

35. SBK Triple Play Database: With Jason Kubel on first and Michael Cuddyer on second—OUT-1, Cuddyer [Casey Blake (5)]; OUT-2, Kubel [Blake (5) to Asdrubal Cabrera (4)]; OUT-3, Redmond [Cabrera (4) to Victor Martinez (3)].

36. SBK Triple Play Database: With Adrian Gonzalez on first and Brian Giles on second—OUT-1, Giles [Jose Castillo (5)]; OUT-2, Gonzalez [Castillo (5) to Ray Durham (4)]; OUT-3, Kouzmanoff [Durham (4) to John Bowker (3)].

37. SBK Triple Play Database: With Yasiel Puig on first and Dee Strange-Gordon on third base—OUT-1, Gonzalez [Michael Brantley (7)]; OUT-2, Strange-Gordon [Brantley (7) to Yan Gomes (2)]; OUT-3 Puig [Gomes (2) to Jason Kipnis (4)].

38. SBK Triple Play Database: With Buster Posey on first, Angel Pagan on second, and Denard Span on third—OUT-1, Crawford [Ryan Zimmerman (3)]; OUT-2, Posey [Zimmerman (3)]; OUT-3, Span [Zimmerman (3) to Anthony Rendon (5)].

39. SBK Triple Play Database: With Kendrys Morales on first and Justin Smoak on second—OUT-1, Smoak [Jeimer Candelario (5)]; OUT-2, Morales [Candelario (5) to Ian Kinsler (4)]; OUT-3, Pillar [Kinsler (4) to Efren Navarro (3)].

40. SBK Triple Play Database: With Tucker Barnhart on first, Freddy Galvis on second, and Nick Senzel on third—OUT-1, Akiyama [Kris Bryant (5)]; OUT-2, Senzel [Bryant (5)]; OUT-3, Barnhart [Bryant (5) to Anthony Rizzo (3)].

Celebrating the Nons

Many "Unofficial" No-Hitters More Fascinating than the "Real" Ones

Stew Thornley

As we are told by the good-hair talking heads on 24-hour sports networks—as well as by any newspaper, electronic fish wrap, podcast, or blog—the 2021 season featured nine no-hitters. But in 11 games a team was held hitless. Why the discrepancy? Two of those games were seven-inning games, and a 1991 committee had declared that for a no-hitter to be "official," it had to contain at least nine hitless innings. An inexplicably strict adherence to this concept is why the lesser number, nine, is usually cited by media members and fans.

This article will cover the various ways these now "non-official" no-hitters have been treated in the past while looking at a number of interesting no-hit games that have been relegated to lesser status.

1991 COMMITTEE ON STATISTICAL ACCURACY

In August 1991, Commissioner Fay Vincent announced the formation of a "committee on statistical accuracy"[1] to settle the issue of whether Roger Maris and Babe Ruth should share the single-season record for home runs. Ruth had commonly been listed as the record holder for a 154-game season and Maris for 162 games. Vincent was influenced by a lengthy Roger Angell article in the May 27, 1991, issue of *The New Yorker* which included this passage:

> There is no wish here to revive the shoutings and buzzings that accompanied the Maris achievement thirty years back, but I think the present commissioner and some brave committee should meet one of these days and quietly wield an eraser, instead of waiting for some young slugger to come along and do it for them with his bat.[2]

Vincent said he told his deputy, Steve Greenberg, "I think Roger [Angell] is right." Vincent added in a 2022 telephone interview, "We couldn't have two sets of records. It was an embarrassment. It smacked of Ford Frick determining that Roger Maris was a poor successor to Ruth."[3]

The committee proclamation the following month of Maris being the sole record holder was well-received. It was offset by an uproar over a concomitant announcement: an "official" definition of a no-hitter as being games of nine innings or more that ended with no hits.[4] The decree lopped from the list those games in which a team was held hitless but came up short of nine innings for the no-hit pitcher. Such games had been truncated for reasons such as darkness, rain, and mutual agreement.

Two no-hitters dropped from the "official list" were ones in which the hitless team did not have to bat in the last of the ninth because it had already won the game. Silver King had done this in 1890: holding Brooklyn hitless but losing the game while pitching for Chicago in the Players' League. Few fans may have been aware of the King game, but most were familiar with a no-hitter pitched by the Yankees' Andy Hawkins July 1, 1990, in Chicago. The game, but not the no-hitter, had blown up in the last of the eighth when the White Sox scored four runs on two walks and three errors. The game made a bigger splash than most no-hitters, leading both news and sports broadcasts that evening and being the top headlines in newspapers the next morning.[5]

Vincent wasn't shy about what he saw as excessive excitement over Hawkins's no-hitter: "I thought it was silly—a reaction by a lot of people who didn't know much about baseball. Within historical context, it was beyond the baseball knowledge of a lot of people, not enough understanding of the history of how many get broken up. The ninth inning is a graveyard for no-hitters."[6]

In recalling the committee activities more than 30 years later, Vincent emphasized he didn't remember much and speculated that "people on the committee may have brought up the no-hitters." Eminent baseball historian David Voigt was a member of the committee.[7] A family friend of Voigt's recalls him having a different recollection. Steve Ferenchick said he once asked Voigt if he thought it was fair to take away so many no-hitters. "I still remember him grimacing

NATIONAL BASEBALL HALL OF FAME LIBRARY, COOPERSTOWN, NY

On May 26, 1959, Harvey Haddix pitched 12 perfect innings, only to lose both the no-hitter and the game in the unlucky 13th.

and saying something like, 'No. We discussed it and a lot of us had the same view I did, that those no-hitters shouldn't be removed from the books. But Fay Vincent came in with his opinion, and the rest of us were basically brought in to rubberstamp it. I wouldn't have changed the rule there but it was his call, not mine.'"[8]

While the Hawkins no-hitter received oversized attention that still resonates, three subsequent no-hitters of this type (full games but with the hitless team not batting in the ninth) have been treated as footnotes: Matt Young of Boston April 12, 1992; Jered Weaver and Jose Arredondo of Anaheim June 28, 2008; and Hunter Greene and Art Warren of Cincinnati May 15, 2022.

PREVIOUS TREATMENT OF NO-HITTERS

Contrary to some reports, no "official" definition of a no-hitter existed before 1991, not that one was needed. *The Sporting News*, in its record books (*One for the Book* and later *The Official Baseball Record Book*) listed all regulation games in which a team was held hitless. The lists included the many times a team was held hitless for fewer than nine innings, and readers in those days were deemed discerning enough to ascribe their opinions to them. Today, people seem to be overly deferential to the 1991 committee definition.

In addition, the *TSN* record books listed all games in which a team was held hitless for at least the first nine innings but got a hit or hits in extra innings. Of course, these really aren't no-hitters; on the other hand,

how many games are more notable than Harvey Haddix pitching 12 innings before having his perfect game and then no-hitter broken up in the 13th?[9]

Not as impressive but still noteworthy is Harry McIntire of Brooklyn having a no-hitter for $10\frac{2}{3}$ innings before giving up a single to Claude Ritchey of Pittsburgh on August 1, 1906. McIntire gave up three more hits and lost the game in 13 innings. A number of pitchers have had a no-hitter through 10 innings, with most of them winning the game at that point. Sam Kimber of Brooklyn did it against Toledo October 4, 1884. George "Hooks" Wiltse of the New York Giants had a perfect game versus Philadelphia July 4, 1908, before hitting a batter; he still completed a 10-inning no-hitter. Cincinnati's Fred Toney's 10-inning no-hitter against Chicago on May 2, 1917, stands out because the opposing pitcher, Jim "Hippo" Vaughn, had held the Reds hitless for the first nine innings. In addition, two pitchers—Francisco Cordova and Ricardo Rincon of Pittsburgh—combined for a 10-inning no-hitter on July 12, 1997, against Houston.

Jim Maloney won a 10-inning no-hitter for Cincinnati at Chicago August 19, 1965; earlier in the season he had also pitched 10 hitless innings before giving up a home run in the 11th inning to Johnny Lewis of New York on June 14 (a game in which Maloney struck out 18 batters). Maloney remains the only pitcher to twice pitch hitless ball over the first 10 innings of a game. Maloney got more support from the Reds in his next no-hitter, a 10–0 win over Houston April 30, 1969. How many no-hitters did Maloney have to this point in his career? In their game stories, the *Cincinnati Enquirer*, *Dayton Daily News*, and *St. Louis Post-Dispatch* referred to Maloney's no-hitter being his third. Jim Ferguson, for the Dayton paper, wrote, "...Maloney was on his way to the record books as one of only five men in the history of baseball to hurl as many as three no-hitters. Sandy Koufax is alone with four such games while Maloney joins Cy Young, Bob Feller and Larry Corcoran, a name from the 1880s, with three." On the other hand, United Press International reporter Vito Sellino labeled the gem as Maloney's second.[10]

So no-hitters were counted by however one wanted to count them.

NOTABLE NONS

Of the true no-hitters of fewer than nine innings, some are distinctive. They fall into several categories determined by several factors, sometimes unique circumstance and sometimes by the attempts of various teams or leagues to cope.

Played to Natural Conclusions

As for games that truly were no-hitters, but fewer than nine innings, some were not shortened but were played to their natural conclusion. The no-hitters by King, Hawkins, Weaver/Arredondo, and Greene/Warren were nine innings although the hitless team batted in only eight of those.

During the period when doubleheaders were scheduled for seven innings under "COVID rules" in 2020 and 2021, two no-hitters took place: Madison Bumgarner of Arizona no-hit Atlanta on April 25, 2021, and Collin McHugh, Josh Fleming, Diego Castillo, Matt Wisler, and Pete Fairbanks of Tampa Bay held Cleveland hitless on July 7, 2021. Both of these occurred in the second games of seven-inning doubleheaders.[11]

In addition, some no-hitters happened in games that, by mutual agreement of the teams, were scheduled for fewer than nine innings. Fred Shaw of Providence did it at Buffalo in the first game of a doubleheader on October 7, 1885; "By mutual consent the clubs played only the innings needed to make a record, and the players, umpire, reporters, and the dozen spectators were glad when the two hours in the cold were ended," wrote the *Buffalo Express*. Jake Weimer of Cincinnati no-hit Brooklyn on August 24, 1906, and won in the last of the seventh when the Reds scored; the second game of a doubleheader, it was scheduled for seven innings by pre-agreement. Howie Camnitz of Pittsburgh held New York hitless on August 23, 1907, in the second game of a doubleheader, scheduled for five innings by agreement of both managers.[12]

Ed Karger of the St. Louis Cardinals pitched a perfect game of seven innings August 11, 1907; the second game of a doubleheader, it was set for seven innings by a prior mutual agreement of St. Louis and Boston.[13]

Resurrection

On June 12, 1959, Mike McCormick of San Francisco carried a no-hitter into the last of the sixth at Philadelphia. After walking two batters, McCormick gave up a single to Richie Ashburn to load the bases. With Gene Freese next up, time was called because of rain, and eventually the game was called. Because it was an uncompleted inning, the game reverted to the last full inning, San Francisco winning 3–0 and McCormick getting his no-hitter back. (A 1962 rule change called for the reversion to occur only if what happened in the top of an uncompleted inning affected the outcome of the game; in 1980, the rules changed to eliminate any reversions by making these suspended games.)[14]

A no-hitter by Jimmy Dygert and Rube Waddell of the Philadelphia Athletics on August 29, 1906, may have been resurrected in similar fashion to McCormick's although it is unclear if a play in the third inning of the game was called a hit or an error. Dygert pitched the first three innings with Chicago's Ed Hahn reaching base in the third when third baseman John Knight fumbled his bunt. Newspaper accounts and box scores differed on if it had been called a hit or error. Waddell relieved Dygert in the fourth—and gave up a run without a hit[15]—and then pitched a hitless fifth. Chicago rallied in the top of the sixth and scored two runs to take a 5–4 lead with a walk, error, and singles by Jiggs Donahue and Billy Sullivan. However, with the Athletics batting in the last of the sixth, the game was called by rain and reverted to the bottom of the fifth, wiping out two White Sox runs and hits.

Uncertainty over the status of the scoring decision on Hahn's third-inning bunt lingered. The game was listed among the no-hitters in *The Sporting News Official Baseball Record Book* of 1974, but by the 1977 edition of the book, it had been removed.

Another disputed no-hitter, also involving Waddell, was on August 15, 1905, when the Athletics beat St. Louis, 2–0, in a game called by rain after five innings. Morning newspapers in St. Louis and Philadelphia noted one hit for St. Louis, the result of Waddell slipping while fielding a grounder, but by the afternoon editions, the hit had been removed from the box scores.

Howie Camnitz of Pittsburgh held New York hitless on August 23, 1907, in a game that both managers had agreed would only be five innings.

First Win for a Forgotten Team

Minnesota's first major-league team—an 1884 St. Paul squad that was one of the last survivors of the minor-league Northwestern League, finishing its season in the now-recognized-as-major Union Association—is an unremarkable story. The nine games it played were all on the road, and St. Paul lost its first four. It played in St. Louis October 5. Charlie Sweeney struck out six St. Paul batters in the first two innings before switching spots with left fielder Henry Boyle. The fielders did well on the slippery grounds except for the fourth inning, when St. Louis made two errors to allow St. Paul to score a run. Heavy rain came down after the fifth inning, causing a delay. The rain stopped but umpire Harry McCaffery deemed the field too wet to play and called the game. St. Paul had a 1–0 win in a game in which it did not tally a hit.[16]

Debuts

Cincinnati's Bumpus Jones, in his first major-league game, no-hit Pittsburg October 15, 1892, and is often credited as the only pitcher to hurl a no-hitter in his debut.[17] However, he was pre-dated in this feat by George Nicol of St. Louis in the American Association. On September 23, 1890, Nicol beat a reorganized and hapless Athletic team of Philadelphia following an en masse resignation of Athletic players a week before when the team couldn't meet its payroll. With the score 21–2 for St. Louis and darkness setting in, the game was stopped after seven innings.

Leon "Red" Ames of the New York Giants pitched his first game in the majors on September 14, 1903, and held St. Louis hitless in the second game of a double-header, which was called after five innings either by darkness or threatening weather, depending on which St. Louis newspaper you choose to rely on.[18]

Last by Darkness

The last game called—not suspended—by darkness was at Wrigley Field September 8, 1985.[19] The last no-hitter stopped by darkness, rather than weather, was the second game of a doubleheader at Braves Field June 22, 1944. Boston's Jim Tobin held Philadelphia hitless over five innings before it was too late to continue under existing light.

OTHER "NON" TIDBITS

In a Montreal at San Diego game June 3, 1995, Pedro Martinez became the only pitcher to have a chance to complete an extra-inning perfect game. Unlike Harvey Haddix—who perpetually knew he would have to keep laboring for at least two more innings for a perfect game—Martinez took the mound with a lead in the last of the 10th. However, he gave up a leadoff double to Bip Roberts before being relieved by Mel Rojas, who retired the final three batters.

Tom Hughes of New York was credited as a no-hit pitcher who gave up the most runs when he lost, 5–0 to Cleveland in the second game of a doubleheader August 30, 1910.[20] However, this was recognized among lists of no-hitters only because he had pitched nine hitless innings before giving up a hit in the 10th and six more in the 11th. Among true no-hit pitchers, Andy Hawkins gave up the most runs in his 4–0 loss to the White Sox July 1, 1990.

CONCLUSION

As luminaries ranging from Leonard Koppett to Dave Smith have stated, "official" means nothing more than "of the office." It does not necessarily mean correct. It doesn't mean that fans, researchers, and historians have to accept Ty Cobb's "official" career-hit total as 4,191 or that he had a higher batting average than Napoleon Lajoie in 1910 or that the historical records of the 1901–60 Washington American League team belong to the 1961–71 Washington Senators.[21] And it certainly does not require the delusion that a regulation game in which a team is held hitless is not a no-hitter.[22]

Vincent acknowledged the controversy over the decision on no-hitters but wasn't fazed by it. He said that he and Bart Giamatti, his predecessor as commissioner, had a philosophy: "Those are the issues that make baseball great, issues that aren't life and death but that generate disagreement and discussion." ∎

Author's Note

Repetitious as they are, the quotation marks around "official" are used intentionally. If readers interpret this overuse as a sign of the author's disdain for an "official" definition, they are invited to make such an inference.

The author appreciates the help of many SABR members, including John Thorn, Scott Merzbach, Steve Ferenchick, Bob Komoroski, Dave Lande, and Steve Gietschier.

Fay Vincent and/or his committee attempted to de-officialize many no-hitters; fortunately several sources still list them. One of the best is Dirk Lammers's site, nonohitters.com. In addition to all the "official" no-hitters listed for the White and integrated leagues (with more coming from Negro Leagues from 1920 to 1948), the site has the so-called "non" no-hitters as well as no-hitters from around the world and no-hitters from the All-American Girls Professional Base Ball League.

Notes

1. Jim Donaghy, Associated Press, "Extra Inning," September 5, 1991, https://apnews.com/article/9a48ac96f06749fa10d0a8d97f2fc8df.
2. Roger Angell, "The Sporting Scene: Homeric Tales" *The New Yorker*, May 27, 1991: 69.
3. Author telephone interview with Fay Vincent, July 18, 2022.
4. Steve Gietschier, "Year in Review: Two Record-Keeping Revisions," *The Sporting News Official Baseball Guide*, 1991: 169, and Donaghy, "Extra Inning," Associated Press, September 5, 1991, https://apnews.com/article/9a48ac96f06749fa10d0a8d97f2fc8df. Gietschier's piece covered the home-run record and the no-hitter definition. Donaghy did not even mention the issue of the record for home runs, even though this had been the focus of news when the committee was announced. Regardless of the committee's decision, in the ensuing years *The Sporting News Complete Baseball Record Book* continued to list the single-season records for home runs for both a 154-game and 162-game season as well as listing all types of no-hitters, including the "non-official" ones.
5. The no-hitter was at the top of the front page—the front page of the entire newspaper, not the sports page—in *USA Today* on July 2, 1990.
6. Interview with Vincent, July 18, 2022. Vincent is correct that many no-hitters get broken up in the ninth. Since 1961, approximately 48 percent of no-hit games carried into the ninth inning have been broken up in the ninth. https://milkeespress.com/lostninth.html.
7. In addition to Vincent and Voigt, then a professor of sociology at Albright College in Reading, Pennsylvania, the other committee members were Rich Levin, director of public relations for the commissioner's office; Michael Bernstein, manager of publishing of Major League Baseball Properties; Seymour Siwoff, general manager of the Elias Sports Bureau; Jack Lang, executive secretary of the Baseball Writer's Association of America; Joe Durso, reporter for *The New York Times*; and George Kirsch, professor of history at Manhattan College in New York.
8. Submission from Steve Ferenchick on sabr-l, the SABR listserv, June 25, 2022.
9. A typically inane exchange between Archie and Meathead on *All in the Family* (Season 3, Episode 17—Archie Goes Too Far, https://www.youtube.com/watch?v=D3mesNGrPcE) centers on whether Haddix did or did not pitch a perfect game. With 25 cents at stake, the pair never resolved the bet.
10. Bob Hertzel, "Maloney Throws No-Hitter!,'" *Cincinnati Enquirer*, May 1, 1969: 61; Jim Ferguson, "Chaney's Fielding Gem Helps Maloney," *Dayton Daily News*, May 1, 1969: 22; "Maloney Takes Casual Approach to No-Hitter," *St. Louis Post-Dispatch* (reference to third no-hitter in caption for UPI Telephoto), May 1, 1969: 1E. Vito Stellino, "Cincinnati's Jim Maloney No-Hits Astros," (UPI), *Raleigh Register* (Beckley, West Virginia), May 1, 1969: 12.
11. Although the *Official Baseball Rules* define a "double-header" as "two regularly scheduled or rescheduled games, played in immediate succession," the term doubleheader is common parlance for two games in the same day and is used here, even though Bumgarner's no-hitter was in the second game of a day-night twinbill.
12. "Good-By Baseball," *Buffalo Express*, October 8, 1885: 2; "All Out Easy," *Cincinnati Post*, August 25, 1906: 6; "Two Wins Put Pirates Back in Second Place," *Pittsburgh Post*, August 24, 1907: 6. Another no-hitter, by Jack Stivetts of Boston versus Washington on October 15, 1892, was called by mutual agreement after five innings to allow Boston to catch a train; however, this was not a pre-game agreement for a set number of innings. King Cole of the Chicago Cubs pitched a truncated no-hitter at St. Louis July 31, 1910, in a game called by a predetermined end time (not a predetermined innings limit) to allow both teams to catch a train to New York.
13. Three other pitchers have perfect games of fewer than nine innings: Rube Vickers of the Philadelphia Athletics versus Washington October 5, 1907 (second game of doubleheader), called by darkness after five innings; Dean Chance of Minnesota versus Boston August 6, 1967,
    called by rain in the last of the fifth; and David Palmer of Montreal versus St. Louis April 21, 1984 (second game of doubleheader), called by rain after five innings.
14. San Francisco had a run scored in the top of the sixth erased, making the final a 3–0 win for the Giants. Prior to this, the erasing of an uncompleted inning that did not affect the game outcome was inconsistent and uncertain. These included several no-hitters although none of them erased a hit that resurrected a no-hitter such as was the case for McCormick. George Van Haltren of Chicago no-hit Pittsburg in a six- or seven-inning game on June 21, 1888; the Chicago and Pittsburg newspapers differed on whether or not the uncompleted seventh inning remained part of the game. King Cole's July 31, 1910, game is also fuzzy as to whether an uncompleted inning was kept on the books. Two pitchers had no-hitters in games in which completed innings apparently were counted: Ed Stein of Brooklyn June 2, 1894, and Elton "Ice Box" Chamberlain of Cincinnati September 23, 1893.
15. Beyond the disagreement on a hit or error on Hahn's batted ball in the third, line scores differ regarding the innings in which runs were scored. The August 30, 1906, (page 13) *Philadelphia Inquirer* shows 012 00 for Chicago and 110 01 for Philadelphia. The August 30, 1906, (page 8) *Scranton Times* has 110 10 for Chicago and 112 00 for Philadelphia. Retrosheet (https://www.retrosheet.org/boxesetc/1906/B08290PHA1906.htm) has a line score similar to that of the Philadelphia paper and also indicates a hit for Hahn.
16. "The St. Paul Unions: Minnesota's First Major League Team" by Stew Thornley, https://stewthornley.net/unions.html.
17. Note on the use of "Pittsburg": In a post on sabr-l June 25, 2022, John Husman cited a page from the Popular Pittsburgh website and wrote, "In 1890, the United States Board of Geographic Names, which was created to bring consistency to the spellings of locations throughout the country, deemed that all cities ending in 'burgh' must drop the 'h' in the spirit of uniformity…Eventually, a special meeting of the U.S. Board of Geographic Names was arranged. On July 19, 1911, the board met. A preponderance of evidence citing Pittsburgh spelled with the 'h' over the decades convinced the board to reinstate the final letter."
18. On Opening Day in 1909 (April 15), Ames had a no-hitter for 9⅓ innings for the Giants against Brooklyn. He lost the no-hitter in the 10th inning and the game in the 13th.
19. The Cincinnati-Chicago game—in which Pete Rose got his 4,191st hit—was stopped by darkness after nine innings with the score tied, 5–5. It was determined that the game would be replayed in its entirety if it was necessary (it was not) to bring the teams back together to determine a division title. However, in 1969 the National League had changed its rules so that regulation games stopped by darkness would be suspended, not called. This happened after a controversial Cubs loss to Montreal June 22, 1969, when the game was called by darkness.
20. ESPN made this oranges-to-apples comparison in its coverage of Andy Hawkins's July 1, 1990, no-hitter, comparing the four runs Hawkins gave up without a hit to the runs Hughes gave up with multiple hits in extra innings, a comparison that is not valid.
21. Tom Mee, who was part of the Minnesota Twins public-relations department from 1961 to 1991, claimed that American League president Joe Cronin in the 1960s declared that the expansion Senators owned the records and history of the Washington Nationals of Walter Johnson, Cecil Travis, and Ossie Bluege. Historians never bought into this manipulation, and in 2020 the Twins even publicly displayed their heritage with banners at their ballpark for the 1924, 1925, and 1933 American League pennants won by the Nationals (1924 also being a world championship).
22. Many of the fewer-than-nine-inning no-hitters featured in the SABR Game Baseball Games Project include a disclaimer with language along the lines of the no-hitter being counted as until 1991, when a committee edict removed them from the ranks. These, of course, are still no-hitters, just not ones "officially" recognized by Major League Baseball.
23. Interview with Vincent, July 18, 2022.

The Death and Rebirth of the Home Team Batting First

Gary Belleville

According to conventional baseball wisdom, the home team enjoys a significant advantage in batting last. But in the early days of big-league baseball, it was not uncommon for teams to choose to bat first.[1] By the time the American League declared itself a major league in 1901, home teams batting first had become a rarity, and by 1914 the practice had completely vanished.

This paper will begin with an overview of the methods used to determine which team batted first in the major leagues of the late 1800s and early 1900s, briefly summarizing the decline in popularity of batting first at home, and then focusing on the 1901–14 period—the dying days of home teams batting first (HTBF). Specific examples will be given to illustrate the various reasons why managers sometimes went against the prevailing winds and sent their team to bat first. This article will also detail the unexpected rebirth of teams batting first in their home ballpark in the twenty-first century. Traditionally, home teams batted first because of tactical or superstitious considerations, although the recent reappearance of the phenomenon was caused by very different circumstances.

Whether or not there is a benefit in batting last is outside the scope of this paper. (For more information on this topic, the reader is invited to review the 2008 study by Theodore L. Turocy of the Department of Economics at Texas A&M University.[2])

METHODOLOGY AND DATA

Retrosheet game log files for 1901–14 were used to calculate the frequency of HTBF and to identify the teams and individuals who used the practice most (and least) often. For select games, contemporary newspaper accounts and Baseball-Reference game logs were used to determine, when possible, why the home team chose to bat first. Retrosheet game log files were also used to ascertain the HTBF games 2007–22, followed by inspection of Baseball-Reference game logs and contemporary newspaper accounts to again establish the circumstances.

DETERMINING WHICH TEAM BATS FIRST (1871–1949)

Baseball's first fully professional organization, the National Association of Professional Base Ball Players, left it up to team captains to determine which team would bat first in its inaugural season of 1871. This typically involved a coin toss, with the winner being given the right to decide if his team batted first ("the ins") or last ("the outs").[3]

That method remained in use until 1877 when the National League—in its second year of existence—made a "radical change."[4] The NL eliminated the coin toss and mandated that the home team must bat *first*. One year later, however, the previous rule was reinstated. "The rule [of always] giving the home club the privilege of going to bat first was abandoned," reported the *Chicago Inter Ocean* in December 1877, without providing a reason for the flip-flop.[5]

The American Association was founded in 1882. In 1885 it got rid of the coin toss, allowing the home team's captain to unilaterally decide which team batted first.[6] The National League followed suit in 1887, and the rule remained that way until after the 1949 season.[7]

THE DECLINE OF HTBF

In the early days of big-league baseball, it was common for a captain to choose HTBF. Games could be played with a single ball, and so being the first team to take swings at a new sphere was believed to be advantageous.[8] However, in the late 1880s Henry Chadwick—the "Father of Baseball"[9]—was a strong proponent of batting last. He passionately advocated his position in print several times in 1888.[10] In the August 8 edition of *Sporting Life*, he excoriated those who chose to bat first. "Will the League captains kindly tell me what advantage the 'first crack at the new ball' in the first part of the first inning yields, which is not similarly at command in the second part of the first inning?" he asked pointedly. "And can anyone of them point out wherein going to the bat first in a match equals the desirable advantage of having a chance for a winning rally which going to the bat last gives a team in the last part of a game? Is not that habit you have all of you got into of sending the visitors to the field first one of the many ruts you have got into?"[11]

It is unclear exactly when the custom of batting last at home became firmly entrenched, although there are several helpful clues.[12] The July 30, 1892, edition of *Sporting Life* pointed out that Brooklyn Grooms player-manager John Montgomery Ward was "sending visiting teams to the bat first on the Brooklyn grounds,"[13] which may have indicated a shift in opinion was underway.[14] Chadwick continued to push for home teams to bat last in the spring of 1894, writing that "sending men to the bat first, in nearly every instance is a weak point of play."[15] Eventually his message got through, because by 1901 teams rarely batted first at home.

THE DEATH OF HTBF (1901–14)

Home teams batted first in only 1.7 percent of major-league games in 1901. Contemporary news sources indicate getting first crack at the new ball was *not* a commonly cited rationale. Instead, teams primarily used the strategy in an attempt to snap a losing streak, or "break the hoodoo," in the parlance of the times.[16]

Between 1901 and 1914, home teams batted first only 70 times, or in 0.4 percent of all major-league games. After 1914 no home team batted first for the remainder of the twentieth century.[17]

Choosing to bat first was often an act of desperation by struggling teams. Only twice in this period did a team that went on to win the pennant bat first at home.[18] Teams went 32–38 (.457) with this strategy between 1901 and 1914, which was considerably worse than the .536 winning average posted by those teams when batting last at home.[19] It is worth noting that the lower winning average may not have been caused by choosing to bat first, but may have had more to do with the difficult circumstances which drove them to try HTBF.[20]

As the chart in Figure 1 shows, HTBF dropped off steadily at the beginning of the twentieth century, effectively ending in 1908. Three outliers 1913–14, two in the AL and one Federal League contest, seemed to be the end of the practice.

MANAGERS AND CLUBS USING THE STRATEGY MOST OFTEN (1901–14)

According to Retrosheet, five men between 1901 and 1914 were responsible for 40 of the 70 examples of HTBF (Table 1). All five were from the National League, so it's not surprising that 49 of the 70 games in which the host club batted first were in the senior circuit.[21]

Figure 1. Games with the Home Team Batting First in the Major Leagues (1901–14)

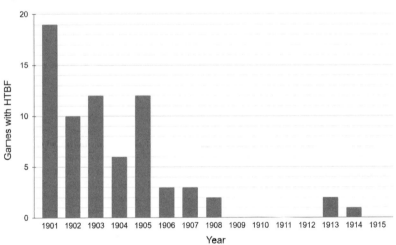

Table 1. Top 5 Managers Batting First at Home (1901–14, * denotes player-manager)

Manager/ Player-Manager	Team(s) from 1901–14	Managerial Career	Home Games Batting First	HTBF Record	Home Games	HTBF %
George Davis*	NY Giants (1901)	1895, 1900–01	7	4–3	71	9.9%
Bid McPhee	Cincinnati Reds (1901–02)	1901–02	4	0–4	113	3.5%
Frank Selee	Boston Nationals (1901) Chicago Orphans/Cubs (1902–05)	1890–1905	11	7–4	325	3.4%
Joe Kelley*	Cincinnati Reds (1902–05) Boston Doves (1908)	1902–05, 1908	7	3–4	334	2.1%
Ned Hanlon	Brooklyn Superbas (1901–05) Cincinnati Reds (1906–07)	1889–1907	11	5–6	522	2.1%

By comparison, it happened 20 times in the American League and only once in two seasons of Federal League play.

On top of being future Hall of Famers, the field generals on this list all broke into the big leagues when it was common for home teams to bat first.[22] For instance, Ned Hanlon made his major-league debut as an outfielder with the National League's Cleveland Blues in 1880, while Bid McPhee's rookie season came in 1882 as a second baseman with the Cincinnati Red Stockings of the American Association.[23]

Aggregating the Retrosheet data by team (Table 2) shows that the top five clubs in HTBF account for 48 of the 70 games, led by the Cincinnati Reds, who did it 15 times between 1901 and 1914. As mentioned earlier, the strategy was not typically used by pennant contenders. In 1901 through 1914, the closest the Reds came to first place was 16½ games in 1903.

The Washington club was responsible for 7 of the 20 American League games with the home team batting first between 1901 and 1913; no other team in the AL did it more than twice.

NOTEWORTHY EXAMPLES OF HOME TEAMS BATTING FIRST (1901–14)

This section will describe some of the more interesting cases of HTBF, starting with the 1901 New York Giants, who were led by 30-year-old player-manager George Davis. Davis chose to send the Giants to bat first at home seven times in 1901, the most by any team in a single season between 1901 and 1914. All seven came in a 42-game stretch between August 8 and September 16, and no other big-league team batted first at home during that period.

The Giants had been in first place as late as June 10, but they had won only 17 of their previous 50 contests heading into the second game of their August 8 doubleheader against Brooklyn. Davis was feeling the heat, and that day the team issued a tersely-worded statement on his future as manager. "Davis will continue to manage the team," it read. "But he has been told that if the team has another 'slump' or demoralized streak he would be deposed and [former Giants skipper Bill] Joyce put in his place as manager."[25] To add to the pressure, Joyce was in attendance at the doubleheader and received a hero's welcome from the fans at the Polo Grounds.[26]

Davis tried to change the Giants' luck by having them bat first in the second game of the twin bill.[27] The ploy had the desired effect, as New York scored two runs in the top of the first and held on for a 4–1 victory, snapping its four-game losing skid. But after the Giants lost their next two home games batting last, the superstitious Davis again attempted to break their "hard luck" by having them bat first at home in the second game of their August 14 doubleheader.[28] They won again, ending another four-game losing streak.

The Giants continued to struggle for the remainder of the season, and Davis chose to bat first at home five more times, including back-to-back home games on September 7 and 9. New York won both times to snap an eight-game losing skid.

The Giants finished the season with a dismal 52–85 record. Seeing the writing on the wall, Davis jumped to the American League for the 1902 season.[29] He never managed in the big leagues again.

Frank Selee had his Chicago Orphans (later Cubs) bat first at home 11 times during his 3½-year run as the team's manager (1902–05). Selee's reasons ranged from the customary—as when he used the strategy to break an eight-game losing streak on August 23, 1902—to the extraordinary. On September 15, 1902, the Cubs batted first against Cincinnati's weakest starting pitcher, 21-year-old Henry Thielman, who had lost 13 of his previous 16 decisions. The *Cincinnati Enquirer* reported that Selee "preferred the first crack at the chilled wing of the Red's [sic] premier loser to a final assault."[30] Chicago scored three runs in the top of the first against an ice-cold Thielman and held on for a 6–3 win.[31]

Selee had a unique reason to send the Cubs to bat first at home on May 15, 1904. Chicago was on a two-game winning streak, although there was another outstanding "hoodoo" to overcome: The Cubs had lost all four Sunday games up to that point of the season.[32] Selee's move worked yet again. "The Chicago Nationals, after a month or more of strenuous effort, have finally succeeded in winning a game of ball on a Sunday," reported the *Chicago Inter Ocean*.[33]

Table 2. Top 5 Franchises Batting First at Home (1901–14)

Franchise	HTBF Games	HTBF Games by Year	HTBF Record
Cincinnati Reds	15	5x (1903), 4x (1901), 2x (1904, 1906, 1907)	6–9
Chicago Orphans / Cubs	12	5x (1902), 3x (1904), 2x (1903), 1x (1905, 1908)	7–5
Washington Senators/Nationals	7	2x (1902, 1903), 1x (1901, 1908, 1913)	4–3
Brooklyn Superbas / Dodgers / Robins	7	6x (1905), 1x (1901)	2–5
New York Giants	7	7x (1901)	4–3

Cincinnati Reds player-manager Joe Kelley had his squad bat first at home five times in 1903 and three more times the next season. After dropping the first two regular-season games in 1903 to the defending National League champion Pittsburgh Pirates, Kelley chose to bat first on April 18 at the Palace of the Fans against Kaiser Wilhelm, who was making his major-league debut. In the top of the first inning, the nervous rookie made a throwing error and surrendered three runs, although he settled down after that to foil Kelley's strategy.[34] Wilhelm tossed a complete game to pick up his first big-league win.

Perhaps spurred on by Wilhelm's difficulties in the top of the first inning, Kelley sent the Reds to bat first the next day against another Pittsburgh hurler making his major-league debut, 21-year-old Bucky Veil. That move failed too, as Veil earned the first of his five career victories in the big leagues.

THE TWENTIETH CENTURY'S FINAL FIVE GAMES WITH THE HOME TEAM BATTING FIRST

In 1908 the home team batted first once in both the National and American Leagues. Just when it looked like the practice had died out, it happened twice more in 1913; one year later the home team batted first for the final time in the twentieth century. A list of the last five games can be found in Table 3.

Although Frank Chance was the player-manager in two of the last five games, one should not conclude that he was a strong proponent of this strategy. He didn't choose to bat first in any of the other home games that he managed between 1905 and 1914.

The 1908 Chicago Cubs' bid for a third consecutive pennant ran into a snag in late June and early July when they were hit with a rash of injuries, knocking them out of first place.[35] They came into their July 16 matchup against the surging New York Giants on a four-game losing streak. In an attempt to "dent the hoodoo," player-manager Chance sent his squad to bat first at the West Side Grounds.[36] In the top of the ninth inning, the Cubs looked like they might snap their losing streak, but Christy Mathewson—who had started showering in the clubhouse on the assumption that he would not be needed—hurried to the mound to snuff out a Chicago rally.[37]

Nearly a month after Chance's gambit, on August 14, manager Joe Cantillon of the seventh-place Washington Nationals also elected to bat first at home. The Nationals were on a two-game winning streak when they faced the Chicago White Sox in the first game of a doubleheader. Cantillon, trying to break a different sort of jinx, chose to bat first against a tough southpaw, Doc White. Although the Nationals had beaten White in Chicago two weeks earlier, he had gone 4–0 with three shutouts in his four starts in Washington so far that season.

"In order to change their luck, the Nationals went to the bat first," reported the *Washington Herald*, "and celebrated the occasion by shoving a run across the plate before White got his true bearings."[38] A 20-year-old Walter Johnson—making his 28th career appearance—made the first-inning run stand up. Johnson carried a no-hitter into the ninth, only to lose it when White led off with a single. The Big Train settled for a two-hit shutout.[39]

Five years passed before another big-league team batted first at home: the struggling New York Yankees.[40] Then tenants of the New York Giants at the Polo Grounds and still eight years from their first pennant in club history, they came into the second game of their June 2, 1913, twin bill against the defending World Series champion Boston Red Sox on an eight-game losing skid. Worse still, the Yankees were 0–12 at the Polo Grounds so far that season and had an 18-game home winless streak against Boston dating back to June 22, 1911.

Desperate times called for desperate measures, and 36-year-old player-manager Frank Chance chose to have the Yankees bat first, hoping to change his team's luck. It failed.[41] "The only benefit derived from the shift," chided *The New York Times*, "was in allowing the spectators to get away from the Polo Grounds a half inning earlier than would have been the case under usual conditions."

Unlike the sad-sack Yankees, the Washington Nationals were expected to contend for the pennant in 1913.[42] But poor play in late May and early June had cost them dearly, and the Nationals came into the second game of their June 26 doubleheader against the league-leading Philadelphia Athletics 13 games out of first place.

The Nationals were on a modest two-game losing streak after

Table 3. The Final Five Games of the Twentieth Century with HTBF

Date	Home Team	Home Manager	Score
July 16, 1908	Chicago Cubs	Frank Chance	Giants 4, Cubs 3
August 14, 1908 (Game 1)	Washington Nationals	Joe Cantillon	Nationals 1, White Sox 0
June 2, 1913 (Game 2)	New York Yankees	Frank Chance	Red Sox 8, Yankees 6
June 26, 1913 (Game 2)	Washington Nationals	Clark Griffith	Athletics 10, Nationals 3
June 25, 1914	Buffalo Buf-feds	Larry Schlafly	Buffeds 6, Rebels 2

being humiliated by the Athletics by a combined score of 25–4 in those two contests. Washington manager (and part owner) Clark Griffith hoped to "change his luck" by sending the Nationals to bat first.[43] Griffith was clearly desperate, because it was the only time he used the strategy in his 20-year managerial career.

It made no difference, as Philadelphia pummeled Washington for a third consecutive game, marking the low point in the Nationals' season. Led by a dominant Walter Johnson, Washington bounced back and went 56–33 the rest of the way to finish in second place, 6½ games behind the Athletics.[44]

The final time a home team batted first in the twentieth century came under bizarre circumstances. Hal Chase, generally regarded by many as the most corrupt player in baseball history, had jumped his contract with the White Sox on June 20, 1914, and signed with the Federal League's Buffalo Buf-feds.[45] He played one road game for Buffalo before White Sox owner Charles Comiskey was granted a preliminary court injunction preventing Chase from playing for any other team.[46]

But Chase still had to be served with the injunction, so he went into hiding, eventually returning to Buffalo on June 25. That afternoon the Buf-feds staged "Hal Chase Day" in an attempt to cash in on the drama. The team had learned that Chase would be served with the injunction as soon as he set foot on the field, so player-manager Larry Schafly informed the umpires that Buffalo was choosing to bat first.[47] The strategy was intended to improve the odds of Chase making at least one plate appearance in front of the large weekday crowd.

Chase batted second for the Buf-feds—he struck out—and remained in the game until the Buffalo sheriff personally delivered the injunction to him as he returned to the dugout after the bottom of the second inning. Less than a month later, Chase's lawyers got the injunction dissolved in court and he returned to action with Buffalo.[48]

CLUBS USING THE STRATEGY LEAST OFTEN (1901–14)

Table 4 lists the five clubs that batted first at home the least often between 1901 and 1914. The skippers of those five teams were largely a newer generation of managers as compared to those in Table 1. Only 3 of the 19 men listed in Table 4 began their major-league managerial careers prior to 1901: John McCloskey (1895), George Stallings (1897), and Patsy Donovan (1897).

1950 RULE CHANGE

Happy Chandler was baseball commissioner for less than six years (1945–51), but his impact on the game was considerable, in particular the pivotal support he provided for baseball's integration.[49] In 1949 Chandler directed the Rules Committee to rewrite the rule book, making it more understandable and helping to ensure that the rules were correctly and uniformly applied. Chandler asked them to rewrite the rules in plain language, define all terms, and regroup the rules in logical sequences.[50] It was the most significant alteration of the rule book since 1904.

The modernization resulted in the removal of the home team's choice to bat first or last, which was considered more of a housekeeping change since the option hadn't been invoked in decades.[51] Specifically, rule 26 was dropped:

Rule 26—Choice of Innings–
Fitness of Field for Play
The choice of innings shall be given to the manager or captain of the home team, …

It was replaced by rule 4.02:

Rule 4.00—Starting and Ending a Game
… 4.02 The players of the HOME TEAM shall take their DEFENSIVE POSITIONS, the first batter of the visiting team shall take his

Table 4. Clubs Batting First at Home the Least Often (1901–14)

Franchise	Managers (1901–14)	HTBF Games
Chicago White Sox	Clark Griffith (1901–02), Jimmy Callahan (1903–04, 1912–14), Fielder Jones (1904–08), Billy Sullivan (1909), Hugh Duffy (1910–11)	0
Boston Americans/ Red Sox	Jimmy Collins (1901–06), Fred Lake (1908–09), Patsy Donovan (1910–11), Jake Stahl (1912–13), Bill Carrigan (1913–14), 5 others	0
Pittsburgh Pirates	Fred Clarke (1901–14)	0
St. Louis Cardinals	Patsy Donovan (1901–03), Kid Nichols (1904–05), John McCloskey (1906–08), Roger Bresnahan (1909–12), Miller Huggins (1913–14), 2 others	1
New York Highlanders/ Yankees	Clark Griffith (1903–08), George Stallings (1909–10), Frank Chance (1913–14), 4 others	1

position in the batter's box, the umpire shall call "Play" and the game shall proceed.

A key member of the Rules Committee was Tom Connolly, who had umpired in both the National (1898–1900) and American Leagues (1901–31) before becoming the junior circuit's umpire-in-chief.[52]

The Associated Press story announcing the rule book enhancements quoted Connolly as saying that he "never heard of a manager wanting to bat first."[53] The statement was surprising considering Connolly had umpired in 7 of the 20 American League games in which the home team batted first between 1901 and 1913, and he was the home plate umpire the last time it happened.[54] The 79-year-old future Hall of Famer could be excused for his imperfect memory. "Shucks, who can remember ever seeing a home club bat first in a game?" asked the *Albuquerque Journal* that off-season. "Not even the oldest inhabitant."[55]

THE REBIRTH OF HOME TEAMS BATTING FIRST

After 92 consecutive seasons with no home teams batting first, MLB quietly made a change that ensured its eventual re-emergence.[56] Starting in 2007, any team that had to relocate a home game to another city would still bat last. Since the team was already penalized by having to play an extra game in front of an unfriendly crowd, it no longer made sense to take away the privilege of batting last.[57]

The change came far too late for the 1991 Montreal Expos and the 1994 Seattle Mariners. On September 13, 1991, a 55-ton concrete slab fell off Montreal's Olympic Stadium, forcing the Expos to play their last 13 "home" games of the season on the road.[58] Montreal's opponents batted last in their home ballpark in each of those games.[59] A similar situation happened in 1994 when the ceiling tiles inside the Kingdome needed to be urgently replaced and the Mariners had to play 13 "home" games on the road.[60]

MLB's revised policy for relocated games resulted in the home team batting first in 44 contests between 2007 and 2022. The yearly breakdown can be seen in Figure 2.

These 44 games came about for a wide variety of reasons, the majority of which would have been incomprehensible to Henry Chadwick 120 years earlier. The different circumstances will be briefly outlined below.

HOME TEAMS BATTING FIRST (2007–19)

A freak 2007 snowstorm dropped 16 to 18 inches of snow on parts of northeast Ohio over the Easter weekend.[61] The cold and snow wiped out the entire four-game series between Cleveland and Seattle on April 6–9, which was the Mariners' only scheduled trip there.[62]

Three of the games were rescheduled for Jacobs Field on what would have been off days for both teams (May 21, June 11, and August 30).[63] The fourth game was played as part a September 26 doubleheader at Safeco Field in Seattle, with the Mariners batting first in the opener.[64] No American, National, or Federal League team had done so since "Hal Chase Day" in 1914.

In 2010 the Group of Twenty (G20) economic summit was held in downtown Toronto.[65] Law enforcement authorities created an extensive security zone in the area, erecting a 10-foot-high fence around the Rogers Centre and restricting the movement of vehicles and pedestrians in the downtown core.[66] The CN Tower and many downtown businesses were closed during the summit, and the Toronto Blue Jays' three-game series against the Philadelphia Phillies on June 25–27 was moved to the City of Brotherly Love.[67]

The Jays wore their home jerseys and batted last in all three games at Citizens Bank Park.[68] It was the first time the Designated Hitter rule was used in a National League ballpark during the regular season.[69]

Almost exactly one year after the G20 summit, a three-game series on June 24–26, 2011, between the Mariners and Florida Marlins was moved from Miami to Seattle because of a June 29 concert featuring the band U2. The Irish rockers were on the final leg of their 360° tour, the highest grossing concert tour of all time.[70] The $25M stage production, complete with

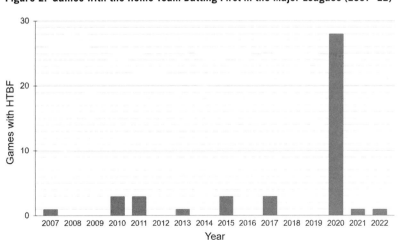

Figure 2. Games with the Home Team Batting First in the Major Leagues (2007–22)

a 300-ton, 167-foot-tall stage, required four days of setup time.[71]

Marlins owner Jeffrey Loria may have lost three home games, but the venue change was likely to his financial benefit.[72] The Marlins were last in National League ticket sales every year between 2006 and 2011, and they were unlikely to draw big crowds for the games against the Mariners.[73] U2, on the other hand, attracted approximately 73,000 fans to Sun Life Stadium.[74]

The series opener on June 24 at Safeco Field was the first time since the DH was instituted in 1973 that National League rules were used in an American League ballpark in the regular season.[75] Mariners pitchers held their own at the plate, batting a combined .250 in the series.

The next time a team batted first at home came in 2013 after the finale of a four-game series between the Reds and San Francisco Giants was rained out on July 4 in Cincinnati. Since it was the Giants' only visit to the Queen City that season and no common off days were suitable as a makeup date, the contest was played as the nightcap of a July 23 doubleheader in San Francisco.[76] Perhaps the most notable aspect of the rescheduled game was that Giants manager Bruce Bochy earned the 1,500th managerial win of his career while wearing a road uniform in his home ballpark.[77]

Tragic circumstances caused the relocation of three games in 2015. Freddie Gray, a 25-year-old Black man from the west side of Baltimore, suffered a broken neck while in police custody on April 12, and died a week later.[78,79,80] Civil unrest broke out after his April 27 funeral, resulting in the postponement of games between the White Sox and Baltimore Orioles on the next two nights.[81,82] The National Guard was called in and a weeklong curfew imposed. On the afternoon of April 29 the gates of Camden Yards remained locked while the Orioles and White Sox played an eerie game with no fans in attendance. It was the first time one of the four major North American sports leagues held a game with no fans present.[83]

The next series—three games versus the Tampa Bay Rays—was moved to Tropicana Field May 1–3.[84] The games were played without the Rays' usual in-game promotions, and the Orioles' traditional seventh-inning stretch song, John Denver's 'Thank God I'm a Country Boy,' was played.[85]

Hurricane Irma caused widespread devastation in South Florida on September 10, 2017, killing hundreds and causing billions in property damage.[86] Although Marlins Park suffered only minor damage, team officials moved the three-game series on September 15–17 between Miami and Milwaukee to Miller Park to avoid straining the resources of police and fire rescue crews.[87,88]

Since the Marlins' extended road trip began three days before the hurricane slammed into Florida, they didn't have their home uniforms with them for the games in Milwaukee; they batted last in their road jerseys.[89] In a lighthearted touch, the Brewers tried to make Miami feel at home by installing neon palm trees in Miller Park's outfield pavilion.

THE PANDEMIC-SHORTENED 2020 SEASON

On March 12, 2020—one day after the World Health Organization (WHO) declared the COVID-19 outbreak to be a global pandemic—spring training came to an abrupt halt.[90] Eventually, baseball restarted in early July, and a 60-game regular season kicked off on July 23 with no fans in the stands.[91]

But after several COVID-19 outbreaks among major-league teams, it was unclear how many of the games could be played in the narrow 67-day period set aside for the regular season.[92,93] One week into the season, the owners and the union agreed to an innovative rule change to help deal with a potential glut of rescheduled games and conserve pitching resources: Doubleheaders would consist of two seven-inning games.[94] The move proved significant, as a whopping 55 twin bills were necessary in 2020.[95]

COVID-19 outbreaks caused the postponement of 45 games during the regular season, with 16 of those games moved to a different city to ensure the regular season was completed on time.[96] Another 12 contests in 2020 were postponed and relocated for other reasons, bringing the total number of games with the home team batting first to 28, or 3.1 percent of regular-season games—the highest percentage since prior to the 1901 season. Incredibly, only two games didn't get played despite the unprecedented challenges.[97]

Since the Canadian and United States governments had closed their border to non-essential travel, playing games in Canada was impossible in 2020.[98] After exploring several options, the Blue Jays made a last-minute decision to play their home games at Sahlen Field in Buffalo, the ballpark normally used by their Triple-A affiliate.[99] But necessary ballpark infrastructure improvements couldn't be completed before Toronto's first home date, so two games against the Washington Nationals on July 29–30 were shifted to the US capital.[100] The Jays batted last, wore their home whites, and heard their seventh-inning stretch song, "OK, Blue Jays," echo across an empty Nationals Park.[101]

COVID-19 wasn't the only hazard affecting play in 2020. Aside from Toronto, no team had more games moved out of its home ballpark in 2020 than the Mariners. In addition to one game being postponed and relocated because of a positive COVID-19 test, the team had to play five more away from T-Mobile Park because of dangerously poor air quality in Seattle.[102,103] Smoke from wildfires on the West Coast elevated the air quality index into the 300s across most of Washington state—anything above 150 is considered unhealthful for everyone, not just "sensitive" groups.[104] The Mariners batted last in two games in San Francisco on September 16–17 and three more in San Diego on September 18–20.

Hurricanes caused two other games to be relocated. First, the threat from Hurricane Isaias bumped a Yankees-Phillies game on August 4 to Philadelphia the next day.[105] Hurricane Laura had a similar effect on an August 26 contest between the Houston Astros and Los Angeles Angels in Houston; it was played as the second game of a twin bill on September 5 at Angel Stadium in Anaheim.[106]

On August 26, six National Basketball Association teams made the decision to not play their postseason games to make a strong statement against racial injustice.[107] The player action came three days after a White police officer in Kenosha, Wisconsin, shot a 29-year-old Black man named Jacob Blake seven times.[108] The boycott soon spread to other professional sports, including baseball. The Milwaukee Brewers, Los Angeles Dodgers, and Seattle Mariners were the first MLB teams to refuse to take to the field, and eventually 11 ballgames were postponed because of the boycott.[109,110]

Two of those games required a change of venue in order to be made up. The Red Sox's decision to sit out their game against the Jays in Buffalo on August 27 resulted in a September 4 doubleheader at Fenway Park.[111] In the second game, the Red Sox batted first at Fenway for the first time in the history of their storied ballpark, which opened in 1912.[112] A change of venue was also required when the Orioles decided not to play their August 27 game in Tampa Bay.[113]

One other game was relocated during the turbulent 2020 season because of a far more traditional postponement: an August 28 game was washed out by rain.[114]

HOME TEAMS BATTING FIRST (2021–22)

The 2021 season featured only one game with a team batting first in its home ballpark. That was the first game of an August 10 twin bill in Anaheim between the Angels and Blue Jays, made necessary because of a rainout on April 11 at TD Ballpark in

Dunedin, Florida, one of three venues the Jays called home in 2021.[115]

The 99-day owners' lockout that began on December 2, 2021, played havoc with the 2022 regular-season schedule.[116] The first eight days of the season were wiped out, forcing makeup games to be played on former off-days and/or turning single games into doubleheaders.[117] The game between the Oakland Athletics and Detroit Tigers that was originally scheduled for April 4 in Oakland was moved to Detroit and played as the first game of a May 10 doubleheader, with the Tigers batting first at Comerica Park. It was the only instance of a team batting first in its home ballpark in 2022.

SUMMARY OF HOME TEAMS BATTING FIRST (2007–22)

After a 93-year absence, teams batted first in their home ballpark a stunning 44 times between 2007 and 2022. The underlying reasons for these games—aside from the 2007 change to how relocated contests were conducted—are summarized in Table 5.

CONCLUSIONS

The rules and customs of the game of baseball are not chiseled in stone. Even basic features like determining which team bats first have evolved over the years without altering the fundamental nature of the game. This insight is particularly relevant as the major leagues enter a new era in 2023 with the introduction of pitch clocks and a ban on defensive shifts.

In the early days of the big leagues, it was common for the home team to choose to bat first and in one season (1877) the National League even mandated the practice. Helped in part by the urging of Henry Chadwick, the strategy became less common in the 1890s, and by 1901 it had become a rarity. Since batting first at home was typically done to break out of a losing streak during this period, elite teams rarely did it. Only twice between 1901 and 1914 did a team that went on to win the pennant choose to bat first at home.

The rule book modernization initiated by Happy Chandler in 1949 eliminated the home team's choice

Table 5. Summary of Reasons for Home Teams Batting First (2007–22)

Reason for HTBF Site Change	HTBF Games
Global Pandemic (player/staff outbreaks, border closure)	18
Extreme Weather (hurricane, snowstorm)	6
Air Quality (wildfire smoke)	5
Racial Injustice (civil unrest, boycott)	5
Economic Summit Security Near Ballpark	3
Game Pre-empted by Concert	3
Rain	3
Owners' Lockout	1

to bat first or last. But starting with the 2007 season, any team that had to relocate a home game to another city retained the privilege of batting last. Since then, a global pandemic, extreme weather, poor air quality, and racial injustice were the most common reasons why teams batted first in their home ballpark. Given that society continues to grapple with these serious issues, it may only be a matter of time before major-league teams bat first at home more times in the twenty-first century than in the previous one.[118] ■

Acknowledgments

The author thanks SABR Games Project Committee Chair John Fredland and two anonymous peer reviewers for providing valuable feedback on early drafts of this article. The author is grateful for the help provided by Retrosheet President Tom Thress. Thanks also to Andrea Gough at the Seattle Public Library for her research assistance.

Notes

1. David Nemec, *The Official Rules of Baseball Illustrated* (Guildford, Connecticut: The Lyons Press, 2006), 51.
2. Theodore L. Turocy, "In Search of the 'Last-Ups' Advantage in Baseball: A Game-Theoretic Approach," *Journal of Quantitative Analysis in Sports* (February 2008). Accessed November 1, 2022: https://www.gambitproject.org/turocy/papers/batfirst.pdf. Turocy concludes that there is no significant strategic advantage to batting first or last. However, he theorized that there may be a psychological advantage to batting last.
3. Nemec, *The Official Rules of Baseball Illustrated*, 51.
4. "Convention of Base-Ball Managers at Cleveland," *Chicago Tribune*, December 10, 1876, 7.
5. "Base Ball Rules," *Daily Inter Ocean* (Chicago), December 7, 1877, 5.
6. Nemec, *The Official Rules of Baseball Illustrated*, 51.
7. The home team's captain also decided which team batted first in the Player's League (1890), American Association (1885–91), and American League (1901–49). Nemec, *The Official Rules of Baseball Illustrated*, 51.
8. Nemec, *The Official Rules of Baseball Illustrated*, 51.
9. Andrew Schiff, "Henry Chadwick," SABR BioProject. Accessed November 9, 2022: https://sabr.org/bioproj/person/henry-chadwick.
10. Henry Chadwick, "Chadwick's Chat," *Sporting Life*, May 9, 1888, 8; Henry Chadwick, "Last at the Bat," *Brooklyn Daily Eagle*, June 29, 1888, 1.
11. Henry Chadwick, "Chadwick's Chat," *Sporting Life*, August 8, 1888, 5.
12. It will be possible to tell precisely when the custom of batting last became firmly entrenched once Retrosheet releases revised game logs prior to 1901.
13. "Editorial Views, News, Comment," *Sporting Life*, July 30, 1892, 4.
14. As of December 2022, the preliminary Retrosheet game log files indicated that National League teams batted first at home 53 percent of the time in 1882, 41 percent in 1894, and just 9 percent in 1898. (Revised Retrosheet game log files for 1871 to 1900 will be released in the coming years. E-mails with Retrosheet President Tom Thress, October 13, 2022.)
15. Henry Chadwick, "Chadwick's Chat," *Sporting Life*, April 14, 1894, 5.
16. "Piatt Goes to Pieces," *Boston Globe*, June 9, 1903, 5.
17. The World Series in 1921 (Giants-Yankees), 1922 (Giants-Yankees), and 1944 (Cardinals-Browns) featured two teams who shared a home ballpark. However, the author does not consider these games to have the home team batting first, since both squads were playing in their home ballpark.
18. Connie Mack had his 1902 Philadelphia Athletics bat first at home on May 15 against Cy Young and the Boston Americans. Player-manager Frank Chance sent his 1908 Chicago Cubs to bat first in a home game against the New York Giants on July 16. It was the last time a National League manager chose to bat first at home.
19. Teams that batted first at home at least once in a season from 1901 to 1914 had a combined record of 1286–1112 (.536) when batting last at home.
20. It is worth reiterating that Turocy concluded that there is no significant strategic advantage to batting first or last. However, he theorized that there may be a psychological advantage to batting last. Turocy, "In Search of the 'Last-Ups' Advantage in Baseball: A Game-Theoretic Approach."
21. It is unclear if manager Bid McPhee or captain Tommy Corcoran made the decision to bat first at home four times during the 1901 season.
22. Frank Selee never played in the major leagues, although his professional baseball career dated back to 1884 in the Massachusetts State Association.
23. Selee began managing in the big leagues in 1890 for the Boston Beaneaters. One year later, he managed rookie outfielder Joe Kelley. George Davis began his big-league playing career in 1890 with the National League's Cleveland Spiders. David Fleitz, "Frank Selee," SABR BioProject. Accessed November 8, 2022: https://sabr.org/bioproj/person/frank-selee.
24. Davis turned 31 on August 23, 1901.
25. "Joyce Reaches Gotham," *Evansville* (Indiana) *Journal-News*, August 9, 1901, 5.
26. Davis was also cheered by the fans when he came to bat, although perhaps not as enthusiastically as Joyce was welcomed. "'Scrappy Bill' Joyce is Again in Town," *Brooklyn Daily Eagle*, August 9, 1901, 10.
27. "Teams Break Even," (New York) *Daily People*, August 9, 1901, 3.
28. "Taylor's Curves Easy," *Boston Globe*, August 15, 1901, 5.
29. Nicole DiCicco, "George Davis," SABR BioProject. Accessed November 9, 2022: https://sabr.org/bioproj/person/George-Davis.
30. "Back to .500 Mark Again," *Cincinnati Enquirer*, September 16, 1902, 4.
31. Thielman only pitched in five more games in the major leagues. His final appearance on a big-league mound was on May 12, 1903.
32. Sunday games usually attracted bigger crowds than games on other days of the week. "Colts Capture the Final Game," *Chicago Tribune*, May 16, 1904, 8.
33. Jack Tanner, "Colts Break the Hoodoo and Win," *Chicago Inter Ocean*, May 16, 1904, 6.
34. "Downed; In a Fighting Game," *Cincinnati Enquirer*, April 19, 1903, 10.
35. Gary Belleville, "July 16, 1908: Christy Mathewson Bolts from the Shower to Preserve Giants' Victory over Cubs," SABR Games Project. Accessed November 17, 2022: https://sabr.org/gamesproj/game/july-16-1908-christy-mathewson-bolts-from-the-shower-to-preserve-giants-victory-over-cubs.
36. Charles Dryden, "Cubs Pipe Fails, and Giants Land," *Chicago Tribune*, July 17, 1908, 6.
37. Belleville, "July 16, 1908: Christy Mathewson Bolts from the Shower to Preserve Giants' Victory over Cubs."
38. "Two From White Sox," *Washington Herald*, August 15, 1908, 8.
39. Johnson was in his first full season in the big leagues in 1908 and he had been inconsistent up to that point. His August 14 outing was his third shutout of his career and the most impressive so far. "Two From White Sox."
40. In the first game in Yankees club history, played on April 22, 1903, in Washington, Senators manager Tom Loftus had his team bat first. The Yankees batted last at American League Park and lost, 3–1. Loftus also had the Senators bat first at home for the first two games of the 1902 season. No American League manager chose to bat first at home more frequently than he did. According to the Retrosheet game log files, Loftus chose to bat first in 1.9 percent of home games between 1901 and 1903. He began managing in the big leagues in 1884 with the Milwaukee Brewers of the Union Association.

41. Chance was in his first and only full season with the Yankees. He also played first base in both games of the doubleheader; the Yankees' regular first baseman, Hal Chase, had worn out his welcome in New York and was traded to the White Sox the previous day. First baseman Babe Borton, who was acquired by the Yankees in the Chase trade, had not yet reported for duty. Martin Kohout, "Hal Chase," SABR BioProject. Accessed November 10, 2022: https://sabr.org/bioproj/person/hal-chase; "Chance Trades Chase to Chicago," *Dunkirk* (New York) *Evening Observer*, June 2, 1913, 7.

42. Mike Grahek, "Clark Griffith," SABR BioProject. Accessed November 10, 2022: https://sabr.org/bioproj/person/Clark-Griffith.

43. "Macks Hit and Score at Will in a Soft Bargain-Day Bill with Senators," *Philadelphia Inquirer*, June 27, 1913, 10.

44. Johnson had a career year in 1913. The 25-year-old went 21–2 for the rest of the season to finish with a 36-7 record and a 1.14 ERA. The extraordinary effort earned him the first of his two American League MVP Awards.

45. Kohout, "Hal Chase."

46. Jack Zerby, "June 25, 1914: Buffalo and the Sheriff Greet Hal Chase on His 'Day' at Federal League Park," SABR Games Project. Accessed November 11, 2022: https://sabr.org/gamesproj/game/june-25-1914-buffaloand-the-sheriff-greet-hal-chase-on-his-day/.

47. Zerby, "June 25, 1914: Buffalo and the Sheriff Greet Hal Chase on His 'Day' at Federal League Park."

48. The court ruled in Chase's favor because his contract with the White Sox lacked mutuality—the team could terminate his contract on 10-days notice, but Chase did not have that ability. Zerby, "June 25, 1914: Buffalo and the Sheriff Greet Hal Chase on His 'Day' at Federal League Park."

49. Terry Bohn, "Happy Chandler," SABR BioProject. Accessed November 11, 2022: https://sabr.org/bioproj/person/happy-chandler.

50. J. G. Taylor Spink, *Baseball Guide and Record Book 1950* (St. Louis: Charles C. Spink & Son, 1950), 93. Accessed November 11, 2022: https://archive.org/details/baseballguiderec1950stlo/page/92/mode/2up?q=Recodified.

51. Perhaps the most significant change to the rule book was the redefinition of the strike zone. The upper portion of the strike zone was changed from the shoulders to the armpits. The lower portion was more precisely defined as the "top of his knees" instead of just "knees." Fritz Howell, "Chandler Predicts Few Players to Be Drafted," *Idaho Falls* (Idaho) *Post-Register*, 11; Spink, *Baseball Guide and Record Book 1950*, 524; J.G. Taylor Spink, *Baseball Guide and Record Book 1948* (St. Louis: Charles C. Spink & Son, 1948), 591. Accessed December 12, 2022: https://archive.org/details/baseballguiderec1948stlo/page/590/mode/2up.

52. Connolly also umpired in one American League game in 1932 (July 31 at Cleveland).

53. Howell, "Chandler Predicts Few Players to Be Drafted."

54. According to Retrosheet data, Connolly also umpired a bunch of National League games in which the home team batted first between 1898 and 1900.

55. Wilbur Bentley, "Angle Shots," *Albuquerque Journal*, January 11, 1950, 12.

56. This is under the assumption that the definition of the "home team" is aligned with the one adopted by Baseball Reference and Retrosheet. By their definition the home team is the one playing in its home ballpark—not necessarily the team batting last. In neutral site games, the home team is the one batting last. E-mails with Retrosheet President Tom Thress, October 13, 2022.

57. David Andriesen, "Home Teams Sweep Doubleheader," *Seattle Post-Intelligencer*, September 27, 2007, D-1.

58. Rory Costello, "Olympic Stadium (Montreal), SABR BioProject. Accessed November 11, 2022: https://sabr.org/bioproj/park/olympic-stadium-montreal.

59. For statistical purposes, all 13 relocated games were considered road games for the Montreal Expos.

60. For statistical purposes, all 13 relocated games were considered road games for the Seattle Mariners. The issues with the Kingdome roof surfaced on July 19, 1994, forcing the Mariners to play on the road for the remainder of the season. They would have played many more "home" games on the road had the players' strike not canceled all games beginning on August 12. Bob Condotta, "Ten Years After the Kingdome Tiles Fell," *Seattle Times*, July 19, 2004. Accessed November 11, 2022: https://archive.seattletimes.com/archive/?date=20040719&slug=tile19.

61. "The Boys of Winter?," *Austin* (Texas) *American-Statesman*, April 10, 2007, C-1.

62. The bad weather also forced the three-game series between Cleveland and the Los Angeles Angels of Anaheim to be moved to a neutral site (Milwaukee) on April 10–12.

63. The addition of a game on May 21 required the approval of the players' union because it forced the Mariners to play games on more than 20 consecutive days. They played on 23 consecutive days (May 15 to June 6).

64. David Ginsburg, "M's Will Make Three Trips to Cleveland for Makeups; but Fourth Game Snowed Out in April Is Moved to Seattle," *The Columbian* (Vancouver, Washington), May 5, 2007, B-5.

65. The Group of Twenty (G20) is an organization comprised of the world's major economies, including the United States and Canada. "Canada and the G20," Government of Canada. Accessed November 13, 2022: https://www.international.gc.ca/world-monde/international_relations-relations_internationales/g20/index.aspx?lang=eng.

66. Ken Fidlin, "The Good," *Toronto Sun*, June 25, 2010, S-31; Jennifer Yang, "A World of Security in the Heart of the City," *Toronto Star*, May 29, 2010, GT-3; Justin Skinner, "Downtowners Looking to Get Out of Town for the Weekend," *City Centre Mirror* (Willowdale, Ontario), June 24, 2010, 1.

67. Kenyon Wallace, "G20 Shuts Down Trains, Jays and Musicals in Toronto," *Edmonton Journal*, June 5, 2010, A-5.

68. "2010/06/25 Recap: PHI 9, TOR 0," YouTube. Accessed November 13, 2022: https://youtu.be/YXgmALFSW3o.

69. The DH was used in World Series games in alternate years between 1976 and 1985. John Cronin, "The Historical Evolution of the Designated Hitter Rule," *The Baseball Research Journal* (Fall 2016): 12. Accessed November 13, 2022: https://sabr.org/journal/article/the-historical-evolution-of-the-designated-hitter-rule.

70. As of November 2022, U2's 360° tour was still the highest grossing tour after adjusting for inflation. It was surpassed in 2019 in unadjusted dollars by Ed Sheeran's Divide tour. Gabrielle Olya, "28 of the Highest-Grossing Concert Tours of All Time," Yahoo Finance, July 21, 2020. Accessed November 14, 2022: https://ca.finance.yahoo.com/news/28-highest-grossing-concert-tours-175633028.html.

71. Jordan Levin, "U2 and Bono: Connecting the Universe," *Miami Herald*, July 1, 2011, B-5.

72. Phil Rogers, "Time to Gaze at Stars," *Chicago Tribune*, June 26, 2011, 3-3.

73. The Marlins briefly escaped the NL cellar in attendance in 2012 with the opening of their new home, Marlins Park. They returned to having the lowest attendance in the league in 2013. As of the end of the 2022 season, the Marlins had not yet escaped the NL cellar in attendance (no fans were allowed during the COVID-shortened regular season of 2020).

74. Sun Life Stadium was originally known as Joe Robbie Stadium. It was the home of the Marlins from 1993 to 2011. Levin, "U2 and Bono: Connecting the Universe."

75. "Late Friday; Mariners 5, Marlins 1," *Fort Worth Star-Telegram*, June 26, 2011, 4-C.

76. Associated Press, "Rain Washes Out Reds-Giants," *Sidney* (Ohio) *Daily News*, July 5, 2013, 13.

77. Janie McCauley, "Reds Split DH After Missed Chances," *Advocate-Messenger* (Danville, Kentucky), July 24, 2013, B-2.

78. Amelia McDonell and Justine Barron, "Death of Freddie Gray: 5 Things You Didn't Know," *Rolling Stone*, April 12, 2017. Accessed November 14, 2022: https://www.rollingstone.com/culture/culture-features/death-offreddie-gray-5-things-you-didnt-know-129327.

79. Kevin Rector and Justin Fenton, "Doctor Defends Autopsy Ruling," *Baltimore Sun*, June 11, 2016, A-1.

80. McDonell and Barron, "Death of Freddie Gray: 5 Things You Didn't Know."

81. "Freddie Gray's Death in Police Custody - What We Know," BBC News, May 23, 2016. Accessed November 14, 2022: https://www.bbc.com/news/world-us-canada-32400497.

82. The April 27-28 games between the White Sox and Orioles were replayed as a May 28 twin bill in Baltimore.

83. Mike Huber, "April 29, 2015: Orioles and White Sox Play for Normalcy in Empty Stadium," SABR Games Project. Accessed November 14, 2022: https://sabr.org/gamesproj/game/april-29-2015-orioles-and-whitesox-play-for-normalcy-in-empty-stadium.

84. Eduardo A. Encina, "Schedule Shifted After Rioting," *Baltimore Sun*, April 29, 2015, B-1.

85. Roger Mooney, "Rays Right at Home Even as Road Team," *Tampa Tribune*, May 2, 2015, S-1.

86. "5 Years Later: Hurricane Irma in Florida," Federal Emergency Management Agency, August 29, 2022. Accessed November 14, 2022: https://www.fema.gov/fact-sheet/5-years-later-hurricane-irma-florida; Associated Press, "Hurricane Irma Caused 400 Senior Deaths in Florida, Study Finds," *Orlando Sentinel*, October 14, 2020, B-5.

87. "Brewers Set to Host Marlins," (Madison) *Wisconsin State Journal*, September 14, 2017, B-2.

88. Steve Wine, "Marlins-Brewers Series Moved to Milwaukee," *Naples* (Florida) *Daily News*, September 14, 2017, C-6.

89. Associated Press, "Stuck on Road, Marlins Lose 6th in Row," *Palm Beach Post*, September 16, 2017, C-5.

90. Dayn Perry, "Timeline of How the COVID-19 Pandemic Has Impacted the 2020 Major League Baseball Season," CBS Sports, July 29, 2020. Accessed November 14, 2022: https://www.cbssports.com/mlb/news/timeline-of-how-the-covid-19-pandemic-has-impacted-the-2020-major-league-baseball-season.

91. The National League Championship Series and the World Series had limited fans in attendance in 2020. All other regular-season and playoff games were played with no fans present. Jordan McPherson, "Prospects Face Major Loss with Minors Canceled," *Miami Herald*, July 1, 2020, A-11; "Fan Friendly: Spectators Return to Park as NLCS Opens in Texas," *Daily Press* (Newport, Virginia), October 13, 2020, B-5.

92. Perry, "Timeline of How the COVID-19 Pandemic Has Impacted the 2020 Major League Baseball Season."

93. Mike Axisa, "Dr. Anthony Fauci Warns Marlins COVID-19 Outbreak Could Put MLB Season 'In Danger'," CBS Sports, July 28, 2020. Accessed November 14, 2022: https://www.cbssports.com/mlb/news/dranthony-fauci-warns-marlins-covid-19-outbreak-could-put-mlb-season-in-danger.

94. Ben Walker, "MLB Will Play 7-Inning Games in Doubleheaders," *Daily Journal* (Flat River, Missouri), August 1, 2020, C-2.

95. The shortened 60-game regular season in 2020 had the most doubleheaders since 1984. Tom Goldman, "Baseball Made It, So Far, through a Pandemic; Football Hopes to Follow," National Public Radio, September 28, 2020. Accessed November 14, 2022: https://www.npr.org/2020/09/28/917707419/baseball-made-it-so-far-through-a-pandemic-football-hopes-to-follow.

96. Goldman, "Baseball Made It, So Far, through a Pandemic; Football Hopes to Follow."

97. The St. Louis Cardinals did not play a game between July 29 and August 15 because of a significant number of COVID-19 cases among players and staff. Only two of the four games between the Cardinals and Detroit Tigers originally scheduled for August 3-6 were played. Jeff Seidel, "Don't Shame the Cards for Virus Outbreak; Praise Tigers for Staying Healthy," *Detroit Free Press*, August 4, 2020, B-1.

98. Mark Davis, "July 30, 2021: Blue Jays Play First Home Game in Canada in Nearly Two Years," SABR Games Project. Accessed November 15, 2022: https://sabr.org/gamesproj/game/july-30-2021-blue-jays-play-firsthome-game-in-canada-in-nearly-two-years.

99. The minor leagues were shut down for the 2020 season because of the pandemic. Associated Press, "Blue Jays Will Play in Buffalo," *Pittsburgh Post-Gazette*, July 25, 2020, WS-5.

100. Laura H. Peebles, "July 29, 2020: Toronto Blue Jays Play 'Home' Opener in Washington, Lose to Nationals," SABR Games Project. Accessed November 15, 2022: https://sabr.org/gamesproj/game/july-29-2020-toronto-blue-jays-play-home-opener-in-washington-lose-to-nationals.

101. "Roundup; MLB Suspends Dodgers' Kelly 8 Games for Throwing at Astros," *Miami Herald*, July 30, 2020, A-16.

102. A three-game series in Seattle scheduled for September 1–3 was canceled because of a positive COVID test in the Oakland Athletics' traveling party. Two of the games were rescheduled in Seattle (September 14 doubleheader), while the other was shifted to Oakland (Game 2 of September 26 doubleheader). Lauren Smith, "Mariners Series Against A's Rescheduled as Doubleheaders Later This Month," *News Tribune* (Tacoma, Washington), September 2, 2020, B-1.

103. Lauren Smith, "Mariners vs. Giants Postponed Due to Poor Air Quality in Seattle," *News Tribune* (Tacoma, Washington), September 16, 2020, B-2.

104. Anything above 100 is considered unhealthy for "sensitive" groups. Brandon Block, "Hazardous Air across Washington Could Last for Days," *The Olympian* (Olympia, Washington), September 16, 2020, A-4; "Air Quality Index (AQI) Basics," AirNow.gov. Accessed November 15, 2022: https://www.airnow.gov/aqi/aqi-basic/.

105. The contest was played as the first game of an August 5 twin bill at Citizens Bank Park. Scott Lauber, "'Weird' Day Ends in Defeat," *Philadelphia Inquirer*, August 4, 2020, D-1.

106. Associated Press, "Angels Strike Early to Earn Doubleheader Split," *Desert Sun* (Palm Springs, California), August 27, 2020, B-3.

107. Brian Mahoney and Tim Reynolds, "Six NBA Playoff Teams Make Bold Statement," *Spokesman-Review* (Spokane, Washington), August 27, 2020, B-2.

108. Christina Morales, "What We Know About the Shooting of Jacob Blake," *The New York Times*, November 16, 2021. Accessed November 15, 2022: https://www.nytimes.com/article/jacob-blake-shooting-kenosha.html; Joe Barrett, "Jacob Blake Shooting: What We Know About the Shooting in Kenosha," *Wall Street Journal*, October 10, 2021. Accessed November 15, 2022: https://www.wsj.com/articles/jacob-blake-shooting-11598368824.

109. Bob Nightengale, "Baseball (Finally) Takes a Stand," *Palladium-Item* (Richmond, Indiana), August 28, 2020, B-1.

110. Three games were canceled on August 26, followed by seven more the next day, and one on August 28.

111. The Blue Jays had decided to play on August 27. "Player Protests," *London* (Ontario) *Free Press*, August 28, 2020, 8; Peter Abraham, "Bradley, Sox Agree to Sit," *Boston Globe*, August 28, 2020, C-1.

112. Associated Press, "Jays: A Win on the Road, a Loss at Home in Fenway Doubleheader," *Toronto Star*, September 5, 2020, S-4.

113. The Rays were planning on playing on August 27. It was rescheduled for the second game of a September 17 doubleheader in Baltimore. Marc Topkin, "The Rays Unite with the Orioles and Opt Not to Play. 'Obviously the World Is Much More Important than Just Sports'," *Tampa Bay Times*, August 28, 2020, C-1.

114. The day after the Twins and Tigers jointly decided not to play their August 27 game in Detroit in support of the racial injustice boycott, their game was postponed because of rain, resulting in the second game of a September 4 doubleheader being played in Minnesota. Omari Sankofa II, "Tigers, Twins Opt for Not Playing," *Detroit Free Press*, August 28, 2020, B-1.

115. The Blue Jays opened the 2021 regular season at their spring-training home in Dunedin before moving back to Sahlen Field on June 1. They played their first game since 2019 at the Rogers Centre on July 30, 2021. Aside from the one game in Anaheim on August 10, the Jays played the remainder of their 2021 home schedule at the Rogers Centre. Mike Harrington, "A Second Home," *The Citizen* (Auburn, New York), June 2, 2021, B-1; Davis, "July 30, 2021: Blue Jays Play First Home Game in Canada in Nearly Two Years."

116. Mike Axisa, "MLB Lockout Ends: What's Next for Baseball as MLBPA, Owners Reach Agreement and Get Ready for 2022 Opening Day," CBS Sports, March 13, 2022. Accessed December 19, 2022: https://www.cbssports.com/mlb/news/mlb-lockout-ends-whats-next-for-baseball-as-mlbpa-owners-reach-agreement-andget-ready-for-2022-opening-day.

117. Three days were also added to the end of the regular season. "MLB Announces Revised 2022 Regular-Season Schedule," MLB.com, March 16, 2022. Accessed December 19, 2022: https://www.mlb.com/news/mlbrevised-2022-regular-season-schedule.

118. With a more balanced schedule having been introduced for the 2023 season, that milestone may be reached even sooner than one might expect. The 2023 schedule had all 30 teams playing each other for at least one series. This decreased the number of home series against each team in the same division from three to two and increased the number of times a team made one and only one visit to a city. The number of divisional games was reduced from 76 to 52 and interleague games were increased from 20 to 46. Non-divisional intraleague games were reduced from 66 to 64. Mike Axisa, "MLB Releases 2023 Schedule: All 30 Teams Will Face Each Other in New Format; Opening Day on March 30," CBS Sports, August 25, 2022. Accessed November 15, 2022: https://www.cbssports.com/mlb/news/mlb-releases-2023-schedule-all-30-teams-will-face-each-other-in-new-format-opening-day-on-march-30.

Strategic Pitch Location

The Role of Two-Pitch Sequences in Pitching Success

John Z. Clay

On the surface, baseball does not appear overly complex. Not only is the sport easy enough for millions of children to understand and play in their Little League games, its charming simplicity is one of the many reasons it was adopted as "America's Pastime." However, as both the interest and capital involved in professional baseball have drastically increased, so too have the measures taken by teams to ensure their victories. Since the dawn of sabermetrics, our vision of baseball has become both much clearer and cloudier: although analysis does reveal many insights, one of them is that baseball is an intricate system that we have only begun to understand.

An important aspect of the game's strategy is the pitch-by-pitch decision making taking place throughout a plate appearance. The nature of this matchup between the pitcher-catcher duo and a batter is sequential. The pitcher acts and is met with a reaction by the batter, a process that iterates until the batter either fails or succeeds to reach base. There are two domains of behavior sequences to consider when analyzing the pitcher vs. batter matchup: the sequential behavior of the pitcher, and the sequential behavior of the batter. I refer to the former, the sequence of strategic decisions that a pitcher makes throughout an at-bat, as *sequential pitch behavior.* A pitcher's sequential pitch behavior can be divided into several subfactors, each concerned with one of the variables over which the pitcher has control. For example, a pitcher may vary the type of pitch thrown (e.g., fastball vs. breaking pitch), the velocity at which it is thrown, or the intended target area of the strike zone. In this paper, I will exclusively discuss *location sequence behavior*—how pitchers use strategic decisions about locations within the strike zone to retire batters.

Any behavior is closely linked to previous behaviors, and to fully understand an action it may be important to consider the influence of the previous action(s). A pitcher's sequential pitch behavior is heavily influenced by their history, and a key factor in determining future pitching behavior is the success of previous behaviors within a certain time period such

as a single game or a series of previous at-bats against a particular batter. The more success a previous behavior brought a pitcher within a time period, the more likely he will be to use it in certain future situations. This is known in psychology as *conditioning.* Due to individual differences in both brain functioning and pitching strategies, it is difficult to determine the correct number of occurrences of previous behaviors (a.k.a. the length of the behavior sequence) to consider when quantifying the influences that led to the current behavior. In this paper I will discuss two-pitch sequences, particularly *two-pitch location sequence behavior*—a behavior sequence containing the strike zone location that a pitch was thrown in, and the location that the following pitch was thrown in.

In the sections below, pitchers will be grouped together according to similarities in their two-pitch location sequence behavior to analyze how these behavior sequences are related to pitching success. The philosophy behind my approach is not unique—grouping players based on the similarities they show in relevant behaviors has been successfully implemented by the titans of sabermetrics. For example, Bill James used his *Similarity Scores* to define the difference between the careers of two players, a method he described in depth in the 1994 book *Politics of Glory.*[1] Similarly, Nate Silver's PECOTA projection system works on the assumption that players who show similar behavior patterns will, on average, have a comparable amount of success.[2] Within this well-explored research philosophy, my approach is unique due to the use of machine learning techniques to analyze specific pitch-by-pitch behavior.

RESEARCH OVERVIEW

The present paper is concerned with the strategic decision-making process that takes place between a pitcher and a batter as they face off throughout an at-bat. I analyze two-pitch sequences of the strike zone locations that pitchers target to investigate how location sequence behavior across a full season relates to performance metrics (batting average against, slugging percentage, etc.).

I present a statistical model to quantify the two-pitch location sequence behavior of pitchers, and subsequently partition them by the similarities they show in their sequential behaviors. Once pitchers are grouped, I test for differences across a range of performance metrics. All topics are discussed in further depth in the following sections.

I am unaware of any other study that does an analysis similar to what is described below. A recent study by Arnav Prasad, presented at the MIT Sloan sports analytics conference, conducted a novel analysis of pitch sequencing using directed graph embeddings to quantify pitcher patterns, after which they group pitcher based on these patterns.[3] However, the author did not associate the pitcher groups with performance metrics as the present study does.

METHOD
Pitchers

Pitch-by-pitch data were collected for every pitcher in the American League who threw more than 1,450 pitches in the 2019 MLB season. The pitch count cutoff was set around the edge of less-often-used starting rotation pitchers and often-used bullpen pitchers. Eighty-seven pitchers were included in the analysis (pitch count range = 1,466–5,228, M = 2,588.71, SD = 863.14). This was a convenience sample. All data were acquired through Baseball Savant's Statcast database on MLB.com.[4]

Data Analysis

Data analysis took the following path: First, each pitcher was defined by a transition matrix derived from their two-pitch location sequence behaviors with a discrete-time Markov chain (DTMC). Second, pitchers were partitioned according to similarities in these behaviors using three different cluster analysis algorithms. Lastly, Analyses of Variance (ANOVAs) were conducted to test for differences in various performance metrics between the pitcher groups created by the cluster analysis. (The method described here is similar to that of Rahman et al., 2018.[5])

Markov chains quantify behavioral sequences by accounting for the probability that one state transitions to another state. DTMC's rely on the assumption that the transition to the next state is solely dependent on the previous state—this is otherwise known as the Markov property. The states in a Markov chain are context dependent. In the current study, the states that pitchers are transitioning between are the strike zone location that the previous pitch was thrown in, and the location of the following pitch. Strike zone locations

were coded by the Statcast database at Baseball Savant online. See Figure 1 for a visualization. (Please note that the Statcast database does not include a tenth zone for undisclosed reasons.)

Pitcher two-pitch location sequence behavior was then defined by a transition matrix containing the probability for each possible state-to-state transition: i.e., the probability of transitioning from location one back to location one, location one to location two, and so on through to location 14 to location 13, and lastly location 14 to location 14. The probability that a pitcher transitioned from location one to location two was equal to the number of times he followed a pitch in location one with a pitch in location two divided by the total number of times he threw a pitch in location one. I added a delimiting state of *begin at-bat* so that the Markov chain would not attribute the first pitch of an at-bat to the last pitch of the previous at-bat. With 13 strike zone location states and one delimiting state, pitcher behavior was defined across their probabilities for all 196 possible state-to-state transitions in a 14 x 14 transition matrix.

After pitchers were defined by their two-pitch location sequence behaviors, they were partitioned with an extended cluster analysis approach. Pitchers were clustered through three different cluster analysis algorithms—k-means, hierarchical, and spectral—after which the variation of information method was used to determine the single best clustering. I will avoid discussing cluster analysis in much depth. (Please see Kettenring's 2006 work for a general overview of the approach.[6] For an example of cluster analysis in baseball research, see Dvorocsik, Sarris, and Camp's paper in the spring 2020 issue of the *Baseball Research Journal*.[7])

Traditional k-means clustering employs the use of an elbow plot to determine the number of groups

Figure 1. Strike Zone Locations

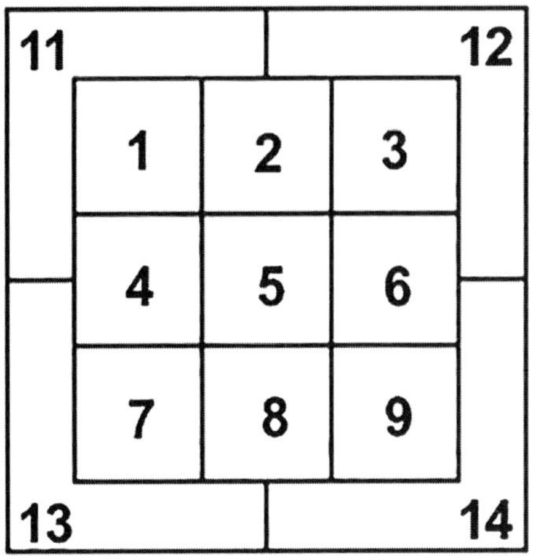

(k) that best fits the data. However, hierarchical and spectral algorithms use other methods. In this method, I use the elbow plot to suggest a range of clusterings from each of the three algorithms. The elbow plot suggested a k range of three to seven, creating fifteen different solutions for grouping pitchers. To determine the best solution, the variation of information technique was used to compare each possible pairing of clusterings and choose the most efficient algorithm/grouping.[8]

RESULTS

Pitchers were first defined by the 14 x 14 transition matrix containing the probabilities they showed for each possible state transition, after which they were partitioned according to their similarities in the 196 transition variables. Subsequent analyses suggested that the most efficient algorithm was k-means clustering with five groups. See Table 1 for the members of each of the five created pitcher groups.

A series of one-way between-subjects ANOVAs were conducted to test for differences in performance metrics between the created pitcher groups. A total of nineteen ANOVAs were performed. To be economic, I will report the specific statistics for only the significant tests. The ANOVAs each met the assumptions for homogeneity of variance, and post hoc comparison p values were adjusted using the Bonferroni correction to control for false positives.

There were no significant differences found between the five pitcher groups for the following performance metrics: Isolated Power (ISO), Batting Average on Balls In Play (BABIP), Slugging Percentage (SLG), Weighted On-base Average (wOBA), Expected Weighted On-base Average (xwOBA), Walks and Hits Per Inning Pitched (WHIP), O-Swing%, O-Contact%, Z-Swing%, hits, total pitches, and at-bats.

Significant differences were found between pitcher groups in seven performance metrics: spin rate, pitch velocity, batted ball exit velocity, surrendered batting average against (BAA), expected batting average against (xBAA), adjusted earned run average (ERA+), and Z-Contact%. For all significant test statistics, see Table 2. For the means and standard deviations of each group in each performance metric, see Table 3. See the following paragraphs for the post hoc comparisons, and Table 4 for a visualization.

Table 1. Players by Group

Pitcher Group							
One (n = 7)	**Two (n = 21)**		**Three (n = 21)**		**Four (n = 14)**	**Five (n = 24)**	
Brett Anderson	Ariel Jurado	Mike Leake	Andrew Heaney	Marco Gonzales	Adam Plutko	Aaron Brooks	Iván Nova
José Suarez	Brad Peacock	Sam Gaviglio	Blake Snell[3]	Matthew Boyd	Asher Wojciechowski	Aaron Sanchez[1]	Jaime Barría
Martín Pérez	Carlos Carrasco	Scott Barlow	CC Sabathia[3]	Mike Minor[2]	Chad Green	Adrian Sampson	Jakob Junis
Nick Ramirez	Edwin Jackson[1]	Shane Bieber[2,3]	Chris Sale	Nestor Cortes Jr.	Dylan Cease	Andrew Cashner	José Berríos[2]
Tommy Milone	Gabriel Ynoa	Spencer Turnbull[1]	Daniel Norris	Thomas Pannone	Gerrit Cole[2]	Charlie Morton[2]	José Leclerc
Wade LeBlanc	Jesse Chavez	Trevor Cahill	Danny Duffy	Tyler Skaggs	Jake Odorizzi[2]	Chris Bassitt	Lance Lynn
Wade Miley[1]	Jordan Zimmermann[1]	Yonny Chirinos	David Price[3]	Yusei Kikuchi	Justin Verlander[1,2,3]	Collin McHugh[1]	Mike Clevinger
-	Jorge López	-	Dillon Peters	-	Liam Hendriks[2]	David Hess	Mike Fiers[1]
-	Kyle Gibson	-	Eduardo Rodriguez	-	Lucas Giolito[1,2]	Domingo Germán	Reynaldo López
-	Luis Cessa	-	J.A. Happ	-	Matt Barnes	Dylan Bundy	Trent Thornton
-	Marcus Stroman[2]	-	Jacob Waguespack	-	Nathan Eovaldi	Félix Peña[1]	-
-	Marcus Walden	-	Jalen Beeks	-	Rick Porcello[3]	Frankie Montas	-
-	Masahiro Tanaka[2]	-	James Paxton[1]	-	Trevor Bauer[3]	Griffin Canning	-
-	Michael Pineda	-	John Means[1,2]	-	Zach Plesac	Homer Bailey[1]	-

1 = has thrown or contributed to a no-hitter
2 = 2019 MLB All Star
3 = Cy Young Award winner

Table 2. Test Statistics for the Significant ANOVAs

Performance Metric	F	p	η^2
Spin Rate	$F(4,82) = 3.73$	.007	.148
Pitch Velo.	7.47	< .001	.267
BB Exit Velo.	2.59	.042	.112
BAA	3.41	.012	.142
xBAA	3.58	.009	.148
ERA+	2.55	.045	.115
Z-Contact%	6.56	< .001	.242

BB Exit Velo. = batted ball exit velocity

Tukey's post hoc analysis found that the average spin rate of Group One was significantly lower than: Group Three, $p = .04$, Four, $p = .003$, and Five, $p = 0.012$. Group One also showed significantly lower batted ball exit velocity than Group Two, $p = .037$. Please refer to Table 3 for the means of each group.

Pitcher Group One had significantly lower average pitch velocity than groups: Two, $p = .003$, Four, $p < .001$, and Five, $p = .004$. Additionally, Group Four showed significantly higher average pitch velocity than Group Three, $p = .003$.

Group Four exhibited significantly lower average BAA compared to Groups One, $p = .048$, and Two, $p = .011$. Group Four also showed significantly lower xBAA than Group Two, $p = 005$. Additionally, Group

Four had significantly higher ERA + than pitcher Group Two, $p = .044$.

Lastly, Group Four showed the lowest overall Z-Contact% and significantly lower average Z-Contact% than Groups One ($p = .029$) and Two ($p < .001$). Additionally, Group Three showed significantly lower Z-Contact% than Group Two ($p = .004$).

DISCUSSION

Pitchers were defined by their two-pitch location sequence behaviors and subsequently grouped together according to their similarities. Upon their grouping, a range of ANOVAs were performed to test for differences in performance metrics. Significant differences were found in six of the ANOVAs, and post

Table 3. Means and Standard Deviations for Each Group

Performance Metric	Pitcher Group - M (SE)				
-	**One**	**Two**	**Three**	**Four**	**Five**
Spin Rate	2029.86 (47.68)	2210.33 (33.45)	2235.09 (28.61)	2309.21 (48.02)	2260.67 (39.57)
Pitch Velo.	85.19 (1.02)	88.48 (.345	87.25 (.42)	89.85 (.67)	88.37 (.39)
BB Exit Velo.	87.9 (.5)	89.48 (.24)	88.63 (.24)	88.88 (.34)	88.72 (.29)
BAA	0.269 (.009)	0.265 (.007)	0.257 (.004)	0.232 (.009)	0.251 (.006)
xBAA	0.263 (.007)	0.263 (.006)	0.251 (.005)	0.229 (.009)	0.253 (.006)
ERA+	95.0 (7.65)	100.38 (4.94)	101.57 (4.43)	126.5 (12.16)	106.71 (5.57)
Z-Contact%	87.23% (.008)	87.84% (.005)	84.04% (.007)	82.51% (.011)	85.58% (.007)
WHIP	1.40 (.058)	1.35 (.045)	1.36 (.042)	1.23 (.059)	1.32 (.031)
ISO	0.197 (.018)	0.200 (.011)	0.191 (.008)	0.183 (.01)	0.190 (.01)
BABIP	0.295 (.009)	0.303 (.007)	0.304 (.004)	0.294 (.009)	0.295 (.004)
SLG	0.466 (.022)	0.464 (.017)	0.448 (.01)	0.415 (.017)	0.441 (.014)
wOBA	0.333 (.011)	0.329 (.008)	0.325 (.005)	0.303 (.011)	0.321 (.007)
xwOBA	0.333 (.007)	0.334 (.007)	0.323 (.006)	0.304 (.010)	0.327 (.007)
Hits	136.0 (15.15)	120.81 (8.32)	129.14 (9.58)	107.07 (10.65)	135.88 (9.61)
O-Swing%	32.33% (.012)	32.07% (.007)	32.12% (.005)	32.13% (.007)	31.26% (.005)
O-Contact%	66.40% (.015)	61.77% (.015)	64.47% (.017)	59.74% (.022)	62.86% (.013)
Z-Swing%	68.37% (.006)	68.09% (.007)	68.81% (.005)	69.39% (.008)	67.79% (.007)

Bold = significant differences found between groups
BB Exit Velo. = batted ball exit velocity

Table 4. Post Hoc Comparisons

Performance Metric	Pitcher Group				
-	**One**	**Two**	**Three**	**Four**	**Five**
Spin Rate	< 3, 4, 5	-	> 1	> 1	> 1
Pitch Velo.	< 2, 4, 5	> 1	< 4	> 1, 3	> 1
BB Exit Velo.	< 2	> 1	-	-	-
BAA	> 4	> 4	-	< 1, 2	-
xBAA	-	> 4	-	< 2	-
ERA+	-	< 4	-	> 2	-
Z-Contact%	< 4	< 4, 3	> 2	> 1, 2	-

All reported differences were significant at p < .05.
BB Exit Velo. = batted ball exit velocity

hoc comparisons found that many of the significant effects included pitcher Groups One or Four. It must be highlighted that testing for significance is a methodology that was devised for non-baseball phenomena, and differences in baseball metrics that do not reach significance may still be highly relevant to the game. In this paper I use significance to highlight the metrics in which the groups showed the largest differences, and to set an informal cut-off for which differences to explore in further depth below.

Many of the performance metrics did not show significant differences between groups. This was expected, as pitchers were classified on a granular level. Given the complexity of baseball strategy, it is unlikely that these low level behaviors would be a major contributor to most metrics of success. Additionally, many of the metrics in which differences were tested for are dependent on several other metrics. For example, the calculation for expected weighted on-base average (xwOBA) is especially intricate. As the complexity of performance metrics increases, granular behaviors such as the ones studied presently are likely to have their effects diluted, hindering any significance that may have been revealed in a less complex metric.

Tests of differences between total pitches and at-bats were included to ensure that no group differed significantly in use. Significant differences were not found between the groups for either variable, suggesting the effects that were found were not a result of pitch level sample size differences.

The ANOVAs did reveal significant differences between pitcher groups in six performance metrics: spin rate, pitch velocity, batted ball exit velocity, BAA, xBAA, and ERA+. Each test offers insight into how two-pitch location sequence behaviors may be related to pitching success. Differences in spin rate and pitch velocity suggest that pitching mechanics are related to how pitchers transition between strike zone locations. Additionally, significant differences in average batted ball exit velocity may suggest that certain location sequence behavior patterns (i.e., the ones shown by Group Two) are less effective than other patterns in limiting batter contact.

BAA, xBAA, ERA+, and batted ball exit velocity are each important performance metrics. The significant differences found between groups in these metrics suggests that two-pitch location sequence behavior may be directly related to metrics indicative of high performance. It must be noted that pitching behavior was not manipulated, and this model and accompanying analyses cannot be used to make direct causal claims. However, the differences found suggest that

successful pitchers on average display different two-pitch location sequence behaviors than pitchers with lower performance. It may be that players who engage in some sequence behavior patterns are also engaging in other actions that are responsible for their success.

It should be noted that pitch location sequence behavior is likely related to the pitch types and movements that pitchers use. Many pitchers favor a specific pitch when the count is favorable for recording an out. For example, pitchers who rely on fastballs are likely to pitch in the higher third of the zone in two strike counts to strike batters out, while pitchers with a refined sinker may utilize the bottom third of the zone more often.

I will now focus on Groups One and Four in more depth.

Pitcher Group One
Group One performed poorly in relation to the other groups (Tables 1–4). Out of sixty-eight career seasons, members of Group One have appeared in two All-Star Games (2.9%), have thrown one career no-hitter (Wade Miley, 2021), and have received zero Cy Young Awards. They showed significantly lower spin rate in relation to three other groups, lower pitch velocity than three other groups, and a higher batting average against than Group Four. Further analysis showed that of the five groups, Group One showed the lowest probability to use 65 out of the 196 (33.16%) possible state transitions. This suggests that there were many two-pitch location sequence behaviors that the pitchers in Group One very rarely used, likely leaving their pitching patterns more predictable than the other groups.

Pitcher Group Four
Opposite to Group One was Group Four, who showed very high performance compared to the rest of the sample (see Table 5). These pitchers have been elected

Table 5. Players in Pitcher Group Four

Pitcher Group Four	
Justin Verlander[1,2,3]	Matt Barnes
Trevor Bauer[3]	Dylan Cease
Gerrit Cole[2]	Nathan Eovaldi
Lucas Giolito[1,2]	Chad Green
Jake Odorizzi[2]	Zach Plesac
Liam Hendriks[2]	Adam Plutko
Rick Porcello[3]	Asher Wojciechowski

1 = has thrown or contributed to a no-hitter
2 = 2019 MLB All Star
3 = Cy Young Award winner

to 21 All-Star Games out of 124 cumulative career seasons (16.9%). Additionally, 5 out of the 11 pitchers from the 2019 MLB All-Star Game included in this sample belonged to this group. Group Four boasts three Cy Young Awards (Justin Verlander, 2011 and 2019; Rick Porcello, 2016), two future Cy Young Awards (Trevor Bauer, 2020; Justin Verlander, 2022), and two future Reliever of the Year Awards (Liam Hendriks, 2020 and 2021). This group has also thrown four career no-hitters, including two of the previous three at the time of this writing (Justin Verlander, September 1, 2019; Lucas Giolito, August 25, 2020). Group Four has also been well compensated for their success. In 2019, Gerrit Cole signed the largest contract for a pitcher in MLB history ($324 million), and his previous team-mate Justin Verlander's 2023–4 contract is currently tied (Max Scherzer) for the highest average annual value (AAV) in MLB history at $43.3 million.

The significant differences found through the ANOVAs, along with the distribution of accolades would suggest that the two-pitch location sequence behaviors that pitchers were grouped by are related to pitching success, and perhaps played a role in how pitchers were able to achieve their success. However, the number of transition probabilities offers some challenges when drawing conclusions on how the groups acted differently from each other. With 196 variables to consider, a comprehensive review would be arduous to write, and even more painful to read. This clustering method offers many options for gathering insights, and I will discuss three here: I will address two specific insights that may be drawn, and then end with a case study.

First, Group Four showed the highest probability for 61 out of the 196 (31.12%) possible state transitions, the highest of the groups. After Group Four, Group One showed the highest probability for the second highest number of transitions (41/196; 20.91%). This suggests that pitchers in Group Four varied their two-pitch location sequence behaviors more than the other groups, which may have made their behavior less predictable to the batter. Similar trends arise when considering how often each group used each two-pitch sequence. Group One showed a higher probability to transition from location five to the end of the at-bat (43.15%) than any other group's probability of making any two-pitch sequence. The highest two-pitch sequence probability for the other groups were as follows: Group Two (41.43%), Group Three (38.52%), Group Four (36.20%), and Group Five (37.56%). Thus, Group Four's highest probability for a *single transition* (i.e., zone location 1 to location 5) was the lowest out of the groups (by a slight

Justin Verlander

margin). In other words, Group Four showed a more equal distribution of two-pitch transitions, and did not rely heavily on any specific sequences.

A closer look at the strike zone locations that pitcher groups most often ended their at-bats with offers additional insight into how Group Four was different from the others. Of the 13 possible transitions of strike zone location that could end an at-bat, Group Four placed last (out of the five groups) in ten, second to last in one, and first in the other two. Not only were they much *more likely* to end their at-bats by attacking strike zone locations seven and 13 when compared to the other groups, they were much *less likely* to end their at-bats in the other locations. Considered in light of the previous findings, these results suggest that while the pitchers in Group Four vary their two-pitch location sequence behavior more than the other groups, they show a higher tendency to focus on a small number of locations towards the end of an at-bat.

CASE STUDY
Justin Verlander's Third Career No-Hitter
All results presented thus far were concerned with data over a full year. I will end with a brief case study of how this model may be used to analyze smaller sections of data: a single game. On September 1, 2019, in Toronto, Ontario, Canada, Justin Verlander threw his third career no-hitter. Upon analyzing his two-pitch location sequence behaviors, three trends are immediately apparent. Verlander threw 120 pitches that day, and with 28 added *begin at-bat* transition variables he showed 148 state transitions. Verlander's 148 two-pitch sequences were distributed across 83 unique transitions. Notably, 52 out of the 83 (62.65%) two-pitch sequences were only used once, and no sequence was used more than five times. Verlander did very well

to avoid pitching predictably, which likely contributed to the Blue Jays' struggles that night.

However, despite this tactical variance, there were certain situations in which Verlander opted to continue previous behavior trends. Out of the 28 batters faced, the first pitch to 13 of them (46.42%) were in strike zone locations three (four first pitches; three to right handed batters and one to left handed batters), 11 (four first pitches; two to both RHB and LHB), or 12 (five first pitches; two to RHB and three to LHB). Additionally, 16 of the 28 (57.14%) plate appearances ended with pitches in locations five (five PA endings; three to RHB and two to LHB), nine (six PA endings; one to RHB and five to LHB), or 14 (five PA endings; four to RHB and one to LHB). See Figure 2 for a visualization—shaded locations were often attacked by Verlander to begin at-bats, while striped locations accounted for over half of the recorded outs.

During his no-hitter on September 1, 2019, Justin Verlander showed *situational variance*—during certain stages of an at-bat he was tactically unpredictable, using many different unique state transitions throughout the game. However, during other stages of the game he remained resolute and continued the behaviors he had success with earlier, e.g., towards the beginning and end of at-bats. These findings continue the trends found in the yearly data—the pitchers in the most successful group showed high variance in their two-pitch location sequence behaviors in some situations, but constrained their behavior in others.

Limitations and Future Directions

The present study had several limitations. First, I am not as much working in the realm of Big Data as I am in quasi-Big Data. Baseball offers a vast wealth of data to pull from, and only analyzing one variable (location) for one year (2019) does not offer as much insight as could be gleaned from a larger data set.

Figure 2. Verlander's Attack Pattern

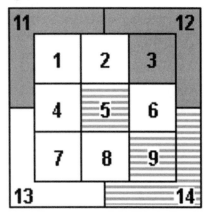

NOTE: 13 of 28 first pitches of the at-bat made in the shaded locations; 16 of 28 final pitches of the at-bat made in the striped locations.

Thus, it cannot be assumed that the pitching behaviors observed here are representative of behaviors displayed by pitchers in other years. Additionally, the year from which the data were collected may be slightly confounding. The 2019 MLB season was marred by a "juiced ball" controversy in which a vocal portion of players and fans believed that the league-issued baseballs were doctored to increase the frequency of home runs. Regardless of whether the baseballs had been tampered with, the belief that they were likely had some influence on pitching behaviors.

The relatively large number of ANOVAs that were conducted increased the risk of encountering both Type I and Type II errors, though the Bonferonni correction was used for pairwise comparisons. More data and follow-up tests are required to test the robustness of the revealed effects.

Lastly, Markov models are drastically simplified abstractions of complex pitching behaviors, as they only consider the transition between two states. Future studies should consider employing more robust methods, such as neural networks or graph network analysis. However, due to the exploratory nature of the present study I opted to use a DTMC for its tractability and ease of explanation.

CONCLUSIONS

The present study presented a model for grouping pitchers by their pitch-by-pitch behavior, and results suggested that certain recorded behaviors may contribute to pitching success. Pitchers in the most successful group showed *situational variance*, in which they pitched stochastically in some situations and more predictably in others. Trends were revealed at both year-level data and through a single game case study. ∎

Notes

1. Bill James, *The Politics of Glory: How Baseball's Hall of Fame Really Works* (Macmillan, 1994), 86–106.
2. Nate Silver, *The Signal and the Noise: Why So Many Predictions Fail—But Some Don't* (Penguin, 2012), 74–107. For a description of the approach PECOTA takes see chapter three.
3. Arnav Prasad, "Decoding MLB Pitch Sequencing Strategies via Directed Graph Embeddings," 15th Annual MIT SLOAN Sports Analytics Conference, 2021.
4. https://baseballsavant.mlb.com.
5. Molla H. Rahman, Michael Gashler, Charles Xie, and Zhenghui Sha, "Automatic clustering of sequential design behaviors," *International Design Engineering Technical Conferences and Computers and Information in Engineering Conference*, Vol. 51739, American Society of Mechanical Engineers, 2018.
6. Jon R. Kettenring, "The practice of cluster analysis," *Journal of Classification* 23, no. 1 (2006) 3–30.
7. Gregory Dvorocsik, Eno Sarris, and Joseph Camp, "Using Clustering to Find Pitch Subtypes and Effective Pairings," *Baseball Research Journal*, Spring 2020.
8. Marina Meilă, "Comparing clusterings—an information based distance," *Journal of Multivariate Analysis* 98, no. 5 (2007): 873–95.

Standardized Peak WAR (SPW)

A Fair Standard for Historical Comparison of Peak Value

David J. Gordon, MD, PhD

When judging the greatness of a baseball player's career by whatever metrics one may put stock in, we weigh them from two perspectives:

1. **Total Value**: How much did they accomplish in their career? How many years did they play at a high level? What career milestones did they achieve?

2. **Peak Value**: How productive were they in their very best seasons? Were they ever regarded over any statistically meaningful time period as one of the top few players in MLB?

The most exalted players in the Hall of Fame (HoF)—Babe Ruth, Willie Mays, Ty Cobb, Walter Johnson, Hank Aaron, Rogers Hornsby, Honus Wagner, Cy Young, etc.—were elite on both counts; one need not overthink their HoF qualifications. But many less exalted players, both inside and outside of the HoF, were elite from one perspective but not the other. At the two extremes, we have "marathoners" like Don Sutton, who compiled elite career totals (324 W, 3,574 SO) in 23 seasons but never came close to winning a Cy Young award, and we have "sprinters" like Sandy Koufax, who won three Cy Young awards and an MVP award in four seasons (1963–66) but pitched only 12 seasons and won only 165 games. Both are worthy Hall of Famers, but they got there by very different paths.

Over the last two decades, the Wins Above Replacement metric (WAR), which combines the contributions of different performance elements, weighted according to their contributions to team wins and adjusted for the environment in which a player's statistics were accrued, has become the metric of choice for global evaluation of player performance.[1,2] WAR is superior to traditional counting stats like HR, RBI, W, and SO because it incorporates many diverse elements of performance that contribute to team wins and adjusts for the environment (league, ballpark, era) in which a given player performed. But while career WAR is a reasonable measure of the total value of a player's accomplishments, we have not had a good measure of peak value.

Jay Jaffe invented a WAR-based composite score called the Jaffe WAR Score (JAWS), which purports to combine total and peak value into a single global performance metric to assess a player's qualifications for the HoF.[3,4] JAWS is the simple average of career WAR (the total value component) and the combined WAR (WAR7) for the player's seven best seasons (the peak value component). The problem with this method is that WAR7 is a poor measure of peak value, especially for pitchers. While hitter usage has remained relatively constant since the advent of the 154-game schedule in the 1890s (with the notable exception of the Negro Leagues), seven seasons has a very different meaning for pitchers of different eras.

In the 1870s, teams played only 2–3 games per week, and 90% of the innings were handled by a single pitcher.[5] Now, 150 years later, we have 13-man pitching staffs (not counting frequent call-ups of fresh arms from the minor leagues) with relief pitchers taking on an ever increasing share of the workload. Today, few individual pitchers accrue as many as 200 IP per season. So, the 11,633 batters faced (BF) by Cy Young in his best seven seasons is more than double the 5,752 BF by Clayton Kershaw in his best seven seasons.[6] In this context, Kershaw's 47.7 WAR7 really represents a *higher* "peak" performance rate per 1,000 BF than Young's 79.1 WAR7 (8.3 versus 6.8 WAR per 1,000 BF).[7] As for relief pitchers, Mariano Rivera faced only 5103 batters in his entire career but still accrued 56.4 WAR—an even better production rate (11.1 WAR per 1000 BF) than Kershaw's peak. However, comparing production rates over disparate numbers of BF is unfair to Cy Young, because this would require Young to maintain peak effectiveness over twice as many BF as Kershaw. We need a peak value measure that compares like numbers of BF for pitchers and like numbers of PA for hitters.

I will now present a new construct called Standardized Peak WAR (SPW), which is designed to compare peak values of players who received vastly differing annual PA or BF opportunities. SPW is standardized to 3,250 PA for batters and 5,000 BF for pitchers. The former number represents five 650-PA seasons for batters, 650 PA being a typical total for a healthy everyday player hitting near the top of the lineup over 150–160 games. The latter number represents five 1,000-BF seasons, where 1,000 BF represents a typical workload for a regular starting pitcher from 1909–88.[8] In the 1880s, pitchers like Charles "Old Hoss" Radbourn, Pud Galvin, and Tim Keefe among others posted insanely high WAR totals (near 20) while amassing 600 + IP and 2500 + BF. Since 2006, only three pitchers—CC Sabathia (1,023 BF in 2008), Felix Hernandez (1,001 BF in 2010), and David Price (1,009 BF in 2014)—have logged as many as 1000 BF in a season. The detailed calculation of SPW and a comparison of rankings by WAR and SPW are presented below.

METHODOLOGY

The Baseball-Reference.com version of WAR for pitchers and for non-pitchers as of December 2022 is the underlying performance metric used in the calculation of SPW.[9] For Negro Leaguers, I have used the comparable WAR values from the Seamheads database, which incorporates statistics from both MLB-certified and uncertified leagues (and thus recognizes the achievements of players of color who played before 1920 and those who played mostly in Cuba and Mexico).[10] I have calculated SPW for every player in the HoF and for every MLB player with career batting or pitching WAR ≥ 30. The calculation of SPW is illustrated

below for two mid-20th century icons, Sandy Koufax (Table 1) and Mickey Mantle (Table 2).

One first calculates "standardized WAR" (sWAR) per 1000 BF for pitchers or per 650 PA for hitters for each season and sorts the seasons in descending order. Then one adds up the WAR for each season until reaching 5,000 cumulative BF or 3,250 cumulative PA. SPW is obtained by interpolating between the cumulative WAR values just before and just after the BF or PA threshold is crossed. For pitchers with < 5,000 BF or non-pitchers with < 3,250 PA, SPW is defined as their career WAR.

Note that the SPW construct cannot combine hitting and pitching stats for a single player within any single season. For players with significant career value as both hitters and pitchers (e.g., Babe Ruth, Martin Dihigo, Bullet Rogan, Wes Ferrell), I have used the higher of their SPW for hitting and pitching.

One could as easily use the FanGraphs version of WAR or other similar metrics for this purpose.[11] Indeed, a similar approach can be applied to any appropriate cumulative (as opposed to rate) stat.

RESULTS: PITCHERS

Values of total pitching WAR and SPW for the 80 pitchers with SPW ≥ 32.0 are listed in Table 3 (opposite). Of the 71 pitchers who have been retired for at least five years, 44 (62%) are in the HoF as of January 2023 (indicated in boldface type). As many as six others (Clemens, Schilling, K. Brown, Cicotte, Finley, and perhaps Pettitte) have been kept out of the HoF by issues unrelated to their accomplishments on the field. (Note that SPW values are not adjusted for alleged PED use.)

Table 1. Calculation of SPW for Sandy Koufax

Year	Age	BF	Season WAR	sWAR	Cumulative BF	WAR
1963	27	1210	10.7	8.84	1210	10.7
1964	28	870	7.3	8.39	2080	18.0
1966	30	1274	10.3	8.08	3354	28.3
1965	29	1297	8.1	6.25	4651	36.4
			SPW		5000	38.46
1962	26	744	4.4	5.91	5395	40.8
1961	25	1068	5.7	5.34	6463	46.5
1955	19	183	0.9	4.92	6646	47.4
1959	23	679	2.2	3.24	7325	49.6
1957	21	444	1.3	2.93	7769	50.9
1960	24	753	1.5	1.99	8522	52.4
1958	22	714	1.2	1.68	9236	53.6
1956	20	261	-0.3	-1.15	9497	53.3

Table 2. Calculation of SPW for Mickey Mantle

Year	Age	PA	Season WAR	sWAR	Cumulative PA	WAR
1957	25	623	11.3	18.14	623	11.3
1956	24	652	11.2	17.18	1275	22.5
1961	29	646	10.4	16.10	1921	32.9
1955	23	638	9.5	14.89	2559	42.4
1963	31	213	2.9	13.62	2772	45.3
			SPW		3250	51.7
1958	26	654	8.7	13.30	3426	54.0
1962	30	502	6.0	11.95	3928	60.0
1953	21	540	5.8	10.74	4468	65.8
1954	22	651	6.9	10.63	5117	72.7
1959	27	640	6.6	10.31	5757	79.3
1952	20	626	6.4	10.22	6383	85.7
1960	28	644	6.4	9.95	7026	92.1
1966	34	393	3.6	9.16	7419	95.7
1964	32	567	4.8	8.47	7986	100.5
1967	35	553	3.9	7.05	8539	104.4
1968	36	547	2.7	4.94	9086	107.1
1965	33	435	1.8	4.14	9521	108.9
1951	19	386	1.5	3.89	9907	110.4

Seven of the listed pitchers (shown in italics) are still active.

Two surprising features stand out from this table. First, the all-time SPW leader is reliever Mariano Rivera, who averaged more than 11 WAR per 1,000 BF over his 5103-BF career. SPW does not generally favor relievers over starters, but Rivera was an exceptional case. Rivera is one of only four relievers with SPW ≥ 32 and is the only one who pitched exclusively as a modern closer. Eckersley spent the first half of his career as a starter before becoming a one-inning closer, while Gossage and Wilhelm were multi-inning relievers, who also started 37 and 52 games, respectively, over the course of their careers. While it is easier for a reliever to post a high sWAR in a single 250-BF season than it is for a starter to do so in a 1,000-BF season, Rivera (who totaled only 5,103 BF in his 19-year career) had to produce at an elite level *without a single bad season* to achieve his 56.4 SPW. No other one-inning reliever has even come close to doing this.

Second, and just as strikingly, 12 of the top 16 SPW totals were posted by pitchers who were active in the twenty-first century, including four who were still active in 2022. In that respect, the SPW leaderboard stands in stark contrast to the career leaderboard for pitching WAR, in which only three of the top 16 pitchers (Clemens, R. Johnson, and Maddux) pitched into the twenty-first century and seven (Young, W. Johnson, Nichols, Alexander, Mathewson, Keefe, and Plank) pitched before 1920. This contrast largely reflects the

elimination by SPW of the opportunity advantage enjoyed by old-time pitchers. However, the modern practice of protecting starters from pitching past the 6th or 7th inning may also tilt SPW in their favor.

Of the 80 pitchers listed in Table 3, 31 (39%) had < 60 career pitching WAR. They fall into the following categories:

1. Three Negro Leaguers: Mendez, Williams, and R. Brown. They were great pitchers, whose career totals—including WAR—underestimate their true body of work, much of which is lost to history.

2. Three active pitchers: deGrom, Sale, and Kluber. Most players (except for late bloomers) come close to attaining their final SPW by their early 30s.

3. Three relievers—Rivera, Gossage, and Wilhelm. It is virtually impossible for any pure reliever—even Rivera—to face enough batters to accrue 60 WAR.

4. The remaining 22 belong to the group I call "sprinters," who pitched brilliantly over 5,000 BF but were prevented by injury or inconsistency from amassing 60 career WAR. Saberhagen, Koufax, and Santana (with six Cy Young awards and an MVP among them) are

Table 3. Pitching Leaderboard for Standardized Peak WAR (SPW)

	Pitchers	WAR	SPW		Pitchers	WAR	SPW		Pitchers	WAR	SPW
1	Rivera, Mariano	56.3	56.43	28	Vance, Dazzy	62.9	38.18	55	Spahn, Warren	92.5	34.00
2	Martinez, Pedro	86.1	53.56	29	Appier, Kevin	54.9	38.09	56	Kluber, Corey	34.7	33.94
3	Johnson, Walter	152.3	49.55	30	Brown, Kevin	68.2	37.95	57	Hubbell, Carl	68.8	33.70
4	Clemens, Roger	138.7	49.44	31	Cone, David	61.6	37.87	58	Perry, Gaylord	93.0	33.66
5	Johnson, Randy	103.5	48.25	32	Eckersley, Dennis	62.1	37.76	59	Adams, Babe	50.2	33.64
6	Grove, Lefty	113.3	46.07	33	Mussina, Mike	82.8	37.69	60	Reuschel, Rick	68.1	33.63
7	Paige, Satchel	61.2	46.03	34	Williams, Joe	50.4	37.38	61	Willis, Vic	67.0	33.51
8	Maddux, Greg	104.8	45.70	35	Waddell, Rube	60.9	37.30	62	Viola, Frank	47.1	33.26
9	Kershaw, Clayton	73.1	43.34	36	Walsh, Ed	63.8	37.12	63	Bunning, Jim	60.4	33.24
10	Verlander, Justin	78.2	42.90	37	Keefe, Tim	89.1	36.69	64	Roberts, Robin	83.0	33.15
11	Scherzer, Max	70.7	42.41	38	Tiant, Luis	65.6	36.47	65	Stieb, Dave	56.5	33.09
12	Halladay, Roy	65.4	41.49	39	Marichal, Juan	61.8	36.28	66	Smoltz, John	66.4	33.00
13	Gossage, Rich	41.6	41.24	40	Newhouser, Hal	60.0	36.20	67	Hernandez, Felix	49.9	32.81
14	Young, Cy	165.6	40.87	41	Nichols, Kid	116.7	35.92	68	Ford, Russ	32.7	32.67
15	Greinke, Zack	71.4	40.49	42	Blyleven, Bert	96.1	35.77	69	Clarkson, John	85.0	32.51
16	Schilling, Curt	80.5	40.41	43	Wilhelm, Hoyt	46.8	35.71	70	Niekro, Phil	97.0	32.49
17	Seaver, Tom	106.0	40.39	44	Wood, Wilbur	52.2	35.69	71	Finley, Chuck	58.3	32.49
18	Mendez, Jose	45.3	40.16	45	Coveleski, Stan	66.6	35.53	72	McDowell, Sam	43.1	32.45
19	deGrom, Jacob	41.1	39.90	46	Cicotte, Eddie	57.9	35.51	73	Guidry, Ron	47.9	32.38
20	Mathewson, Christy	100.4	39.65	47	Lee, Cliff	42.5	35.37	74	Plank, Eddie	87.5	32.32
21	Saberhagen, Bret	58.9	39.42	48	Oswalt, Roy	49.9	35.06	75	Glavine, Tom	73.9	32.24
22	Alexander, Pete	116.2	39.19	49	Feller, Bob	65.2	34.69	76	Hudson, Tim	56.6	32.23
23	Gibson, Bob	81.7	38.97	50	Buffinton, Charlie	60.7	34.57	77	Langston, Mark	50.0	32.17
24	Sale, Chris	45.6	38.79	51	Brown, Mordecai	57.2	34.46	78	Hamels, Cole	58.0	32.13
25	Santana, Johan	51.1	38.70	52	Brown, Ray	38.7	34.38	79	Hahn, Noodles	46.0	32.06
26	Carlton, Steve	84.1	38.55	53	Rijo, Jose	35.0	34.32	80	Pettitte, Andy	60.7	32.02
27	Koufax, Sandy	53.1	38.46	54	Bond, Tommy	61.0	34.23				

illustrative examples. This group of 22 pitchers has not been favored by HoF voters; Koufax and Mordecai Brown are the only Hall of Famers among them.

On the other side of that coin, we find 18 pitchers with SPW < 32 who sustained their value long enough to compile at least 60 WAR. They are listed in ascending order of the ratio of SPW/WAR (expressed as a percent)

in Table 4. Two-thirds (12) of these pitchers are in the HoF, and Sabathia will be a strong HoF candidate when he becomes eligible in 2025. While the pitchers at the bottom of this list either barely made the 60-WAR cutoff or barely missed the 32 SPW cutoff, the top 12 pitchers could aptly be considered "marathoners."

The contrast between the two prototypes—sprinters and marathoners—is illustrated in Figures 1 and 2, which graphically represent the season-by-season

Table 4. Other Pitchers with Career Pitching WAR ≥ 60

Pitchers	WAR	SPW	Ratio	Pitchers	WAR	SPW	Ratio
1 Galvin, Pud	83.3	30.54	37%	10 Palmer, Jim	67.6	29.18	43%
2 Ryan, Nolan	83.6	31.94	38%	11 John, Tommy	62.1	26.95	43%
3 Jenkins, Fergie	82.2	31.73	39%	12 Lyons, Ted	66.8	29.42	44%
4 McCormick, Jim	76.0	29.35	39%	13 Faber, Red	67.7	31.42	46%
5 Mullane, Tony	61.0	23.73	39%	14 Rusie, Amos	65.2	30.84	47%
6 Mathews, Bobby	62.3	25.23	40%	15 Drysdale, Don	61.3	29.79	49%
7 Welch, Mickey	63.1	25.62	41%	16 Buehrle, Mark	60.0	29.54	49%
8 Sutton, Don	68.3	27.76	41%	17 Sabathia, CC	61.8	31.57	51%
9 Radbourn, Old Hoss	73.2	31.49	43%	18 McGinnity, Joe	61.9	31.85	51%

Figure 1. Pedro Martinez vs Eddie Plank

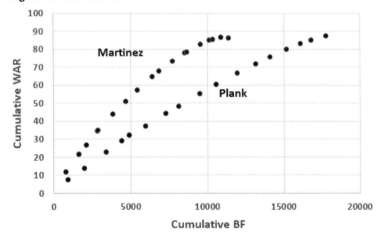

Figure 2. Mariano Rivera vs 3 HOF Starters

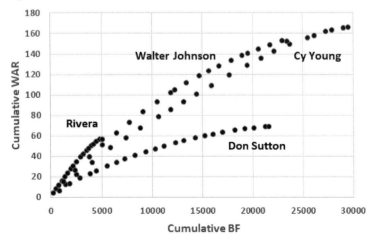

accrual of WAR, with seasons ordered by descending WAR per 1000 BF as in Table 1. Figure 1 shows the cumulative WAR accrual trajectories of two Hall of Famers who posted similar career pitching WAR almost 100 years apart, Pedro Martinez (86.1 WAR in 1992–2009) and Eddie Plank (87.5 WAR in 1901–17). Although both men exceeded the 60 WAR threshold, they followed very different tracks to get there. Martinez posted a 53.6 SPW—the best of any starting pitcher—topped by 21.5 WAR in 1,652 BF (265 composite ERA+) in 1999–2000. Eddie Plank mustered only a 32.3 SPW with 16.4 WAR in 2,383 BF in his two best seasons (1904 and 1908). Yet, while Martinez burned out in his early 30s, Plank pitched effectively to age 41 and eventually accumulated more WAR than Martinez. Both were legitimate Hall of Famers, but Pedro is the one on the short list for the best of all time.

Figure 2, which compares the career WAR accrual trajectories of Mariano Rivera and three HoF starters—career pitching WAR leaders Cy Young and Walter Johnson and classic "marathoner" Don Sutton, illustrates the remarkable fact that Mariano Rivera managed to amass more WAR than anyone else in history in any combination of seasons totaling 5,000 BF. Of course, this does not imply that Rivera had a better overall career than Young or Johnson, who went on to face an additional 24,565 and 18,405 batters, respectively, and amass an additional 124.7 and 102.6 pitching WAR beyond their SPW. Rivera faced only 103 batters beyond 5,000 BF and accrued no additional WAR beyond his SPW. We can never know what Rivera might have done as a starting pitcher with an extra 15,000 BF to work with—not as well as Johnson or Young perhaps, but almost certainly better than "super-compiler" Don Sutton, who faced 16,528 more batters than Rivera with only 12 more WAR to show for it. Rivera also clearly outshone "sprinter" Sandy Koufax (Table 1), who faced almost twice as many batters (9497) in his career while amassing 3.2 fewer pitching WAR than Rivera. Also, on Rivera's side of the ledger are his stellar 0.70 ERA and 0.759 WHIP in 527 BF in postseason competition (which do not factor into WAR calculations), which were even better than his in-season 2.209 ERA and 1.0003 WHIP, which in turn rank 13th and 4th, respectively, on the all-time pitching leaderboards. Furthermore, Rivera compiled his stats in the so-called "Steroid Era," while Young and Johnson each pitched for at least 11 years in the pitcher-friendly Deadball Era.

Finally, there are 15 HoF pitchers with total WAR < 50 and SPW < 30, well beyond striking distance of the 60 WAR and 32 SPW thresholds. They include:

- Three Negro Leaguers: Andy Cooper, Leon Day, Hilton Smith. They each have < 3000 BF on record.

- Four modern relief pitchers: Rollie Fingers (6942 BF), Trevor Hoffman (4388 BF), Lee Smith (5388 BF), Bruce Sutter (4251 BF). Not being Mariano Rivera, none could accrue more than 28 WAR in so few BF.

- Eight others: Charles Bender, Jack Chesbro, Burleigh Grimes, Jesse Haines, Catfish Hunter, Jim Kaat, Rube Marquard, Jack Morris. They simply did not have either the total or peak WAR to make the grade, despite more than ample BF totals.

RESULTS: POSITION PLAYERS (NON-PITCHERS)

The SPW results for non-pitchers are less surprising than those for pitchers, since their WAR values are generally not distorted by huge opportunity disparities across different eras. Still, the SPW leaderboards for non-pitchers with SPW ≥ 32, which are broken down by position in Tables 5–7 (see pages 42 and 43), give prominence to several nineteenth century players whose stats were diminished by the shorter schedules they played, catchers (who generally receive fewer PA per season than other players), players like Williams and DiMaggio, who missed several prime seasons in wartime military service, and—most significantly— pre-1947 players of color, who were confined to the Negro Leagues. As in Table 3, Hall of Famers as of January 2023 are shown in boldface type, and active players are in italics.

Because there were fewer C and 2B with SPW ≥ 32 than other IF and OF, I have extended the leaderboards for those positions to SPW ≥ 30; the extra players are shaded gray.

Of the 152 non-pitchers with SPW ≥ 32 (unshaded portions of Tables 5–7), 131 players have been retired for at least five years; 100 (76%) of them are in the HoF as of December 2022. Six others (Bonds, A. Rodriguez, J Jackson, McGwire, Giambi, and Sosa) have been kept out of the HoF by allegations unrelated to their accomplishments on the field. The list of Hall of Famers includes 11 players who were elected as Negro Leaguers, including two—Oscar Charleston and Josh Gibson—whose SPW values place them among the top 10 peak hitters in MLB history.

The 52 (34%) of these players with < 60 career WAR fall into the following categories:

1. Nine Negro Leaguers: Gibson, Lloyd, Stearnes, Hill, Wilson, Moore, Irvin, Suttles, and Leonard. These were great players, whose career totals—including WAR—underestimate their true body of work, much of which is lost to history. But we have at least 3,250 recorded PA for each of them—enough to earn them a place on the SPW leaderboard. All but Moore are in the HoF.

2. Ten active players: Betts, Judge, Correa, Longoria, Arenado, Goldschmidt, Machado, Donaldson, Harper, J. Ramirez. Most will likely finish with ≥ 60 WAR.

3. Ten catchers: Gibson (who also appears in the first list), Piazza, Bennett, Campanella, Ewing, Mauer, Dickey, Bresnahan, Cochrane, and Schang. Indeed, only four catchers (Bench, Carter, Rodriguez, and Fisk) have ≥ 60 career WAR, since most need frequent rest and many break down in their early 30s.

All except Mauer (not yet eligible), Bennett, and Schang are in the HoF.

4. The remaining 24 are the "sprinters," who played brilliantly over 3,250 PA but were prevented by injury or inconsistency from amassing 60 career WAR. Prominent examples are Gordon, Greenberg, and Keller, whose careers were curtailed by wartime military service, and Kiner, Sisler, Tulowitzki, and Wright, who were derailed by injury in their early 30s. This group of 24 hitters has fared better than their pitching counterparts with HoF voters; nine of the 21 eligible players (41%) are in the HoF.

The SPW tables do show some mildly surprising results. For example, among outfielders Mantle outranks Aaron, Ted Williams outranks Mays, and among infielders Banks outranks Ripken, although the second player in all three pairings has the higher career WAR. However, modern players do not dominate the SPW

Table 5. SPW Leaderboards for Catchers and 1B

	Catchers	WAR	SPW	1B	WAR	SPW
1	Gibson, Josh	57.0	51.16	Gehrig, Lou	113.6	47.37
2	Carter, Gary	70.2	37.63	Pujols, Albert	101.7	43.67
3	Bench, Johnny	75.1	36.81	Foxx, Jimmie	92.3	43.04
4	Piazza, Mike	59.5	36.46	Brouthers, Dan	79.8	42.90
5	Bennett, Charlie	38.8	35.99	Connor, Roger	84.3	41.75
6	Campanella, Roy	46.4	35.02	Anson, Cap	94.4	40.34
7	Fisk, Carlton	68.5	34.84	Sisler, George	54.8	39.47
8	Ewing, Buck	48.0	34.52	Allen, Dick	58.7	37.67
9	Mauer, Joe	55.2	33.56	Mize, Johnny	70.7	37.44
10	Rodriguez, Ivan	68.7	33.52	McGwire, Mark	62.1	36.86
11	Dickey, Bill	56.4	33.34	McCovey, Willie	64.5	36.67
12	Bresnahan, Roger	42.0	32.74	Bagwell, Jeff	79.9	36.58
13	Cochrane, Mickey	49.9	32.51	Helton, Todd	61.8	35.83
14	Schang, Wally	47.9	32.00	Votto, Joey	64.3	35.45
15	Gene Tenace	46.8	31.70	Chance, Frank	46.0	35.02
16	Thurman Munson	46.1	31.04	Giambi, Jason	50.5	34.50
17	Buster Posey	44.8	30.78	Cabrera, Miguel	67.7	34.06
18	Gabby Hartnett	55.9	30.66	Thome, Jim	73.1	34.05
19	Yogi Berra	59.4	30.47	Thomas, Frank	73.8	33.96
20	Bill Freehan	44.8	30.21	Goldschmidt, Paul	58.5	33.92
21				Greenberg, Hank	55.5	33.81
22				Suttles, Mule	36.2	32.98
23				Leonard, Buck	32.8	32.80
24				Terry, Bill	56.5	32.64

Table 6. SPW Leaderboards for Other Infielders

	2B	WAR	SPW	SS	WAR	SPW	3B	WAR	SPW
1	Hornsby, Rogers	127.3	54.32	Wagner, Honus	130.8	52.49	Schmidt, Mike	106.9	44.81
2	Morgan, Joe	100.4	47.71	Rodriguez, Alex	117.6	44.40	Brett, George	88.6	41.76
3	Lajoie, Nap	106.9	47.40	Lloyd, John Henry	52.5	43.30	Wilson, Jud	44.7	40.21
4	Collins, Eddie	124.4	44.87	Wells, Willie	61.6	41.49	Santo, Ron	70.5	40.02
5	Robinson, Jackie	66.2	43.37	Banks, Ernie	67.7	41.41	Mathews, Eddie	96.1	39.34
6	Utley, Chase	64.5	39.13	Ripken, Cal	95.9	40.95	Boggs, Wade	91.4	38.50
7	Carew, Rod	81.2	38.41	Vaughan, Arky	78.0	40.95	Beltre, Adrian	93.5	38.42
8	Gehringer, Charlie	84.8	37.66	Boudreau, Lou	63.3	39.44	Baker, Home Run	62.8	37.30
9	Grich, Bobby	71.1	37.39	Glasscock, Jack	62.0	38.37	McGraw, John	45.7	36.39
10	Cano, Robinson	68.1	35.11	Yount, Robin	77.4	37.26	Jones, Chipper	85.3	35.53
11	Sandberg, Ryne	68.0	35.08	Jennings, Hughie	42.3	37.06	Boyer, Ken	62.8	35.17
12	Frisch, Frankie	71.8	34.77	Davis, George	84.9	36.55	Robinson, Brooks	78.5	35.05
13	Gordon, Joe	55.8	34.11	Tulowitzki, Troy	44.5	36.10	Rolen, Scott	70.1	34.84
14	Dunlap, Fred	37.1	33.18	Larkin, Barry	70.5	35.74	Longoria, Evan	58.1	34.15
15	Alomar, Roberto	67.0	31.62	Correa, Carlos	39.5	35.71	Arenado, Nolan	52.2	34.13
16	Knoblauch, Chuck	44.6	31.59	Trammell, Alan	70.7	35.67	Bell, Buddy	66.3	33.90
17	Zobrist, Ben	44.5	31.49	Moore, Dobie	35.5	35.50	Martinez, Edgar	68.4	33.26
18	Whitaker, Lou	75.1	30.99	Wallace, Bobby	70.3	34.62	Machado, Manny	52.0	32.84
19	Stanky, Eddie	41.4	30.89	Garciaparra, Nomar	44.3	34.29	Donaldson, Josh	46.7	32.81
20	Biggio, Craig	65.5	30.23	Appling, Luke	77.6	34.21	Bando, Sal	61.5	32.52
21	Pedroia, Dustin	51.9	30.15	Cronin, Joe	64.7	34.18	Wright, David	49.2	32.32
22	Childs, Cupid	44.4	30.01	Smith, Ozzie	76.9	32.79	Ramirez, Jose	40.3	32.18
23				Fletcher, Art	47.1	32.36			
24				Dahlen, Bill	75.2	32.01			

Table 7. SPW Leaderboards for Outfielders

	OF	WAR	SPW		OF	WAR	SPW		OF	WAR	SPW
1	Ruth, Babe	162.7	61.42	19	Hill, Pete	46.8	41.16	37	Lofton, Kenny	68.4	34.61
2	Bonds, Barry	162.8	55.94	20	Betts, Mookie	56.4	40.75	38	Keller, Charlie	43.8	34.09
3	Charleston, Oscar	79.3	54.04	21	Torriente, Cristobal	60.1	40.41	39	Cedeno, Cesar	52.9	33.96
4	Williams, Ted	122.0	53.47	22	Ott, Mel	110.8	39.00	40	Hamilton, Billy	63.2	33.89
5	Mays, Willie	156.1	52.76	23	Robinson, Frank	107.2	38.68	41	Beltran, Carlos	70.1	33.89
6	Cobb, Ty	151.4	52.47	24	Delahanty, Ed	69.6	38.68	42	Lynn, Fred	50.2	33.59
7	Mantle, Mickey	110.2	51.66	25	Walker, Larry	72.7	38.63	43	Goslin, Goose	66.4	33.48
8	Trout, Mike	82.4	49.15	26	Snider, Duke	65.9	38.61	44	Lemon, Chet	55.6	33.42
9	Speaker, Tris	134.8	45.82	27	Simmons, Al	68.2	38.28	45	Irvin, Monte	38.1	33.26
10	Musial, Stan	128.6	45.41	28	Kaline, Al	92.9	37.99	46	Wynn, Jim	55.7	33.21
11	Henderson, Rickey	111.1	45.27	29	Heilmann, Harry	72.5	37.15	47	Sosa, Sammy	58.6	33.14
12	Yastrzemski, Carl	96.5	43.83	30	Judge, Aaron	36.9	36.70	48	Bautista, Jose	36.7	32.75
13	Clemente, Roberto	94.8	43.24	31	Jackson, Reggie	74.0	36.26	49	Gwynn, Tony	69.2	32.61
14	DiMaggio, Joe	79.2	42.67	32	Doby, Larry	65.6	36.13	50	Raines, Tim	69.4	32.54
15	Griffey, Ken	83.8	42.56	33	Dawson, Andre	64.8	35.26	51	Stargell, Willie	57.5	32.48
16	Aaron, Henry	143.0	42.21	34	Edmonds, Jim	60.4	35.13	52	Harper, Bryce	42.5	32.40
17	Jackson, Shoeless Joe	62.2	41.60	35	Kiner, Ralph	48.1	34.76	53	Smith, Reggie	64.5	32.38
18	Stearnes, Turkey	51.9	41.21	36	Jones, Andruw	62.7	34.72	54	Williams, Ken	43.0	32.06

leaderboard for hitters as they do for pitchers; the lofty historical rank of active mid-career players Trout and Betts is noteworthy but hardly surprising.

There are 28 non-pitchers with career WAR > 60 whose SPW falls below 32 (Table 8).

The 10 players at the bottom of this list either barely made the 60 WAR cutoff or barely missed the 32 SPW cutoff. But the top 18, including such luminaries as Pete Rose and Derek Jeter, can be aptly described as marathoners. Sixteen of the 28 players listed (57%) are Hall of Famers, but only Rose, Killebrew, and Suzuki ever won an MVP award. Ichiro will likely be elected when he becomes eligible in 2024, and Rose would be in the HoF already but for his gambling. The HoF candidacies of Ramirez, Palmeiro, and perhaps Sheffield have lost traction due to their PED-related histories. Ramirez, Sheffield, and Abreu remain on the BBWAA HoF ballot; Whitaker and Dwight Evans have received significant recent support from the Veterans Committee.

Figure 3 (analogous to Figure 1) compares the career WAR accrual trajectories of two hitters with similar career WAR totals—Joe DiMaggio with 79.1 WAR over 7672 PA in a 13-year career shortened by injuries and three years of wartime military service and Pete Rose, who amassed 79.6 WAR in more than

twice as many (15,890) PA spread across 24 seasons, the last seven of which were at or below replacement level. Both had legitimate HOF credentials (setting aside Rose's disqualification), but DiMaggio was far and away the more impactful player in his prime.

Finally, there are 37 HoF non-pitchers with total WAR < 50 and SPW < 30—well beyond striking distance of the 60 WAR and 32 SPW thresholds. They include:

- Five catchers: Ferrell, Lombardi, Mackey, Schalk, Santop. (Mackey and Santop also appear on the Negro League list.) WAR consistently undervalues catchers.

- Six Negro Leaguers: Bell (6747 PA). Brown (2324 PA), Dandridge (2547 PA), Johnson (4345 PA), Mackey (4340 PA) and Santop (1977 PA). The statistical records are skimpy for all except Cool Papa Bell. I have not counted Buck O'Neil (elected largely for his non-playing contributions), nor Bud Fowler or Frank Grant (almost no data).

- Twenty-eight others: Baines, Bottomley, Brock, Combs, Cuyler, Duffy, Evers, Fox, Hafey,

Table 8. Other non-pitchers with Career Hitting WAR ≥ 60

	Catchers	WAR	SPW	1B	WAR	SPW
1	Gibson, Josh	57.0	51.16	Gehrig, Lou	113.6	47.37
2	Carter, Gary	70.2	37.63	Pujols, Albert	101.7	43.67
3	Bench, Johnny	75.1	36.81	Foxx, Jimmie	92.3	43.04
4	Piazza, Mike	59.5	36.46	Brouthers, Dan	79.8	42.90
5	Bennett, Charlie	38.8	35.99	Connor, Roger	84.3	41.75
6	Campanella, Roy	46.4	35.02	Anson, Cap	94.4	40.34
7	Fisk, Carlton	68.5	34.84	Sisler, George	54.8	39.47
8	Ewing, Buck	48.0	34.52	Allen, Dick	58.7	37.67
9	Mauer, Joe	55.2	33.56	Mize, Johnny	70.7	37.44
10	Rodriguez, Ivan	68.7	33.52	McGwire, Mark	62.1	36.86
11	Dickey, Bill	56.4	33.34	McCovey, Willie	64.5	36.67
12	Bresnahan, Roger	42.0	32.74	Bagwell, Jeff	79.9	36.58
13	Cochrane, Mickey	49.9	32.51	Helton, Todd	61.8	35.83
14	Schang, Wally	47.9	32.00	Votto, Joey	64.3	35.45
15	Gene Tenace	46.8	31.70	Chance, Frank	46.0	35.02
16	Thurman Munson	46.1	31.04	Giambi, Jason	50.5	34.50
17	Buster Posey	44.8	30.78	Cabrera, Miguel	67.7	34.06
18	Gabby Hartnett	55.9	30.66	Thome, Jim	73.1	34.05
19	Yogi Berra	59.4	30.47	Thomas, Frank	73.8	33.96
20	Bill Freehan	44.8	30.21	Goldschmidt, Paul	58.5	33.92
21				Greenberg, Hank	55.5	33.81
22				Suttles, Mule	36.2	32.98
23				Leonard, Buck	32.8	32.80
24				Terry, Bill	56.5	32.64

Hodges, Kell, Kelly, Lazzeri, Lindstrom, Manush, Maranville, Mazeroski, McCarthy, Oliva, J. Rice, Rizzuto, Roush, Schoendienst, Thompson, Traynor, L. Waner, Ward, Youngs. They simply did not have either the total or peak WAR to make the grade, despite more than ample PA totals.

IMPACT OF PED

I have noted above that the SPW ≥ 32 leaderboards (Tables 3–7) contain several players who have been implicated as PED users. We do not have reliable timelines of PED usage for most of these players, but the chronologies for Bonds (who allegedly began using PED in 1999) and Clemens (who allegedly began using in either 1997 or 1998) are well documented.[12,13] In Figures 4–5, the overall career WAR accrual trajectories for Clemens and Bonds are compared to the truncated trajectories that include only their pre-PED seasons.

Clemens's SPW fell from fourth (49.4) to eighth (45.1) among all pitchers when his 1997–2007 seasons are excluded. Bonds's SPW fell from second (55.8) to 14th (46.9) among all non-pitchers after his 1999–2007 seasons, which include his four best seasons (2001–4), are excluded. The "PED years" clearly inflated Bonds's SPW more than that of Clemens. However, even without his alleged steroid seasons, Bonds's SPW still outstrips such luminaries as Eddie Collins, Lou Gehrig, Tris Speaker, Rickey Henderson, Stan Musial, Mike Schmidt, Henry Aaron, Mel Ott, and nearly everyone else who ever played MLB. Like Clemens, Bonds did not need steroids to place him among the greatest players of all time.

DISCUSSION

Peak as well as total value has always been considered in the HoF selection process. As Bill James has phrased it, we think of "black ink"—triple crowns, ERA titles, etc.—and major awards. when we anoint our Hall of Famers.[14] We esteem the accomplishments of players like Sandy Koufax, who spent a half-decade among the elite players in baseball, even though their career totals may not be especially impressive. However, while WAR has given us a comprehensive (if imperfect) metric for career value, we have lacked a fair and unbiased quantitative measure of peak value. Jaffe's WAR7, which he uses to calculate JAWS, is a poor indicator of peak value because the WAR values for a player's best seven seasons are often based on widely differing numbers of opportunities to produce value, i.e., PA for hitters or BF for pitchers.

Obviously, WAR systematically undervalues players whose careers were confined to the Negro Leagues. The HoF has been addressing this issue systematically by delegating it to a special committee with appropriate resources and historical expertise. SPW validates most of their selections where sufficient data exist.

The biggest issue for other hitters is the systematic undervaluation of catchers by career WAR (which is only partially addressed by SPW). However, HoF voters have done a pretty good job of using subjective criteria to honor catchers with < 60 WAR who had high peak value. The only glaring omission is nineteenth century catcher Charlie Bennett whose late-career effectiveness was hampered by injuries and who ultimately lost his leg in a train accident. HoF voters have also done a reasonably good job of honoring other worthy high-peak hitters like Greenberg, Sisler, and Kiner, who fell well short of 60 WAR.

The absence of a standardized measure of peak value has been far more problematic for pitchers due to the huge historical disparity in the distribution of BF. Jaffe's unstandardized WAR7 grossly overestimates the peak value of nineteenth century pitchers (who often pitched 400–650 innings per season) and underestimates the peak value of relief pitchers (who now pitch about 60 innings per season) and modern starters (who now pitch 180–200 innings per season). While HoF voters have recognized the inadequacy of WAR-based metrics for relief pitchers, they have overlooked the elite peak performance rates of pitchers like Johan Santana, Bret Saberhagen, Kevin Appier, and David Cone, who did not compile impressive career totals. Jaffe himself has recently introduced a fudge factor to modify the calculation of JAWS to correct for these inequities (s-JAWS and r-JAWS).[15] But if we really want a fair and unbiased estimate of peak value, we need to replace the seven-season construct by one based on a standard yardstick of a fixed number of PA or BF. That is what Standardized Peak WAR does.

The specific choices of 3,250 PA and 5,000 BF to be the yardsticks for computing SPW, intended to represent five full-time seasons for the typical mid-twentieth century player, are somewhat arbitrary. They are meant to be a large enough body of work to exclude the "flashes in the pan" who have one or two flukish seasons, but short enough to include great players who received limited opportunities to accrue WAR. If I had chosen 4,550 PA and 7,000 BF to align more closely with Jaffe's WAR7, Negro Leaguers and relief pitchers would not have fared as well.

When we compare the leaderboards for SPW with those for WAR, we see some striking differences. First, we see the Negro League hitting and pitching stars assume their rightful place among the all-time greats. Josh Gibson's 51.2 SPW leads all catchers by far, despite his modest 57.0 career WAR. Oscar Charleston's 54.0 SPW ranks behind only Ruth, Hornsby, and Bonds among all hitters. On the pitching side, Satchel Paige's 46.0 SPW ranks seventh, behind only Rivera, Martinez, W. Johnson, Clemens, R. Johnson, and Maddux.

Second, we see modern starting pitchers—even active ones like Kershaw, Verlander, Scherzer, and Greinke—move to the fore. While their diminished workloads hold back their values of WAR, WAR7, and JAWS, their peak value (as measured by SPW) is probably enhanced by being better rested than their workhorse predecessors. Still, the best of the old-timers—W. Johnson, Young, Grove, Mathewson, Alexander, etc.—hold their own on the SPW leaderboard.

Third, we see 14 catchers with SPW $\geq$ 32, versus only four with WAR $\geq$ 60 and five with JAWS $\geq$ 50. However, I would argue that catchers are still undervalued by SPW—just not as badly. I don't think WAR captures the full defensive value of catchers, who are the only defenders except pitchers who have a hand in every pitch. Yadier Molina is widely predicted to be a first-ballot Hall of Famer, but his SPW is only 26.4.

Fourth, a relief pitcher, Mariano Rivera, tops the SPW pitching leaderboard. However, even SPW can do little for most modern one-inning relievers. In terms of WAR per 1,000 BF, Billy Wagner (38.6) is the most impressive of any post-1990 closer except Rivera. But this is based on only 27.8 WAR in only 3,600 BF (the equivalent of about 1.3 Hoss Radbourn seasons). Wagner has received significant HoF support, but I am not convinced that his total value is enough to warrant his selection for the HoF.

SPW is not meant to be a stand-alone stat to determine who belongs in the HoF. Quantity as well as quality still matters. One could follow in Jaffe's footsteps and combine WAR and SPW to form a comprehensive JAWS-like statistic. Unfortunately, the contribution of SPW, which ranges only up to 61.4 (for Babe Ruth), would be swamped in a simple average by the contribution of WAR (which exceeds 160 for Bonds, Ruth, and Young). I prefer my own invention, the Gordon Career Value Index (CVI), which begins with WAR and awards extra credit for all seasons in which WAR > 5.0 per 650 PA or 1,000 BF.[16] An added advantage of CVI is that, unlike SPW, it incorporates both hitting and pitching value in a single metric and thus gives full credit to two-way players and good-hitting pitchers.

Although WAR is the best comprehensive performance metric we have, it has limitations. The methodology for calculating WAR is opaque and differs across platforms. Also, since Baseball-Reference.com periodically tweaks their WAR calculations, many of the SPW values in this article may have changed by the time you read it. The positional adjustments and defensive component of WAR for non-pitchers are somewhat arbitrary and do not necessarily reflect the state of the art. I also believe that WAR undervalues the defensive value of catchers and overly penalizes designated hitters for their absence of defensive value.

The key point of this analysis is that the evaluation of any player's qualifications for the HoF should include the height of their performance peak—not just career totals. JAWS does not do this well because its measure of peak value reflects widely varying numbers of BF or PA. The SPW methodology introduced here standardizes peak WAR to 5,000 BF for pitchers and 3,250 PA for non-pitchers. Thus, one can fairly compare the SPW of players of all eras—those who played 60-game or 162-game schedules, those who played 12 or 24 years, those who lost substantial time to injuries or military service, those who spent much or all of their careers in the Negro Leagues, and pitchers who started 90% or 15% of their team's games or even those who pitched only in relief. ■

References

1. Baseball-Reference.com WAR Explained, https://www.baseball-reference.com/about/war_explained.shtml.
2. Keith Law, *Smart Baseball*, Harper Collins, 2017, 183–203.
3. Jay Jaffe, *Cooperstown Casebook*, St. Martin's Press, 2017, 22–27.
4. Baseball-Reference.com, Jaffe WAR Score System (JAWS), https://www.baseball-reference.com/about/jaws.shtml.
5. David J. Gordon, *Baseball Generations*, Summer Game Books, 17–38.
6. Baseball-Reference.com, https://www.baseball-reference.com.
7. Baseball-Reference.com, Starting Pitcher JAWS Leaders, https://www.baseball-reference.com/leaders/jaws_P.shtml.
8. Baseball-Reference.com, Year-by-Year Top-Tens Leaders & Records for Batters Faced, https://www.baseball-reference.com/leaders/batters_faced_top_ten.shtml.
9. Baseball-Reference.com, Year-by-Year Top-Tens.
10. Seamheads Negro League Database, Wins Above Replacement, 1886–1948, https://www.seamheads.com/NegroLgs/history.php?tab=metrics_at&first=1886&last=1948&lgID=All&lgType=All&bats=All&pos=All&HOF=All&results=100&sort=Tot_a.
11. FanGraphs, https://www.fangraphs.com.
12. Mark Fainaru-Wada and Lance Williams, *Game of Shadows*, Gotham Books, 2006.
13. Frederick C. Bush, SABR Biography of Roger Clemens, https://sabr.org/bioproj/person/b5a2be2f.
14. Bill James, *Whatever Happened to the Hall of Fame?: Baseball, Cooperstown, and the Politics of Glory*, Fireside Books, 1994, 1995.
15. Baseball-Reference.com, Jaffe WAR Score System (JAWS).
16. David J. Gordon, Using Career Value Index (CVI) to Evaluate Hall of Fame Credentials of Negro League Players, *Baseball Research Journal*, Fall 2022, 51:112–21.ß

The Relationship Between WAR and the Selection of Annual Performance-Based Awards

Ben Alter

It has been over 20 years since Baseball Prospectus developed the statistic "Wins Above Replacement Player" (WARP), and 12 years since Sean Smith's Wins Above Replacement (WAR) was first posted on Baseball-Reference.com.[1] WAR now is widely recognized as a useful metric for assessing a ballplayer's overall performance.

Several performance-based awards are given to players each year, with three of them based on balloting by the Baseball Writers Association of America (BBWAA): the Most Valuable Player Award, the Cy Young Award, and the Rookie of the Year Award.[2] If balloters cast their votes for the players with the best statistics (and WAR is a valid measurement of their performances), then the top vote getters should be the non-pitchers with the highest WARs and the pitchers with the highest pitching WARs (pWARs). This paper explores the relationships between WAR and the winners of the three ballot-based performance awards over the years.

THE MVP AWARD AND WAR

The BBWAA has chosen MVP awards for each league since 1931. Previous incarnations of the MVP award include the Chalmers Award, which was given out from 1911 to 1914, and League Awards, which were given out from 1922 to 1929. The winners of these awards are not included in this study, mainly because previous winners were not eligible to win again, invalidating one of the bases of this study.

The BBWAA does not offer a clear definition of what "most valuable" means, leaving the judgment to the individual voters. Among its official criteria are the player's "strength of offense and defense," the number of games played, and the player's "general character, disposition, loyalty and effort."

Initially, one BBWAA writer in each city with a team filled out a ten-place ballot, with ten points for the recipient of a first-place vote, nine for a second-place vote, and so on. The BBWAA began polling three writers in each league city in 1938, and reduced that number to two in 1961. Beginning in 1938 more weight was given to the first-place vote, increasing it from 10 points to 14.

Several previous studies have tried to identify the statistical drivers that correlate well with MVP balloting, including Wood (1999), whose dataset also begins in 1931, and Hanrahan (2003), which uses 1938 as its starting date. Silver (2003) was an early study using sabermetrics as its basis, which used WARP3, a derivative of WARP.

This paper assesses the relative weight placed on individual-based statistics, team-based statistics that are not used to determine bWAR, and subjective factors. MVP winners since 1931 are grouped by decade and then by their bWAR ranking. Excluded from this analysis are instances where relievers were named league MVP, because relievers invariably have much lower bWARs than non-pitchers and starting pitchers.[3]

Figure 1 shows how often the players in the top five in bWAR in their league have been the MVP. In the

Figure 1. Relationship Between MVP Winners and bWAR (Excluding Relievers)

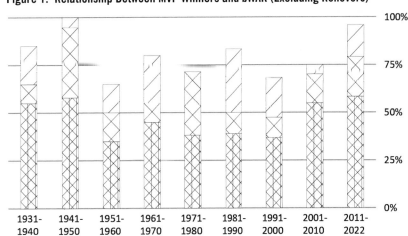

59

first 20 years of the modern MVP award, it was quite common for the MVP to be in the top 5 in bWAR. Only MVP winners Frankie Frisch (1931), Mickey Cochrane (1934), Gabby Hartnett (1935) and Marty Marion (1944) were not in the top 5 in bWAR.

MVP winners with bWARs outside the top 10 became much more common in the 1970s. Table 1 lists the 12 MVP winners since 1970 who finished outside the top 10 in bWAR. Nine of these MVP awardees played for division-winning teams. The three exceptions—Jeff Burroughs, Andre Dawson, and Ryan Howard—led the league in RBIs, a team-dependent statistic not used in calculating bWAR.

Table 1. MVP Winners Who Did Not Finish in the Top 10 in bWAR (Excluding Relievers), 1970 to Present

Year	League	MVP Winner
1970	AL	Boog Powell
1974	AL	Jeff Burroughs
1974	NL	Steve Garvey
1976	AL	Thurman Munson
1979	AL	Don Baylor
1979	NL	Willie Stargell (Award co-winner)
1987	NL	Andre Dawson
1995	AL	Mo Vaughn
1996	AL	Juan Gonzalez
1998	AL	Juan Gonzalez
2006	AL	Justin Morneau
2006	NL	Ryan Howard

MVP winners with relatively low bWAR-related metrics all but disappeared by 2008. In the last 15 seasons, only one MVP winner (Bryce Harper in 2021) failed to finish in the top 5 in bWAR (Harper finished ninth among non-pitchers). Sixteen of the last 28 MVPs led their league in bWAR.

How have the league leaders in bWAR fared in MVP balloting? Figure 2, which shows how frequently the league leader in bWAR finished in the top 5 in MVP balloting, has many similarities to Figure 1. It shows the same drop in the 1950s, fewer players in the 1960s, and even fewer in the 1980s. The relationship between MVP winners and bWAR leaders has been even more pronounced in the last 12 years than the relationship between top MVP vote-getters and bWAR. All 26 MVP winners dating back to 2010 have been in the top three in bWAR.

Whereas there is an increased preference for players with high bWARs, in certain time periods there was an even higher preference for players with high offensive WARs (oWARs). Figure 3 shows how often players in the top 5 in oWAR for their league have won the MVP award. Voters clearly leaned toward high oWAR in the 1960s, the 1980s, and the 2000s. Since 2011, the difference between bWAR and oWAR in MVP balloting has all but disappeared

In summary, MVP voters have long used offensive statistics to inform their choices for the MVP award (excluding pitchers). In the "Analytical Age" (James 2020), their choices continue to be aligned with offense, although they are more closely aligned with bWAR, which also takes into account defensive metrics and does not take into account team-based statistics. The reason for this change may be the increased awareness and general acceptance of bWAR as a valid statistic for measuring a player's performance.

THE CY YOUNG AWARD AND pWAR

From 1956 to 1966, the BBWAA issued just one Cy Young Award per year, after which awards were given to one pitcher in each league. In 1956 and 1957, Cy Young Award winners were ineligible to win a second time. Writers voted for only one pitcher until 1970, when each writer was allowed to vote for three pitchers, with the first-place vote worth five points, the second-place vote three points, and the third-place vote one point.

As shown on Figure 4, pitchers who led their league or were close to the league lead in wins, a team-based statistic, usually won the Cy Young Awards for most of the award's existence (the graph excludes relievers who received the Cy Young Award, since relievers are rarely among the league leaders in wins).[4] This dynamic changed in 2010, when Felix Hernandez won the Cy Young Award with just 13 wins. Jacob deGrom in 2018 and 2019 and Corbin Burnes in 2021 won the Award with 10, 11, and 11 wins, respectively, suggesting that the pattern has permanently changed. An exclamation point was added to this dynamic when Kyle Wright, the only 20-game winner in 2022, finished a distant tenth in Cy Young balloting.

Conversely, starting in the mid-1980s (long before the Analytical Age), there has been a pronounced increase in the alignment between Cy Young balloting and the metrics that are used to calculate pWAR, as shown on Figure 5 (page 62). In the last five years, five of the ten Cy Young award winners (deGrom in 2018 and 2019, Burnes in 2021, as well as Trevor Bauer in 2020 and Sandy Alcantara in 2022) have not finished in the top 5 in wins. Wins and pWAR are clearly going in different directions.

THE ROOKIE OF THE YEAR AWARD AND bWAR

The BBWAA has selected Rookies of the Year since

Figure 2. Relationship Between Players with the Highest bWAR and MVP Balloting (Excluding Pitchers)

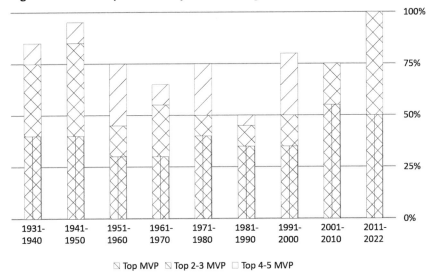

Figure 3. Relationship Between Players with the Highest oWAR and MVP Balloting (Excluding Pitchers)

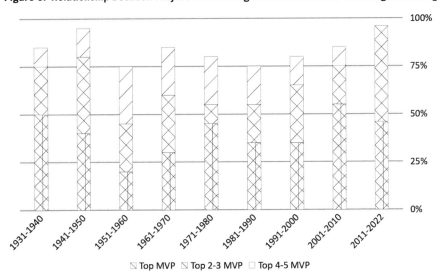

Figure 4. Ranking of Wins by Cy Young Award Winners (Excluding Relievers)

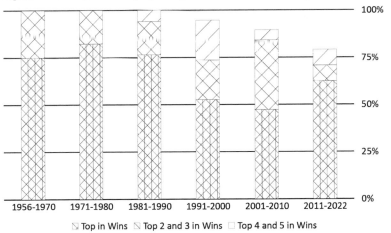

Figure 5. pWAR Rankings of Cy Young Award Winners

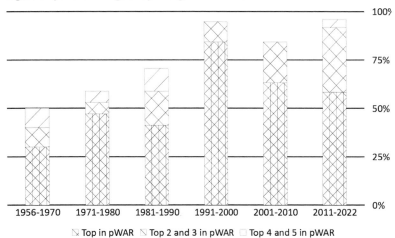

□ Top in pWAR □ Top 2 and 3 in pWAR □ Top 4 and 5 in pWAR

1947. In the first two years of the award, only one player was chosen from both leagues. Starting in 1949, ROY awards have been given in each league. Until 1957, the term "rookie" was undefined, and voters were given discretion regarding who qualified as a rookie. In 1971, rookies were defined as players with fewer than 130 at-bats, 50 innings pitched, or 45 days on the active roster of a major league club (excluding time in military service or on the injury list) before September 1. Since 1980, voters have named three rookies on their ballots, with five points going to their first-place choice, three points to their second-place choice, and one point to their third-place choice.

How do the ROY winners shape up with regard to bWAR? Since the number of rookies receiving votes has varied widely and there is no handy list of players who are rookies in a given year, the ROY winners are compared only with the other rookies who received votes that year.

Table 2 shows the percentage of ROY winners who had the highest bWAR among vote-getters. From 1949 to 1981 and from 1992 to 2001, roughly half the ROY winners had the highest bWAR among vote-getters. Of particular note is the huge jump in ROY winners with the highest bWAR since 2010.

Table 2. Percentages of Rookies of the Year with the Highest bWAR

Interval	First in bWAR
1949–60	46%
1961–70	50%
1971–80	45%
1981–90	35%
1991–2000	50%
2001–10	30%
2011–22	71%

Table 3 shows the difference between the bWAR of the ROY winner and the vote-getter with the highest bWAR (excluding years in which vote-getter with the highest bWAR won). As with Table 2, Table 3 shows a drastic decrease in the difference between vote-getters with the highest bWAR and the bWAR of the seven ROY winners from 2011 to 2022 who didn't have the highest bWAR.

Table 3. Average Difference Between the ROY Winner and the Rookie with the Highest bWAR Who Received ROY Votes

Interval	Average distance from leader
1949–60	1.2
1961–70	1.1
1971–80	1.9
1981–90	1.6
1991–2000	1.4
2001–10	1.5
2011–22	0.6

In conclusion, rookies with relatively high bWARs fared far better in ROY balloting in the past twelve years than in the previous 62 years. As in the case of the MVP award, this change aligns with the increased awareness and general acceptance of bWAR as a valid statistic for measuring a player's performance.

CONCLUSIONS

In the last 12 years, votes for the MVP and Rookie of the Year awards have become closely aligned with performance as measured by modern sabermetrics, specifically by bWAR and pWAR. These alignments correspond to the date when bWAR was first posted on Baseball-Reference.com. The Cy Young Award, which has been aligned with the metrics taken into account by pWAR since the mid-1980s, has since 2010 shown a decreased alignment with a pitcher's win total, a team-based statistic that is not used in calculating pWAR. The timing of these changes with the increased availability of bWAR statistics is most likely causational. ∎

References

Baseball Almanac. 2008. Rookie of the Year Award/Jackie Robinson Award.

Baseball-Reference.com. Last accessed on November 16, 2022.

Baseball-Reference.com. WAR Comparison Chart, accessed on October 26, 2022.

Baseball-Reference.com. WAR Explained, accessed on October 26, 2022.

Baseball Writers Association of America website: bbwaa.com, accessed on October 26, 2022.

Cely, Monte (2007). "The Cy Young Award: Individual or team recognition?" *Baseball Research Journal*, No. 35, 48–51.

Gillette, Gary and Pete Palmer, 2007. *The ESPN Baseball Encyclopedia* (Fourth ed.). New York: Sterling Publishing Co., 1763.

Hanrahan, Tom, 2003. An MVP voting model (Part I). *By the Numbers*, Vol. 13 No. 3, 18–28.

James, Bill, 2020. "Three looks at the MVPs." billjamesonline.com/three_looks_at_the_mvps/, accessed on October 29, 2022.

Kepner, Tyler. 2011. "Where Do You Find Value? Discussing the M.V.P. Criteria." *The New York Times*, SP3.

Silver, Nate, 2003. "Lies, Damned Lies: WARPed MVP voting." Baseball Prospectus.

Vass, George, 1998. "History of the rookie award filled with controversy." *Baseball Digest*. 57 (7): 26.

Wood, Rob, 1999. What drives MVP voting? *By the Numbers*, Vol. 9 No. 1, 12–17. [10].

Notes

1. Baseball Reference (bWAR) and FanGraphs (fWAR) have similar but different versions of WAR (bWAR and fWAR, respectively). This paper uses Baseball Reference's bWAR.

2. Other awards given to players, such as Gold Glove Awards, Silver Slugger Awards, and Rolaids Relief Man Awards, are either not done by balloting, or the results of the balloting are not provided to the public; therefore, the basis of these awards are not amenable to quantitative analysis.

3. James (2020) does a similar analysis, also employing Win Shares in the analysis. The conclusions of that analysis are similar to the conclusions of this study. It also should be mentioned that some people believe that pWAR undervalues the contributions of relievers.

4. Cely (2006) analyzes the relationship between the Cy Young Award and other conventional statistics, such as ERA, strikeouts, and WHIP. It also investigates the relationship between the Cy Young Award and team performance.

Trades from Hell

A Tale of Two Cities

William Shkurti

The major league baseball clubs of Cleveland and Cincinnati have much in common. They call the same state home. Both have established a proud tradition that dates back to the nineteenth century, and have enjoyed success and endured failure. They are mid-market teams who can afford to compete when managing resources wisely, but can't afford to buy their way out of their mistakes.

In the 1960s both teams traded away popular home-grown slugging outfielders. The Indians traded away Rocky Colavito, and the Reds traded away Frank Robinson. In both cases the fan base reacted negatively. Both players thrived for their new teams while their old teams continued to struggle. And both trades are still ubiquitous today on lists of "worst trades of all time."

Yet within a short period of time after these two trades were consummated, the fates of these two clubs diverged. The Cincinnati Reds bounced back to enjoy a dominant decade of success as the Big Red Machine. The Cleveland Indians descended into a pattern of futility that lasted 35 years. Veteran Cleveland sportswriter Terry Pluto even wrote a book about it, titled *The Curse of Rocky Colavito*.[1]

But the "common wisdom" in baseball isn't always the whole truth. Using the tools of modern-day sabermetrics, such as Wins Above Replacement, we take a fresh look at the fates of the two ballclubs in the wake of the trades and demonstrate how and why they diverged. We will begin with the Colavito trade, then the *second* Colavito trade, followed by the Robinson trade. From there we will examine some other management decisions that shaped the outcome in surprising ways. It will reveal new insights about how the business of baseball and the sport of baseball intersect, not only back then, but what it portends for the present day.

COLAVITO I: "THEY WON'T COMPLAIN IF WE WIN"

In 1959 the Cleveland Indians made a surprisingly strong run for the American League pennant. Although the team fell five games short behind the champion Chicago White Sox, they put on a great show that captured the hearts of Cleveland fans. Nearly 1.5 million of them paid their way into Municipal Stadium, reversing a four-year trend of declining attendance and ending speculation about a franchise relocation to Minneapolis.

Credit for the resurgence went to general manager Frank Lane, known as "Frantic Frank" and "Trader Lane" because of his obsession with trading players. In fact, many of the players Lane brought into Cleveland via trades contributed to the team's 1959 success.[2] Rather than rest on his laurels, Lane engaged in another trading frenzy to improve the club for the 1960 season. Gone were the team's best all-around player (Minnie Minoso), its winningest pitcher (Cal McLish), and its most promising rookie (Gordy Coleman). But the trade that rocked the fan base most occurred just before opening day when Lane shipped AL 1959 home-run champ Rocky Colavito to Detroit for AL 1959 batting champ Harvey Kuenn.

Rocky Colavito had been a Cleveland Indian since he was signed in 1951. He showed consistent power while working his way through the farm system. He put up good power numbers as a part-time outfielder in 1956 and as a starter in 125 of 153 games in 1957. After manager Joe Gordon installed him as the regular right fielder in 1958, he blossomed. He batted .303 with 41 home runs and 113 RBIs. His On Base Plus Slugging of 1.024 ranked him third in the American League behind only future Hall of Famers Ted Williams and Mickey Mantle.

His popularity among the Tribe faithful grew accordingly. A handsome young man with a modest demeanor, he attracted a loyal following among young people.[3] During the 1959 pennant run, he had tied Harmon Killebrew for the league lead in homers with 42 and was one shy of Jackie Jensen for the lead in RBIs with 111. He cemented his hold on Cleveland fans on a muggy June night in Baltimore when he became only the second American League player to hit four home runs in a nine inning game. The other was Lou Gehrig.[4]

All this made his Topps baseball card the most valuable piece of cardboard in Northeast Ohio in the summer of 1959. But while Colavito's power numbers stayed strong in 1959, his batting average dropped from .303 to .257. Lane said he wanted the team to be more balanced and less dependent on home runs. He traded Colavito to Detroit for Harvey Kuenn on April 17, 1960. The fans objected. "They won't holler if we win," Lane retorted.[5]

But they didn't win. Many of the players Lane traded for didn't produce: young pitchers didn't come through and the team lacked punch. They finished fourth in 1960 at a disappointing 76–78, 21 games out. Attendance plummeted by more than 500,000.

Then in December of 1960, Lane traded away Harvey Kuenn to the Giants for pitcher Johnny Antonelli and right fielder Willie Kirkland. Kirkland was even more of a home-run-or-nothing player than Colavito. That was too much for Indians ownership and when Lane asked for a contract extension they refused. Lane left Cleveland to work for a kindred spirit, Charlie Finley in Kansas City. Meanwhile Colavito thrived in Detroit, while Antonelli and Kirkland flopped in Cleveland. Kirkland was himself traded away for aging outfielder Al Smith in 1963.

Table 1 documents the ugly outcome of this trade using Wins Above Replacement (WAR) as calculated by Baseball Reference[6]. It covers the period 1960–64. The results of this trade are unambiguous. Colavito contributed 21 WAR for Detroit and Kansas City over that five-year period.

The players Cleveland received in exchange managed to contribute a total of only four, thus this trade cost the team a net of 17 wins over five years. And even that number is distorted by Colavito's off season in 1960, which was probably driven by him pressing too hard after the trade.

As lopsided as this trade looks, it's important to keep it in context. Between 1960 and 1964 the Cleveland Indians finished with a cumulative record of 392–409, a total of 113 games out of first. So, a switch of 17 games would have been nice, but would not have turned a perpetual also-ran into a contender on its own. But unfortunately for Cleveland fans, this would not be the worst of the fallout from this trade.

Table 1. Colavito Trade I Balance Sheet (1960–64)

Year	Colavito WAR	Replacement WAR	Replacement Sub Total	Net to Cleveland
1960	1.1	Kuenn 2.4	2.4	1.3
1961	7.6	Kirkland 2.8, Antonelli -1.1	1.7	-5.9
1962	5.7	Kirkland 0.1	0.1	-5.6
1963	2.9	Kirkland 0.8	0.8	-2.1
1964	4.1	Smith -0.9	-0.9	-5.0
Total	**21.4**		**4.1**	**-17.3**

COLAVITO II: TRADE FROM HELL ON STEROIDS

Gabe Paul took over the reins as Cleveland's general manager just before the start of the 1961 season. In ten years as Cincinnati's GM, he had rebuilt their farm system and gained a reputation as a solid baseball executive. He was credited with building the Reds team that went on to win the National League pennant in 1961. But he would struggle to achieve success with Cleveland.[7]

Paul decided the team had endured enough turmoil with Lane's constant shuffling of players, so he decided to stay with the team Lane had put together for the 1961 season They fared no better, finishing fifth, 30 games out. To make matters worse, players Lane had traded away made very visible contributions to their new teams. Rocky Colavito had a near MVP season in Detroit, and former Indians Norm Cash, Don Mossi, Hank Aguirre, and Dick Brown helped the Tigers make a serious run for the pennant.

The only team standing between Detroit and the championship was the New York Yankees. The Bronx Bombers featured former Tribe farmhand Roger Maris, who proceeded to beat Babe Ruth's single season home run record. Meanwhile, former Tribe prospect Gordy Coleman provided a big bat that helped Gabe Paul's former team capture the National League flag.

Embittered Indians fans continued to show their disgust. Home attendance dropped by another 225,000 in 1961 to a weak 726,000. While Paul changed managers twice (from Jimmy Dykes to Mel McGaha in 1962 and McGaha to Birdie Tebbetts in 1963) and shuffled players, his team couldn't break .500. Attendance continued to fade. In 1963 it dropped yet again to a dismal 563,000, second to last in the major leagues, behind only the perennially pathetic Washington Senators.

In 1964 the Indians finished sixth, 20 games out. Attendance ticked up slightly to 653,000, but the team was losing money, and unhappy investors started looking at moving the team to greener pastures like Seattle, Oakland, or Dallas.[8] Paul decided the best change to stabilize the franchise was to bring back Rocky Colavito. Colavito had been traded by Detroit to Kansas City after the 1963 season and had done well there. Kansas City was not interested in trading with Cleveland, but Chicago was. So, Paul engineered a three-way deal where Kansas City shipped Colavito to Cleveland on January 20, 1965, while Cleveland shipped veteran catcher John Romano and two promising but untried rookies—outfielder Tommie Agee and pitcher Tommy John—to Chicago.

At first the trade paid off. In 1965 Colavito batted .287 with 26 home runs and a league-leading 108 RBIs. His presence seemed to energize the hitters around him, many of whom had career years, or near career years. Combined with a corps of young pitchers, the Indians improved to 87–75 (their first winning season since 1959), only 15 games out of first. That brought 935,000 fans back to the ballpark, the best results in five years.

The resurgent Tribe then started off 1966 with a great deal of excitement, but it would not last. Colavito hit 30 home runs, but his batting average dropped 49 points to .231 and he knocked in only 72 runs. The next year after 191 at-bats he was batting only .241 with five home runs and 21 RBIs, and was traded to Chicago on July 29. The Tribe floundered, finished fifth in 1966 and eighth in 1967. Attendance fell again, to 903,00 in 1966 and 663,00 in 1967.

Meanwhile, once again the players Cleveland had traded away blossomed. John Romano had two decent years as a part-time player for Chicago, then was traded to St. Louis where he played very little, then retired. Tommy John would go 14–7 in 1965 on his way to a stellar 26-year career with 288 lifetime wins and 62 WAR. Tommie Agee won the 1966 American League Rookie of the Year with an incredible season where he batted .273, scored 98 runs, hit 22 home runs, knocked in 86 runs, and stole 44 bases. Chicago later traded him to the Mets where he helped the 1969 Miracle Mets get to the World Series and finished sixth in NL MVP voting. Overall, his 12-year career netted 25 WAR.

If you add all these up, Cleveland traded away 92 WAR over the next 25 years and received a meager 5.5 in return—certainly a disaster that belongs in the Worst Trades of All Time pantheon. That said, the comparison might be a little unfair. No one could have foreseen Tommy John's long career and the revolutionary reconstructive ligament surgery that prolonged it. Another way to look at this would be to assess the trade over its first five years to make it comparable to the first Colavito trade as shown in Table 2.

Compared to Colavito I, which cost Cleveland a net of 17 games over five years, Colavito II cost 32. The Frank Robinson trade completed a year later would produce yet another contrast.

ROBINSON: "NOT A YOUNG 30"

Frank Robinson debuted in left field with the Cincinnati Reds in 1956, the same year

Colavito arrived in Cleveland. The 20-year-old hit 38 home runs, drove in 83 and batted .290 to capture the National League Rookie of the Year award. His OPS that year trailed only future Hall of Famer Duke Snider among all National League regulars and exceed that of future Hall of Famers Hank Aaron and Willie Mays. He went on to produce Hall of Fame numbers over the next nine years. In 1961 he bashed 37 home runs, drove in 124 and batted .323 while leading the Reds to the National League pennant and capturing the MVP award.

Robinson continued to produce after the 1961 season, but the Reds failed to repeat as champs. Owner and general manager Bill DeWitt decided the Reds' Achilles Heel was poor pitching, so he traded Robinson to Baltimore for pitcher Milt Pappas and two other players after the end of the season on December 9, 1965. The fans were not pleased. DeWitt later described Robinson as "not a young 30," his age at the time of the trade, a statement he would live to regret.[9] Robinson responded, at age 30 in 1966, by winning the American League Triple Crown, the MVP award, and leading the Baltimore Orioles to a World Championship.

That finished Bill DeWitt in Cincinnati (the Reds with Milt Pappas finished seventh, 18 games out in 1966). He sold the team and went on to greener pastures. Ironically, it was DeWitt who as GM of the Detroit Tigers fleeced Frank Lane for Rocky Colavito in exchange for Harvey Kuenn.

Meanwhile Robinson continued to perform at a high level for the Orioles until they traded him in 1971. In 1975 he made history as major league baseball's first Black manager—with the Cleveland Indians. In 1982 Frank Robinson was elected to the Hall of Fame. All this helped cement this trade as one of the worst trades in history.

William Schneider argues in an article written for the 2020 Baltimore issue of *The National Pastime* that this trade is not as lopsided as it seems.[10] Using WAR

Table 2. Colavito Trade II Balance Sheet (1965–69)

Year	Colavito WAR	Traded WAR	Traded Sub Total	Net for Cleveland
1965	3.3	Romano 2.7, John 1.4, Agee -0.2	3.9	-0.6
1966	2.0	Romano 2.5, John 3.0, Agee 6.4	11.9	-9.9
1967	0.2	John 1.6, Agee 4.6, Romano -0.3	5.9	-5.7
1968		John 5.6, Agee -0	5.6	-5.6
1969		John 5.1, Agee 5.2	10.3	-10.3
Total	**5.5**		**37.6**	**-32.1**

NOTE: Because batting WAR for pitchers is so small, only pitching WAR is included here and on the other tables.

similar to the comparison involving Colavito, Table 3 tracks the trade over the six years until Robinson was traded by the Orioles. While Robinson did in fact have a strong six years in Baltimore (+ 32.4 WAR), the players Cincinnati received in exchange accumulated + 24.5 WAR over the same period.

Milt Pappas contributed 5.7 WAR before he was traded by new GM Bob Howsam as part of a multiplayer deal that included reliever Clay Carroll. Carroll contributed 7.7 WAR over the next four years. Howsam also

Disgruntled Cleveland fans protest Frank Lane's trade of Rocky Colavito in April 1960.

traded outfielder Dick Simpson, who came over in the Pappas deal, for Alex Johnson, who contributed 6.5 WAR before being traded for Jim McGlothlin, who contributed 4.6. and Pedro Borbon, who didn't contribute much in 1969 or 1970, but would in future years. Overall, the players traded for Robinson contributed only 8.5 WAR less than Robinson over six seasons.

BOTTOM LINE

Table 4 displays the WAR of the players the trading team received in exchange for Robinson and Colavito in the first column. The second column shows what Robinson and Colavito produced for their new teams. The third column shows the net over the life of the trade. The final column shows the net on an annualized basis.

Table 4. Impact of the Colavito and Robinson Trades

Trade	WAR Gained	WAR Traded Away	Net	Net Annualized
Colavito I 1960–64	4.1	21.4	-17.3	-3.5
Colavito II 1965–69	5.5	37.8	-32.3	-6.5
Robinson 1966–71	23.9	32.4	-8.5	-1.4

This comparison shows the trades hurt both clubs, but the impact of the Colavito trade(s) hurt Cleveland more, particularly the second one. One has to wonder if Cleveland was in fact cursed. When Robinson was traded to Baltimore, he was supposedly an "old" 30. He went on to give Baltimore six great seasons (32 WAR) and then went on to play for five more seasons to age 40 (11 more WAR). Colavito was 31 when he returned to Cleveland. He didn't smoke, drink, or carouse and never missed significant playing time due to injury or ill health, which should have made him a "young" 31. He only lasted two more years with Cleveland before being washed up at 33.

Still, even this difference is not enough to explain the diverging path of these two clubs. In the first four years after the second Colavito trade (1965–68), the Cleveland club won an average of 82 games a year and drew an average of 840,000 fans. In the four years after the Frank Robinson trade (1966–69), the Cincinnati Reds averaged 84 wins a year and drew an average of 860,00 fans annually. But over the next four-year period, the fortunes of the two clubs diverged. The Indians dropped to

Table 3. Frank Robinson Trade Balance Sheet, 1966–71

Year	Robinson WAR	Replacement WAR	Replacement Sub Total	Net to Cleveland
1966	7.7	Pappas 2.7, Baldschun -0.1, Simpson -0.5	2.1	-5.6
1967	5.4	Pappas 4.1, Baldschun 0.1, Simpson 0.0	4.2	-1.2
1968	3.7	Pappas -1.1, Johnson 3.1, Carroll 2.9, Cloninger -0.5, Woodward -0.3	4.1	0.4
1969	7.5	Johnson 3.4, Carroll 0.9,Cloninger -1.9, Woodward 0.5	2.9	-4.6
1970	4.8	McGlothlin 3.4, Carroll 2.1, Cloninger 1.6, Woodward 0.5, Borbon -0.5.	7.1	2.3
1971	3.3	McGlothlin 1.2, Carroll 1.8, Cloninger 0.2, Woodward 0.4, Borbon -0.1.	3.5	0.2
Total	32.4		23.9	-8.5

67.5 wins a year between 1969 and 1972 and average ticket sales fell to 640,000 annually. The Reds racked up 94 wins a year from 1970 to 1973 and drew an average of 1,730,000 fans a year. Cincinnati continued to do well the remainder of the decade, while Cleveland stumbled through two more decades of lackluster performance and became the laughingstock of the league. What was going on?

SEEDS OF DESTRUCTION

In the mid-1950s the Cleveland Indians had stood at the summit of the baseball world. Powered by general manager Hank Greenberg's rich farm system, between 1950 and 1956 they won more games than any other team in either league except for the New York Yankees and Brooklyn Dodgers. They drew more fans than any team other than the Yankees. And they made more money than any other team but the Yankees and Dodgers. That made their owners, a consortium of local businesspeople, very happy.[11]

In 1954 they beat the Yankees to the American League Championship by winning a record 111 games. The upcoming talent in their farm system promised a bright future. But beginning with the 1954 World Series, their fortunes began to slump. They lost four straight to the New York Giants. They missed out on returning to the World Series in 1955 when a late season slump cost them the pennant. In 1956 they finished second again to the Yankees, but this time by nine games. The fans seemed bored with a slow and aging team that was becoming less competitive. Attendance fell below one million for the first time since the end of World War II.

Since 1949 the team had been owned by a consortium of local businesspeople. At the end of the 1956 season, the club was still profitable and still owned by local investors, but some of the members of the consortium decided to cash out. One of those who decided to stay in was investment banker William Daley, who became the single largest shareholder with 55% of the outstanding stock. Initially Daley and the remaining owners stressed continuity. For example, they kept GM Hank Greenberg in charge and made him a minority partner. But after a disastrous 1957 season where the team fell to sixth place, 21.5 games out, and home attendance dropped for the third year in a row to a miserable 722,000, Daley and the others had a change of heart.[12]

They forced out Greenberg and turned to Frank Lane, who had just orchestrated a rebound for the St. Louis Cardinals. The Cardinals had finished seventh with a home attendance of 850,000 in 1955, the year Lane took over. Two years later, after a flurry of trades, the Cardinals soared to second and drew 1.2 million fans. But Lane's relationship with Cardinals president Gussie Busch had deteriorated over Busch's worries that Lane's win-now philosophy was trading away too many of the team's top prospects. That made Lane both eager and available. The Indians' owners jumped on it, promising him what Gussie Busch wouldn't, a free hand in player moves.[13]

As discussed previously, this strategy appeared to work in the short run as attendance rebounded in 1959. But Lane wore out his welcome after trading Colavito and Gabe Paul succeeded him but was unable to show improvement on the field or at the gate. The owners restructured financially in 1962. They sold Paul a 20% ownership share, but that didn't change anything.

After four years of declining attendance, Daley and the others pressed Paul to cut expenses as a way of protecting their investment.[14] Paul did this in a number of ways and a big axe fell on player development. This reached a fever pitch in the 1963 and 1964 seasons. Paul's trade to bring back Rocky Colavito temporarily reversed the attendance slide, but underlying structural problems remained.

During the 1966 season the Daley consortium decided it was time to sell the team. Cleveland businessman Vern Stouffer, himself a member of the consortium since 1962, stepped up. Stouffer made his money in the food business, including a very popular line of frozen TV dinners.

Stouffer promised to rebuild the team's decaying farm system and put the franchise back on a winning track. He immediately began to put money back into scouting and player development. To finance his purchase of the team, he sold his food company to Litton Industries, a California conglomerate that made—among other things—the microwave ovens used to heat his TV dinners. Instead of taking the proceeds in cash, Stouffer took it in Litton stock. After all, that stock had increased in value the last 13 years in a row, so he would have the best of both worlds: a baseball team to own and a separate source of growing income.

But three years later, Litton fell on hard times: the stock crashed and took Stouffer's fortune with it. Stouffer in turn pressed management to cut costs and the farm system took another financial hit. In 1972 Stouffer ended up selling the team to Nick Mileti—also local but also under-financed—and the Indians' woes continued.[15]

The arc of this sad story is clearly revealed in Table 5. It compares the number of minor league affiliates in this period between the Cleveland Indians and Cincinnati Reds, according to Baseball Reference.

Table 5. Number of Minor League Affiliates, 1960–72

Year	60	61	62	63	64	65	66	67	68	69	70	71	72
Cleveland	8	5	7	6	5	5	5	5	5	6	5	4	4
Cincinnati	8	8	6	6	5	6	7	6	6	6	6	6	6

The number of farm clubs is by itself not a perfect measure of a given team's player development, which also includes scouting, coaching etc., but in the absence of more complete data it should be a pretty good indicator. At the beginning of the sixties both Cleveland and Cincinnati maintained eight teams, which put them in the top third of all 16 major league franchises.

Most major league teams, including Cleveland and Cincinnati, reduced the number of affiliates early in that decade for both financial reasons and in response to expansion from 16 major league teams to 20. But the most significant inflection points come in 1964 and 1971. In 1964 Cleveland winnowed its system down to five teams as a result of pressure from the owners' consortium to cut costs. Then in 1971 they dropped to four with a second round of cuts in response to an edict from new owner Vernon Stouffer. Indians farm director Hank Peters warned Stouffer that cuts in player development were a form of extended suicide; the results wouldn't show up immediately, but would with a vengeance in three to five years. In fact the more severe downward spiral in Cleveland's fortunes began in 1969, five years after the first permanent round of cuts ordered by the Indians' owners.[16]

Cincinnati, on the other hand, remained relatively stable at around six affiliates from 1963 on. This was not by accident. Even though the Reds endured some lean years at the gate after the Robinson trade, the ownership maintained a strong player development system. Bill DeWitt kept intact the productive farm system Gabe Paul had developed during his time as owner-general manager 1960–66. When Bob Howsam took over as GM after DeWitt sold the club in 1966, he put even more money into scouting and player development.[17]

During the time frame 1963–70, the Reds farm system produced the likes of Pete Rose, Tony Perez, Lee May, Gary Nolan, Johnny Bench, Dave Concepcion, and Don Gullett, all of whom became part of the highly successful Big Red Machine of the seventies. That extraordinary collection of talent captured six division titles, four National League Championships and two World Series 1970–79.

The Cleveland farm system produced a number of good players in the first half of the sixties, including future All-Stars Sam McDowell, Luis Tiant, Tommy John, Sonny Siebert, Steve Hargan, Tommie Agee, Max Alvis, and Vic Davalillo. Unfortunately for the Indians, once the 1964–65 cost reductions set in, the pipeline started to dry up. The only All-Star caliber players produced by the Cleveland farm system to debut between 1967 and 1970 were catcher Ray Fosse and outfielder Richie Scheinblum. Over the next decade, the farm system produced a handful of star players like Chris Chambliss, Buddy Bell, and Dennis Eckersley, but came nowhere close to what was needed.

If you trade for a star player and he produces, that's still just one player. But if you have a strong farm system, it can produce multiple players. The advantage of a strong stream of rookies is their cumulative effect. For example, the Indians' home grown All Stars that came up to the majors between 1962 and 1964 added an average of 16 WAR annually between 1964 and 1966—and that's without Agee and John, who were developed by Cleveland but traded. Running the same calculation for the Cincinnati Reds rookie classes of 1965–68 (Perez, May, Nolan and Bench) shows an average of 18 WAR annually from 1969 to 1971, and that's without Pete Rose, who came up in 1963. This suggests a strong farm system can produce at least an additional 16–18 WAR annually, much more than any one star.

More than any other factor, the starving of the farm system explains Cleveland's lean years after the 1960 Rocky Colavito trade. These reductions were justified at the time as necessary because of lack of fan support at the box office. It would stay that way until the Jacobs brothers bought the team in 1986 and started rebuilding the player development operation.[18]

The financial side of major league baseball teams has always been notoriously opaque, because the teams are generally privately owned and free of financial reporting requirements. Yet a significant amount of evidence has emerged since then that raises the question as to whether the cutbacks in the 1960s were really necessary.

A FINANCIAL SHELL GAME

In 1956 the Daley consortium bought the Cleveland Indians for nearly $4.0 million. In 1966 they sold it for $8 million, doubling their money.[19] This translates to an annual return of 7.2% when inflation averaged less than two percent annually.[20] Quite a good deal if you can get it!

What is missing from this calculation, though, are year-to-year operating results. For example, if the team keeps losing money due to low attendance, investors may have to put in additional cash just to pay the bills. In the example above, if the team lost a million dollars a year for four years, the investment return would be zero, even if the investors could sell the team for four million more than they paid initially. This is what the investors claimed happened to them in the low attendance years like 1963 and 1964 where losses of more than a million dollars a year forced them to cut player development expenses and think about moving the team.[21]

A baseball team is ultimately a business, not a charity, so it can't absorb losses indefinitely. But what we do know now is the definition of "losses" is somewhat elastic and likely exaggerated. In his excellent 1995 study, former sports reporter Jack Torry used publicly available information to put these figures into context. He documented how baseball teams in this era, including the Indians, got IRS approval for a tax writeoff to offset depreciation of their players. Once this is taken into account, the so-called losses are much less.

Using information presented in 1957 and 1958 Congressional hearings on baseball's antitrust exemption, Torry pointed out that in 1956, instead of the team losing $167,000 as it claimed, the team was able to write off $700,000 in depreciation which meant a $167,000 paper loss was actually a $500,000 profit. Torry also calculated the team's paper loss of $1.2 million in 1963 was more like $300,000 after tax adjustments.[22]

A loss is still a loss, but these losses can also be offset in years when the team makes a profit. For example, the team did acknowledge a profit of $609,000 when it drew 935,000 fans in 1965.[23] Indians' management never publicly discussed how much profit they made from the 1959 attendance surge of 1.5 million fans, but it must have been substantial.

We don't know what the real break-even point was for the Indians ballclub in this period, but we do know that in 1957 the team signed Frank Lane to a contract that guaranteed him a bonus for every fan over 800,000.[24] Presumably the Indians' business savvy owners would not have shared profits with Frank Lane or anyone else if there were not profits. That suggests a break-even point of about 800,000. That number is consistent with the report of a $609,000 profit from an attendance figure of 935,000 described above.

If we examine the home attendance figures for the entire eleven years of the Daley Syndicate's ownership, it shows some fluctuations, but attendance for those eleven years averages out to 824,000 annually, or just about break-even. The 1956–66 syndicate included some of the wealthiest men in Cleveland with an estimated net worth of over $100 million. And some of them, including Daley, had already pocketed significant profits from their earlier holdings.[25] And when Vern Stouffer sold the Indians in 1972, he got back $10 million, two million more than he paid six years earlier.[26] This was less than the return the previous investors enjoyed, but still a lot better than return on investment from his Litton stock.

So instead of trying to wring every penny of profit out of a struggling franchise, the Indians owners could have decided to protect the talent pipeline and accept more risk and less profit for themselves, which is what Bill DeWitt and Bob Howsam did in Cincinnati. We don't know the details about the Reds' internal finances in this period, but we do know owner/general manager DeWitt bought the team for $4.6 million in 1962 and sold it to a local consortium for $7.0 million in December 1966.[27] By comparison the Cleveland Indians sold for $8 million in August 1966 as described above, which means at least in the eyes of its new owner, Cleveland was an even better investment than the Cincinnati Reds. But it was the Reds' management that understood what it took to nurture that investment.

CONCLUSION

In this document we used the tools of sabermetrics, particularly Wins Above Replacement (WAR), to examine two trades that are regarded as two of the worst ever: Cleveland's trade of Rocky Colavito for Harvey Kuenn in 1960 and Cincinnati's trade of Frank Robinson for Milt Pappas and others in 1966. Both trades triggered significant blowback from their fan bases at the time, but the eventual impact on both teams was quite different.

Colavito for Kuenn: This trade deserves the scorn heaped upon it, but more for the second trade than the first. The first cost the Indians 3.5 games annually over the five years of its life. In a desperate attempt to undo the damage, Cleveland brought Colavito back in an even worse trade that cost the team 6.5 victories annually over six years and even more thereafter.

Robinson for Pappas et al: The fan base scorned this deal as well. Frank Robinson did turn in some Hall of Fame worthy seasons in his six years with Baltimore, but the cost to the Reds was mitigated to a large degree because they received enough talent in return to limit the loss to less than two victories annually for six years.

After the first Colavito trade, the Indians fell into a slump that lasted 35 years. Cincinnati rebounded within four years of the Robinson trade to establish a legendary team in terms of the Big Red Machine. It is tempting to attribute this to the differing outcomes of these two series of trades. But they alone are not sufficient to explain the divergent outcome of these two teams.

What explains this outcome better are the different paths chosen by the teams' senior leadership. Money troubles, actual and imagined, prompted Cleveland's ownership to direct management to systematically disinvest in what had been a productive farm system. Cincinnati's ownership and management worked together to protect, then enhance, their player development system. This difference can easily account for 16-18 wins annually over multiple years, or the difference between Cincinnati's Big Red Machine and decades of frustration in Cleveland.

Baseball has changed a lot since the 1960s, with more expansion, free agency and multiple layers of postseason playoffs, but a fundamental truth remains. The surest path to sustained success is a foundation built on players you sign, develop, and advance. Few have been better at it in recent years than the Cleveland Guardians. ■

Notes

1. Terry Pluto, *The Curse of Rocky Colavito* (New York: Simon and Schuster, 1994).
2. For more about Lane's stormy tenure in Cleveland see Warren Corbett, "Frank Lane," SABR Biography Project, accessed October 17, 2022. https://sabr.org/bioproj/person/frank-lane-2.
3. For a good description of Colavito's rise and the fans' growing attachment to him see Pluto, 39–42.
4. David Nemec and Scott Flatow, *Great Baseball Feats, Facts, Figures* (New York: Penguin Books, 2008), 258.
5. Hal Lebovitz, "Swaps Leave Fearless Frankie on Spot," *The Sporting News*, April 27, 1960, 3.
6. These figures posted online as of March 23, 2023.
7. Warren Corbett, "Gabe Paul," SABR Bio Project, accessed October 18, 2022. https://sabr.org/bioproj/person/gabe-paul.
8. David Bohmer, *Cleveland Guardians team ownership history*, SABR Team Ownership Project, accessed October 18, 2022. https://sabr.org/bioproj/topic/cleveland-guardians-team-ownership-history.
9. Rob Neyer, *Rob Neyer's Book of Baseball Blunders* (New York: Simon and Schuster, 2006),140.
10. William Schneider, "Frank Robinson and the Trade that Ignited Two(!) Dynasties," *The National Pastime: A Bird's Eye View of Baltimore* (Phoenix, SABR, 2020). Online version accessed October 18, 2022. https://sabr.org/journal/article/frank-robinson-and-the-trade-that-ignited-two-dynasties.
11. "Franchise Page" at Baseball-reference.com and Bohmer.
12. Bohmer.
13. Hal Lebovitz, "Tribe Fans Whoop Over New Chief Lane," *The Sporting News*, November 20, 1957, 3.
14. Bohmer.
15. Bohmer.
16. Pluto, 189–90.
17. Mark Armour, "Bob Howsam," SABR Bio Project. Accessed October 23, 2022. https://sabr.org/bioproj/person/bob-howsam.
18. Bohmer.
19. Bohmer.
20. U.S. Bureau of Labor Statistics, CPI Inflation Calculator, accessed October 24, 2022. https://www.bls.gov/data/inflation_calculator.htm.
21. Bohmer.
22. Jack Torry, *Endless Summers: The Fall and Rise of the Cleveland Indians* (South Bend, Indiana: Diamond Communications, Inc., 1995), 70, 94.
23. Torry, 103.
24. Bohmer.
25. Torry, 69, 93.
26. Bohmer.
27. "DeWitt Sold Reds to 13-member Cincinnati Group," *Official 1967 Baseball Guide*, (St. Louis, Sporting News,1967), 172–73.

Quantifying the Effect of Offseason Contract Extensions on Short-Term Player Performance

Muyuan Li, Greg Plithides, and Max Plithides

Over the past generation, sabermetricians have expended a great amount of time and energy studying the effects of free agency and long-term contracts on player performance (Maxcy, Fort, and Krautmann 2002; Krautmann and Solow 2009; Krautmann and Donley 2009; Hakes and Turner 2011; Martin et al. 2011; O'Neill 2014; Paulsen 2020). However, they have spent far less time studying the effect of big offseason contract extensions on performance the following season. Here, an "offseason contract extension" is defined as any new contract signed during the offseason that adds additional years to a player's contract with his current team.

Over the past decade, this line of inquiry has become increasingly important, as more contract extensions are being made and increasing amounts of money are being dedicated to these agreements. In the 2019–20 offseason alone, pre-free agency player extensions amounted to an enormous $1.7 billion (Sawchik 2019). Since 2020, many young stars including Wander Franco (21), Fernando Tatis Jr. (22), and Francisco Lindor (27) have foregone free agency to sign long-term deals with their clubs in excess of $200 million (MLBTR 2022). Yet a data deficiency regarding the short-term effects of these deals creates a suboptimal information environment that handicaps both teams and agents during negotiations.[1] Agents, players, and teams have thus negotiated many recent megaextensions without large-N empirical data on their short-term performance effects. Given the billions of dollars at stake, there is an urgent need to address this dearth of empirical data.

We explore this topic through the lens of two competing hypotheses: that (*H1*) *signing a pre-free agency offseason contract extension that buys out at least one year of free agency will hurt a player's performance in the following season*, and that (*H2*) *signing a pre-free agency offseason contract extension that buys out at least one year of free agency will benefit a player's performance in the following season*. These hypotheses are mutually exclusive and derived from unique theoretical foundations. *H1*, which we refer to as the *Negative Performance Hypothesis*, derives from the concepts of shirking and stress-impairment.[2] *H2*, which we call the *Positive Performance Hypothesis*, takes its inspiration from the psychological concept of positive reinforcement.[3]

We test these two hypotheses using a data set of all pre-free agency offseason contract extensions that bought out at least one year of free agency since September 2001 ($N = 182$). Notably, the offseason criterion excludes those extensions signed in-season. We choose to exclude these in-season extensions because (1) they make up less than ten percent of all extensions, and (2) they have their own unique characteristics since the season played after and before the extension is signed is the same. We first treat the timing of a contract extension as a random occurrence and consider ex-ante and ex-post wins above replacement (WAR) and games played (G).[4] We next run a second set of model specifications using WAR per game (WAR/G) in lieu of WAR to account for the possibility of injuries. Finally, we weaken the as-if random assumption and run two new model specifications—one comparing WAR, G, and WAR/G post-extension to a player's averages over the previous three seasons, and another comparing a player's performance post-extension to their performance two years before the extension. The idea here is to remove from the equation the player's choice as to the timing of when to negotiate an extension.[5]

THEORY

Much of the literature regarding long-term contracts hints at the role of shirking in poor production from players. "Shirking" here is not meant in a pejorative or layman's sense; teams often encourage shirking as an economically rational form of asset protection for players who they have just signed to long-term deals. Significant evidence supports the notion that shirking in this non-pejorative sense may impact player performance. O'Neill (2014) finds that hitters generally boost their performances during contract years before performing worse when under a long-term contract. Work by Maxcy, Fort, and Krautmann (2002) demonstrates a nearly identical phenomenon at play among pitchers. It shows that pitchers with nagging injuries may be more likely to be placed on the injured list while under long-term contract. The study by Martin, Eggleston, Seymour and Lecrom (2011) similarly evokes the idea of the contract-year phenomenon as evidence of economically strategic behavior that may be attributed to shirking.

More recently, Paulsen (2020) goes beyond merely hinting at the role of shirking in causing poor player performance. By using a player fixed-effects estimation strategy, Paulsen (2020) eliminates much of the uncertainty caused by multi-collinearity concerns in existing player data.[6] Paulsen (2020) also addresses alternative explanations for the observed shirking, such as teams signing improving players to multiyear contracts or players facing an adjustment process when joining a new team. Even when alternative explanations are considered, Paulsen (2020) still finds that shirking behavior principally drives the generally inverse association between years left on a contract and a player's performance.

Still, a disconnect exists between scholars' findings and the testimony of players. Players rarely cite shirking as the cause of their down seasons. Rather, they commonly attribute negative performances following extensions to the increased psychological stress that comes with money and job security. As Jason Kipnis explained to reporters in 2014:

> I might have taken [my extension] the wrong way. There's one of two ways to go about it. There's 'Hey, I have the security and the money now I can go out and just play the game of baseball.' I took the way, where, 'I've got this money, I've got to live up to it.' So I might have pressed at the beginning and tried to do too much. In hindsight that could have hurt me and played a little part of [my down] season.
>
> (Gleeman 2014)

Kipnis's logic, while not supported by research, makes intuitive sense. One would expect large contracts to increase stress levels for already well-paid professionals. According to both physicians and psychologists, stress-distracted athletes generally suffer more injuries than their undistracted counterparts and require more time off as a result (Schultz and Schultz 2015, 265–66; Reardon et al. 2019). They may also feel pressured to perform well, causing them to counterproductively try too hard—what Kipnis calls "pressing"—creating suboptimal outcomes on the field. Yet irrespective of

whether the cause is stress or shirking, both point to worse performance following an offseason contract extension. This brings us to Hypothesis 1.

Hypothesis 1—Negative Performance: Signing a pre-free agency offseason contract extension that buys out at least one year of free agency will hurt a player's performance in the following season.

Conversely, there is at least one reason to believe that an offseason contract extension may benefit a player's performance in the following season. A contract extension coming off a good season could serve as a form of positive reinforcement. Positive reinforcement refers to the introduction of a desirable or pleasant stimulus after a behavior where the desirable stimulus reinforces the behavior, making it more likely that the behavior will reoccur (Doggett and Koegel 2012). Money qualifies as a positive stimulus, and observers often assume that when organizations extend players, buying out several years of free agency, they are expressing faith in or *rewarding* their previous performance.[7] This brings us to our second hypothesis.

Hypothesis 2—Positive Performance: Signing a pre-free agency offseason contract extension that buys out at least one year of free agency will benefit a player's performance in the following season.

Finally, we also offer the caveat that neither H1 nor H2 may be valid. Signing a pre-free agency offseason contract extension that buys out at least one year of free agency may simply not affect player performance in the following season. While we do not expect this, we must account for the possibility and label this outcome our null hypothesis.

METHODOLOGY

To arbitrate between the two hypotheses and their null, we create an original data set ($N = 182$) of all pre-free agency offseason extensions signed between January 2000 and June 2022 that bought out one or more years of free agency. We begin with an open-source data set from MLB Trade Rumors (2022), which includes all contract extensions signed during the period in question. We then hard-code whether each extension occurred during the regular season and add data on the number of years of free agency bought out, including potential options years.[8] Finally, we permute our data set by adding open-source data on player performance from Baseball Reference (2022a, 2022b).

In particular, we collect data on WAR, games played, and WAR/G as critical measures of performance. WAR sums up a player's performance holistically in a single summary statistic, making it ideal for parsimonious statistical analyses.[9] Games played measure a player's ability to stay healthy and speaks to their psychological state,[10] since research shows that shirking and/or stress-distracted athletes generally take more time off with injuries (and suffer more injuries) than their motivated and undistracted counterparts (Schultz and Schultz 2015, 265–66; Reardon et al. 2019).[11] Finally, WAR/G allows us to evaluate performance using an "injuries as random" assumption. While scholars have found little evidence to support the notion that injuries occur randomly (e.g. Timmerman 2007), athletes often speak about injuries as products of chance (Sawchik 2019). WAR/G thus allows us to consider that "baseball players have accidents," and that "stuff happens in life, and sometimes people get hurt and there is not always a reason for it" (Schultz and Schultz 2015, 265).

We also measure the independent and dependent variables—ex-ante and ex-post performance, respectively—in different model specifications using the three measures of play quality outlined. In each model specification, the season following the signing of the contract extension is used to measure short-term ex-post performance. Yet it is less obvious how ex-ante performance should be measured when contract extensions are signed. We therefore model the independent variable (IV) using three different specifications for the sake of transparency.

To begin with, we measure ex-ante performance (the IV) in terms of the season preceding the extension. We prefer this measure of the IV because the comparison makes the most casual and intuitive sense. Under this scenario, the timing of an extension is taken to be as-if random in relation to player performance. This permits us to conceptualize the signing of a contract as a treatment effect occurring within a natural experiment. Yet the as-if random assumption requires further justification, since "the plausibility of as-if random assignment stands logically prior to the analysis of data from a natural experiment." (Dunning 2012, 235)

We therefore seek here to justify the as-if random assumption on two grounds: observations from agents and players and previous research. While extensions of players following good seasons may receive positive press coverage—creating the perception that extensions generally serve as rewards for positive performances—there is surprisingly little large-N data to support this notion. Former MVP Shohei Ohtani, for instance, signed a two-year contract following a -0.4 WAR season in 2020. Similarly, Francisco Lindor signed a

$341 million deal following a .750 OPS season in 2020, and in 2011, the Reds inked Nick Masset to a 2-year extension following a down season in which he posted his lowest single-season ERA since 2008. There is thus little reason observationally, in the absence of large-N data, to expect that contract extensions would solely follow good or bad seasons.

One agent described teams' willingness to negotiate extensions at almost any point in a player's career as bordering on predatory:

> Every time the teams see a seam in the defense [resistance to signing an extension], they exploit the shit out of it.... . The teams have scouting reports on agents.... . They have heat maps. They know our tendencies, they know who will go to arbitration, who won't, whose business is failing and [who] need[s] to vest their fees.
>
> (Sawchik 2019)

Previous research (Krautmann 2018) also provides passing credence to the logical and observational intuition that performance and extension timing are unrelated. Based on previous statistical analysis, players are most likely to be extended when they have one year remaining on their existing contract (Krautmann 2018). Notably, that is *not* a performance-based selection effect. While that means that contracts are not offered entirely randomly, they are likely offered on an as-if random basis *relative to performance*. Essentially, while contract timing may involve much ruminating on a case-by-case basis, on average it is statistically as-if random vis-à-vis performance.

In the interest of transparency, we test our theory with a weakened as-if random assumption by considering a three-year average of previous performances, along with performance in the season two years before the extension.[12] Players who did not have a two- or three-year history in the majors were excluded from these analyses. We break our data into three groups: hitters, all pitchers, and starting pitchers.[13,14] Displaying our data this way allows consideration of heterogeneous effects. Finally, controls are collected for and included in the dataset.[15]

RESULTS

Table 1 presents the difference-in-means results for player performance in the seasons before and after an extension was signed. We observe nontrivial statistical evidence at the 95% level for the Negative Performance Hypothesis across most measures of performance irrespective of position. Players commonly perform at a lower level following the signing of an offseason extension. We thus reject the Positive Performance Hypothesis and the null hypothesis, given our strong belief that the timing of extensions is as-if random with regards to performance and our preference for the IV measure used in Table 1.

There is a notable post-extension drop-off in WAR, games played, and WAR/G. However, the level of drop-off varies by position. WAR shows the least heterogeneity, with extensions causing players of all stripes to be worth (on average) about one win less (batters' coefficient: -1.265; pitchers' coefficient: -1.146; starters' coefficient: -1.232). In terms of games played, there is a large amount of variance between positions. Pitchers are much more likely to miss starts due to injury in the season following the signing of an extension (coefficient: -2.857, $p < 0.0280$). Relief pitchers show an even greater drop-off, although the sample size is small and their usage is heavily situation-dependent.[16]

We suggest three possible reasons for the drop-off in games among pitchers. First, pitching is a high-stress activity that can cause permanent damage to the body. It follows that financially secure pitchers might rationally shirk more to protect their long-term health, and that management may have a significant part in actively encouraging such shirking as a form of long-term asset protection. Second, pitchers appear much less frequently than hitters and may therefore be under greater stress when they do come into the game. Greater stress correlates directly to heightened injury risk and longer injury recovery time (Schultz and

Schultz 2015, 265–66; Reardon et al. 2019). Finally, the possibility of regression to the mean must be acknowledged here with regards to health. While contract extension timing may be reasonably assumed to be as-if random with regards to performance, far less research has been done on its relation to health. Pitchers may simply be more likely to be extended coming off of a healthy season creating unforeseen selection effects.

To address this concern, for our third specific measure of performance, we utilize WAR on a per game basis. The WAR/G difference-in-means metrics measure whether there is still a drop-off if we treat injuries as random events rather than products of a player's psychological state. As can be seen clearly, the WAR/G metric reveals evidence of a drop-off similar to the previous two. The -0.009 per game drop in batters' average performance comes out to -1.458 wins lost over the full course of a full season. Similarly, the -0.038 lost by pitchers per start comes out to -1.254 WAR over the course of thirty-three starts. Essentially, even if all injuries were caused by uncontrolled misfortune, healthy players would still play noticeably worse the season after receiving a contract extension.

All three metrics support the Negative Performance Hypothesis when the baseline for ex-ante performance is considered as performance in the season preceding the extension. However, while we strongly believe in the as-if random assumption that this finding relies on, others may be more skeptical. What happens when we remove the as-if random assumption by using longer-term baselines for measuring ex-ante performance?

Table 1. Difference-in-Means Between the Preceding and Post-extension Performance

	WAR	Games	WAR per Game
Extension Effect (Batters)	-1.265***	-4.046	-0.009
95% C.I.	(-1.863 to -0.667)	(-12.397 to 4.305)	(-0.014 to -0.005)
p-Values	p < 0.0000	p < 0.3407	p < 0.0000
Observations (n_1)	109	109	109
Extension Effect (All Pitchers)	-1.146**	-5.151*	-0.031*
95% C.I.	(-1.928 to -0.364)	(-10.244 to -0.058)	(-0.058 to -0.005)
p-Values	p < 0.004	p < 0.0475	p < 0.02241
Observations (n_2)	73	73	73
Extension Effect (Starters)	-1.232**	-2.857*	-0.038*
95% C.I.	(-2.125 to -0.339)	(-5.400 to -0.314)	(-0.068 to -0.009)
p-Values	p < 0.0073	p < 0.0280	p < 0.0117
Observations (n_3)	56	56	56

*p < .05   **p < .01   ***p < .001

NOTE: Difference in means confidence intervals (C.I.s) are calculated using the pooled standard deviations ($\sigma_{p,i}$), a score statistic (z), and the square roots of the sample sizes × 2. The z-value is set to 1.96 for the 95% C.I. $p < 0.0000$ values occur due to rounding.

Table 2 indicates that there is no statistically significant correlation between pre-extension and post-extension performance according to most measures of performance. The one exception is games played by batters, which seem to increase. We attribute this to a number of players in the sample who were rookies in year one of their three-year averages. We next turn to performance in the season two years before the extension.

The results in Tables 2 and 3 are almost identical. Games played increases significantly for batters once again, this time with an even more significant p-value ($p < 0.0053$). Removing all rookies from the data confirms that they are driving this finding. The p-value ($p < 0.2154$) is now no longer significant. Players of all stripes play similarly after receiving an offseason extension and in the season two years beforehand.

The findings in Tables 2 and 3 are noteworthy. While we stand by our as-if random assumption, if future studies show it to be false, then our findings would instead support the null hypothesis. This adds a significant wrinkle to what would otherwise be a decisive finding in support of the Negative Performance Hypothesis.

CONCLUSION

This article demonstrates that on average—contingent on performance and extension timing being uncorrelated—signing an offseason extension that buys out one or more years of free agency causes a substantial

Table 2. Difference-in-Means Between the Three-year Average and Post-extension Performance

	WAR	Games	WAR per Game
Extension Effect (Batters)	-0.193	9.284*	-0.002
95% C.I.	(-0.813 to 0.417)	(0.769 to 17.799)	(-0.006 to 0.003)
p-Values	p < 0.5400	p < 0.0328	p < 0.4115
Observations (n_4)	88	88	88
Extension Effect (All Pitchers)	0.188	1.431	0.002
95% C.I.	(-1.015 to 0.639)	(-6.757 to 3.894)	(-0.032 to 0.026)
p-Values	p < 0.6534	p < 0.5955	p < 0.8369
Observations (n_5)	58	58	58
Extension Effect (Starters)	0.184	0.630	0.003
95% C.I.	(-1.123 to 0.755)	(-3.344 to 2.083)	(-0.036 to 0.030)
p-Values	p < 0.6974	p < 0.6452	p < 0.8371
Observations (n_6)	46	46	46

*p < .05   **p < .01

NOTE: Difference in means confidence intervals (C.I.s) are calculated using the pooled standard deviations ($\sigma\, p,i$), a score statistic (z), and the square roots of the sample sizes × 2. The z-value is set to 1.96 for the 95% C.I. $p < 0.0000$ values occur due to rounding.

Table 3. Difference-in-Means Between Performance in the Season Two Years Before Extension and Post-Extension Performance

	WAR	Games	WAR per Game
Extension Effect (Batters)	-0.261	13.118**	0.000
95% C.I.	(-0.364 to 0.886)	(3.938 to 22.298)	(-0.004 to 0.005)
p-Values	p < 0.4117	p < 0.0053	p < 0.9025
Observations ($n7$)	102	102	102
Extension Effect (All Pitchers)	0.052	1.544	0.001
95% C.I.	(-0.753 to 0.857)	(-7.281 to 4.193)	(-0.026 to 0.029)
p-Values	p < 0.8987	p < 0.5953	p < 0.9161
Observations ($n8$)	68	68	68
Extension Effect (Starters)	0.098	0.481	0.001
95% C.I.	(-0.0857 to 1.053)	(-2.951 to 3.912)	(-0.032 to 0.033)
p-Values	p < 0.8387	p < 0.7816	p < 0.9625
Observations ($n9$)	52	52	52

*p < .05   **p < .01

NOTE: Difference in means confidence intervals (C.I.s) are calculated using the pooled standard deviations ($\sigma\, p,i$), a score statistic (z), and the square roots of the sample sizes × 2. The z-value is set to 1.96 for the 95% C.I. $p < 0.0000$ values occur due to rounding.

drop in player performance the following season. The underlying theory is that by simultaneously facilitating shirking and ramping up stress, extensions hurt short-term ex-post performance.

However, there is an important caveat to this finding. Using performance from the three-year average, and the season two years before the contract extension, the results demonstrate that the Negative Performance Hypothesis is not robust enough to withstand weakening of the as-if random assumption. If player performance were to determine extension timing, this paper would support the null hypothesis rather than the Negative Performance Hypothesis. We therefore encourage further research into the relationship between performance and extension timing.

These findings also suggest other areas for future research. First, our dataset excludes players who sign in-season extensions in order to minimize selection effects.[17] Future research could examine in-season extensions more closely as an uncommon but financially lucrative subset of extension.[18] Second, the results for pitchers and hitters vary substantially. Although we offer several possible explanations, future sabermetricians should examine the potential causes of this discrepancy in more detail to elucidate further contract-response differences between pitchers and hitters. Third, we recommend that researchers examine the possibility that players' performances may improve in the second year following a new contract extension. While players may generally see a decrease in performance one year after signing a new contract extension, regression to some performance-based mean may be more likely by year two of a new contract extension. Current projections systems certainly assume such regression. We thus suggest that the value of extensions beyond the first year be tabbed for further investigation. Finally, researchers should consider expanding our sample size to include players who were extended but whose free agent years were not bought out. Given the increasing frequency of extensions that buy out arbitration years, this could provide valuable data to front offices on whom to go to arbitration with and whom to extend. This study thus points to a broader research agenda with the potential to have a significant real-world impact. ∎

Notes

1. Sub-optimal information environments benefit nobody. See Tomlinson and Lewicki (2015).
2. Rational shirking is derived from rational choice theory and behavioral economics. Stress-impairment is grounded in neuropsychology and medicine.
3. Positive reinforcement is rooted in behavioral psychology.
4. An event is considered "as-if random" when its occurrence is unassociated with some variable of interest. In this case, we posit that extension timing is uncorrelated with a player's performance in the preceding season. Contract extensions are obviously not a completely as-if random occurrence in a player's career, but we begin with strong simplifying assumptions before relaxing them later.
5. We discuss at length why we believe the timing of extensions to be uncorrelated with performance in the methods section, but more research is needed in this area.
6. A fixed-effects model refers to a regression model in which group means are fixed (non-random). In Sabermetrics, this type of model is valuable for analyzing data that includes multiple seasons from a single player.
7. See, for instance, Fansided staff writer Scott Rogust's description of Fernando Tatis's recent extension as a "reward" for an "incredible 2020 season" (Rogust 2022).
8. The coding process was generally straightforward with two exceptions. First, extensions signed on the first and last days of the season are coded as "offseason," due to the inability to collect down-to-the-minute data. Second, extensions signed after opening days in other countries but before opening days in North America are also coded as "offseason," since overseas opening days involve only two teams and often occur far in advance of their North American counterparts.
9. WAR is pro-rated in our data set for the shortened 2020 season.
10. Games played are pro-rated in our data set for the shortened 2020 season.
11. For relief pitchers, games played are also largely a product of managerial decisions.
12. Faith in the as-if random assumption is decisive in determining how one should interpret our results. We still include our null alternative specification results, however, because we believe in the value of research transparency.
13. We classify Shohei Ohtani as a hitter.
14. We classify a player as a starter if he made fewer than thirty-six appearances in a regular season and started at least one game.
15. Controls are not used in our in-paper analysis to avoid introducing statistical bias into our natural experiment's difference-in-means results. That said, controls were collected, and the full dataset with controls is available upon request.
16. Relief pitchers are not shown on their own in the data, but the drop-off can be inferred from the difference between the games played difference-in-means results between starting pitchers and "pitchers" generally.
17. Pre-season preparation, after all, cannot be undone by signing a contract.
18. In-season extensions can be very large. José Ramírez, for instance, just signed a 5-year $124 million extension in-season.

References

Baseball-Reference.com. 2022a. "Daily Updated Batting WAR Data (in CSV)." Baseball-Reference.com, V2.2. Accessed July 23, 2022. https://www.baseball-reference.com/data/war_daily_bat.txt.

———. 2022b. "Daily Updated Pitching WAR Data (in CSV)." Baseball-Reference.com, V2.2. Accessed July 23, 2022. https://www.baseball-reference.com/data/war_daily_pitch.txt.

Doggett, Rebecca, and Lynn Koegel. 2012. "Positive Reinforcement." In Encyclopedia of Autism Spectrum Disorders, edited by Fred R. Volkmar, 2299. New York, NY: Springer.

Dunning, Thad. 2012. Natural Experiments in the Social Sciences: A Design-Based Approach. New York, NY: Cambridge University Press.

Gleeman, Aaron. 2014. "Jason Kipnis Thinks Pressure of Contract Extension Led to Poor Season." NBC Sports. https://mlb.nbcsports.com/2014/09/11/jason-kipnis-thinks-pressure-of-contract-extension-led-to-poor-season.

Hakes, Jahn Karl, and Chad Turner. 2011. "Pay, Productivity and Aging in Major League Baseball." Journal of Productivity Analysis 35 (1): 61–74.

Krautmann, Anthony C. 2018. "Contract Extensions: The Case of Major League Baseball." Journal of Sports Economics 19 (3): 299–314.

Krautmann, Anthony C., and Thomas D. Donley. 2009. "Shirking in Major League Baseball Revisited." Journal of Sports Economics 10 (3): 292–304.

Krautmann, Anthony C., and John L. Solow. 2009. "The Dynamics of Performance over the Duration of Major League Baseball Long-Term Contracts." *Journal of Sports Economics* 10 (1): 6–22.

Martin, Jason A., Trey M. Eggleston, Victoria A. Seymour, and Carrie W. Lecrom. 2011. "One-Hit Wonders: A Study of Contract-Year Performance Among Impending Free Agents in Major League Baseball." *NINE: A Journal of Baseball History and Culture* 20 (1): 11–26.

Maxcy, Joel G., Rodney D. Fort, and Anthony C. Krautmann. 2002. "The Effectiveness of Incentive Mechanisms in Major League Baseball." *Journal of Sports Economics* 3 (3): 246–55.

MLB Trade Rumors. 2022. "Extension Tracker." MLB Trade Rumors. Accessed July 23, 2022. https://www.mlbtraderumors.com/extensiontracker.

O'Neill, Heather M. 2014. "Do Hitters Boost Their Performance During Their Contract Years?" *The Baseball Research Journal* 43 (2): 78–85.

Paulsen, Richard J. 2020. "New Evidence in the Study of Shirking in Major League Baseball." *Journal of Sport Management* 35 (4): 285–94.

Reardon, Claudia L., Brian Hainline, Cindy Miller Aron, David Baron, Antonia L. Baum, Abhinav Bindra, Richard Budgett, et al. 2019. "Mental Health in Elite Athletes: International Olympic Committee Consensus Statement." *British Journal of Sports Medicine* 53 (11): 667–99.

Rogust, Scott. 2022. "Fernando Tatis Jr Has the Moves On and Off the Field." Fansided, February. https://fansided.com/2022/02/18/fernando-tatis-jr-moves-off-off-field-video/.

Sawchik, Travis. 2019. "What's Behind MLB's Bizarre Spike in Contract Extensions?" FiveThirtyEight, April. https://fivethirtyeight.com/features/whats-behind-mlbs-bizarre-spike-in-contra ct-extensions.

Schultz, Duane, and Sydney Ellen Schultz. 2015. *Psychology and Work Today: An Introduction to Industrial and Organizational Psychology*. 10th ed. New York, NY: Routledge.

Timmerman, Thomas. 2007. "It Was a Tough Pitch: Personal, Situational, and Target Influences on Hit-by-Pitch Events Across Time." *Journal of Applied Psychology* 92 (3): 876–84.

Tomlinson, Edward C., and Roy J. Lewicki. 2015. "The Negotiation of Contractual Agreements." *Journal of Strategic Contracting and Negotiation* 1 (1): 85–98.

2023 Jerry Malloy Negro League Conference
July 20-23 | Detroit, MI

Featuring research presentations, panels, discussions and a banquet with prominent African American players from different eras, the Jerry Malloy Negro League Conference is the only symposium dedicated to preserving and promoting Black baseball history.

Black baseball has a long history in Michigan, especially centered in the Motor City. Among the original entrants to the Negro National League in 1920 was Tenny Blount's Detroit Stars, managed by Pete Hill and anchored by Big Bill Gatewood on the mound. The Detroit Wolves and Motor City Giants also played in Mack Park and Hamtramck Stadium. In addition to the well-known Turkey Stearnes (pictured), other star players included catcher Bruce Petway, the speedy Jimmie Lyons and the powerful Edgar Wesley.

This year's event will be hosted at various venues throughout Detroit, including Wayne State University, Hamtramck Stadium, Comerica Park, and the Detroit Historical Museum.

Register today at sabr.org/malloy

The 1877 National League's Two Cincinnati Clubs

Were They In or Out, and Why the Confusion?

Woody Eckard

In 1877 the National League began the season on April 30 with six clubs. However, in mid-June, the Cincinnatis disbanded for reasons only partly related to their poor on-field performance. A second Cincinnati club was quickly organized under different ownership and stronger financial backing. It began play less than three weeks after the first disbanded and was able to complete the first club's league schedule.

Nevertheless, controversy swirled around the issue of whether either club qualified for league membership. The league failed to clarify their status, even though its Constitution was quite clear in both cases. This suggests that the sustained ambiguity may not have been accidental. The matter was complicated by the fact that the success of the fledgling league was by no means assured, particularly given the ongoing economic depression of 1873–79.[1]

Then in December, both teams were disqualified and their games were excluded from the championship reckoning, i.e., they were not counted in the final standings. And for decades thereafter, published records generally were based on five members.[2] Today, of course, Cincinnati is included in the 1877 National League standings as a single combined club with the records of the other five clubs adjusted accordingly.[3] In 1968, the Special Baseball Records Committee restored both clubs to official status.[4]

This article reviews the history of this unique episode, focusing on the key question of why league officials allowed the ambiguity to persist. It has received little attention, perhaps because of its erasure by the Records Committee. It may also have been overshadowed by the Louisville game-throwing scandal that came to light at the end of the 1877 season.

THE TWO CLUBS

In 1876, the National League's inaugural year, the Cincinnati Reds finished dead last in an eight-team circuit with a dismal 9–56 record. But in the first few months of 1877, local newspapers were waxing optimistic with reports of club management attempting to field a better team in the revamped six-club league.

The Reds were owned and managed by Josiah L. Keck, with financial backing derived from the meat-packing firm of J.L. Keck & Brothers.

But then the well ran dry. A March 27 report in the *Cincinnati Daily Star* stated that "J.L. Keck & Bro. was announced to be in a critical condition yesterday," perhaps a victim of the Depression.[5] Two days later the *Cincinnati Enquirer* reported that "The Red Stocking Base-Ball Club now feel as if they have no backing, and talk of disbanding."[6] Then, on April 8, the *Enquirer* announced that "J.L. Keck & Brothers is no more," its property having been sold to satisfy creditors.[7]

Nevertheless, on April 26 Josiah Keck attended the National League pre-season director's meeting representing the Cincinnati Club.[8] Apparently alternative financing had been secured. The Reds then began their season on schedule, winning their first game against the Louisvilles on May 10. But it was downhill from there. By June 16, their record was three wins and 14 losses, having lost seven straight since June 2.

This was enough for Keck, who decided to disband the club. Per the June 17 *Enquirer*: "Consultation with… the Club last evening confirms the belief that the

Before joining the new Cincinnati club, Charley Jones played two games for William Hulbert's Chicago club.

proprietors...are ready to throw it [i.e., disband]."[9] A June 19 *Chicago Tribune* article titled "The Cincinnatis Go to Pieces" reports: "Keck, the former head, ... said he had no money to go on."[10] An *Enquirer* report, also on the 19th, stated that "members of the Cincinnati Club...were...released from their contracts."[11]

Keck's financial difficulties had another impact with broader implications. The club had failed to pay the $100 annual league membership dues that had a June 1 deadline. As seen here we quote from the relevant sections of the 1877 National League Constitution.[12] Article VI clearly states that the penalty for non-payment is membership forfeiture. It also states that the League Secretary must notify all member clubs "at once."

Relevant Sections of the 1877 National League Constitution[13]

Article III. Membership.
Section 4. ...election [to membership] shall take place at the annual meeting...provided that should any eligible club desire to join the League after...the meeting and *before the commencement of the ensuing championship season*, it may make application in writing to the Secretary...[emphasis added].

Article VI. Dues and Assessments.
Section 1. Every club shall pay...on or before the first day of June...the sum of One Hundred Dollars...*and any club failing [to comply] shall thereby forfeit its membership*...and the Secretary of the League *shall at once notify all League clubs* of such forfeiture of membership [emphasis added].

However, for unspecified reasons, League President William Hulbert and Secretary-Treasurer Nicholas Young kept Cincinnati's non-payment and its apparent non-member status secret until the disbandment, i.e., for more than two weeks. On June 25, a *Brooklyn Daily Eagle* article observed, "Young should have notified the League clubs at once; but Chicago was the only club that knew of it, none of the others having received a notification of [the payment] failure until the 19th."[14] Melville, in his 2001 book *Early Baseball and the Rise of the National League*, suggests that Young's inaction was actually at Hulbert's request.[15]

Almost immediately after the first Cincinnati Club disbanded, a movement began to organize a replacement. The above-mentioned June 17 *Enquirer* article

that reported the impending disbandment also mentioned that "a stock company of eight or ten of Cincinnati's wealthiest men stand ready and anxious to take the Club off Mr. Keck's hands."[16] Five days later, on June 23, a *Cincinnati Star* report indicated that a consortium was up and running.[17] The new management had signed seven players from the old club, including five regulars; had closed a contract to rent the Reds' ball park; and were communicating with league clubs regarding their position in the NL. The principals in the new organization were J.W. Neff and E.M. Johnson, both of Cincinnati. Nevertheless, Hulbert, ever the opportunist, "borrowed" star player Charley Jones for two games with his Chicago club in late June before the new Cincinnati club was a done deal, and also hired away two other players.[18]

A key issue was whether the new club could simply step in and finish the old club's championship schedule. On June 19, the *Cincinnati Enquirer* observed "It would be self-robbery to any one of the League Clubs to deny its consent for the Cincinnati Club to remain in the League."[19] The reason, of course, is that denial could mean foregoing the related revenue. The five other 1877 members were the Bostons, Chicagos, Hartfords, Louisvilles, and the St. Louis Club. (The Hartfords played their "home" games in Brooklyn in 1877, the Mutuals having been booted from the league.)

But such approval need not involve formal admission to the league. After all, in the late 1870s league clubs played many games with non-league clubs as exhibitions, albeit with less fan interest. On June 22, the *Chicago Tribune* reported: "The [Cincinnati] Club will play out its schedule of games if taken back into the League. If not, *it will play the schedule[d] games anyhow*, with such of the League clubs as may wish it" (emphasis added).[20] In the former case, the games would count in the championship standings, generating greater ticket sales; in the latter, they would not count, discouraging sales. Unfortunately, newspaper reports often conflated the two situations, confusing public understanding.

In fact, league rules forbade the admission of new clubs after the start of the championship season. Article III of the Constitution stipulates that the admission of new clubs must occur "before the commencement of the...championship season." Thus, the new Cincinnatis could play out the old club's schedule, but not as a member of the league.

The new club played its first NL opponent, Louisville, on July 3. After an early September team "reorganization" that involved replacing four starters, it completed its schedule on October 6 with a record of 12 wins and 28 losses, not much better than the old club. The combined record was 15 wins and 42 losses, ten games behind fifth-place Chicago. The November 10 *Clipper* presents a detailed season summary of game results for the "Old Team," the "New Team," and the "Reorganized Team."[21]

AMBIGUOUS STATUS

Soon after the first club disbanded, a telegraph poll of the other clubs was conducted by the league, ostensibly to solicit approval for the new club as a replacement. On June 24, the *Enquirer* reported, "The Cincinnatis will be readmitted into the League—the five Clubs unanimously having voted to receive them."[22]

It was clear from the poll that the new club would be allowed to play out the old club's schedule. But, despite the wording in the *Enquirer* report, the championship-versus-exhibition status for the games was not made clear. For example, the July 9 Louisville *Courier-Journal* observed: "The League has not yet decided whether all the games of the Old Reds shall be thrown out or whether the new organization is to be admitted [to full membership] and its games counted. ...no action has yet been taken upon the proposed admission of the new Reds..."[23]

The *Clipper* of July 14 presented a more detailed critique of the Cincinnati Club's ambiguous status (Figure 1), specifically calling for a "definite statement" of clarification from the league.[24]

Newspapers reported NL standings in various ways after July 3. As noted by Pietrusza (1991), "So great was the confusion that some newspapers printed League standings featuring the rebuilt team, but others did not."[25] Many papers published separate standings, with and without Cincinnati. In the former case, the records of the two clubs were combined, assuming that, if admitted to the league, the new club would "inherit" the old club's record. For example, Figures 2 and 3 show dual standings from the July 15 *Chicago Tribune* and August 6 *Cincinnati Enquirer*, respectively.[26] The *Clipper* of September 1 was still reporting dual standings (Figure 4) noting: "Long before this the League should have given the public to understand [whether] this club—the new nine—was in the League or not."[27]

THE NL'S CONUNDRUM

Certainly, the failure of the first Cincinnati Club presented a challenge. At the end of 1876 the NL had expelled the Mutuals of Brooklyn and Athletics of

Figure 1. The *New York Clipper* of July 14, 1877, describing the unclear status of the new Cincinnati club vis-à-vis the National League.

THE CHAMPIONSHIP RECORD.

The first week's play of the second Western tour of the Boston and Hartford Clubs has not improved the position of either club, especially the Hartfords, who have thus far lost all four of the games they have played—two with St. Louis and two with the Louisvilles. The Boston nine offset their Chicago defeat with two victories over Cincinnati; but it is questionable whether the latter will be of any use to them, as it is uncertain yet whether they will be counted on the regular record as legal games. The League ought to hold a meeting at once to settle the status of the new Cincinnati Club. At present the public do not know whether its games are merely exhibitions, or whether they are legal contests which are to be counted in the list of championship games; and the sooner the present mixed condition of things in the League arena is put a stop to by a definite statement *from* the Association in regard to the existing status of the new Cincinnati Club, and the counting of the games of the disbanded nine, the better for the interests and credit of the League. The record up to July 8, inclusive, is as follows:

	Boston.	*Louisville.*	*St. Louis.*	*Hartford.*	*Chicago.*	*Cincinnati.*	*Games Won...*
Boston	.	4	1	2	4	4	15
Louisville	0	..	2	4	3	5	14
St. Louis	3	2	..	3	3	3	14
Hartford	3	2	2	..	3	2	12
Chicago	1	1	5	1	..	3	11
Cincinnati	0	2	1	0	1	..	4
Games lost	7	11	11	10	14	17	70

Figure 2. Dual league standings from the *Chicago Tribune* of July 15, 1877.

THE CHAMPIONSHIP.

The past week has made no very great changes in the list, and the Bostons still lead, though they are not firm enough in the saddle to stand much of a shaking by the Whites this week. There is nothing like a decisive lead anywhere, and is not likely to be for a month to come. The following table is made up on the assumption that the Cincinnati games will none of th[e]m be counted. This is getting to be the general opinion as far as can be judged from exchanges:

CLUBS.	*Boston....*	*St. Louis....*	*Louisville...*	*Hartford...*	*Chicago....*	*Games won.*
Boston	..	2	4	2	4	12
St. Louis	4	..	2	3	3	12
Louisville	2	2	..	4	3	11
Hartford	3	2	2	..	4	11
Chicago	1	5	1	2	..	9
Games lost	10	11	9	11	14	55

The recapitulation is:

Clubs.	*Won.*	*Lost.*	*Played.*
Boston	12	10	22
St. Louis	12	11	23
Louisville	11	9	20
Hartford	11	11	22
Chicago	9	14	23

As a matter of information, and for the satisfaction of such as believe that the League is somehow going to let both Cincinnati Clubs' games count, the following table, comprising all the games played by everybody has been prepared:

Figure 3. Dual league standings from the *Cincinnati Enquirer*, August 6, 1877.

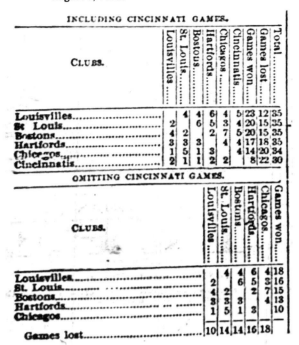

Figure 4. Evaluation of Cincinnati's ambiguous status and dual league standings from the *New York Clipper*, September 1, 1877.

There is considerable talk in certain quarters about the counting of the Cincinnati Club games. Long before this the League should have given the public to understand whether this club—the new nine—was in the League or not. It is asserted that the League has accepted the $100 entrance fee of the new nine, and on this account it is insisted that the Cincinnatis must be in the League. A few facts, however, upset this theory. The club of May last did not pay their entry-fee at all, and, therefore, were not at any time legally in the championship arena. This draws their games out of the count. And as regards the new club, a reading of the League Constitution shows two things, viz., that no club can enter the League except at the annual meeting in December, unless in the case of a club's being organized after such meeting, and "before the championship season begins," and that, therefore, the new Cincinnati Club, not being in the League—despite the acceptance of the entry-fee—their games cannot be counted. All this is well known to the League Board, and to their secretary; and allowing the new club to play their games as if they were regular contestants in the championship arena does not look like fair dealing with the public. To show what might have been the record had the Cincinnati Club teams been legal contestants, we present below a table showing all the games played:

	Boston.	Brooklyn.	Chicago.	Cincinnati.	Louisville.	St. Louis.	Games won.
Boston.............	..	4	7	8	6	2	27
Brooklyn...........	5	..	4	6	5	3	23
Chicago............	1	3	..	6	2	8	20
Cincinnati.........	1	2	2	..	1	2	8
Louisville.........	4	6	6	5	..	6	27
St. Louis..........	6	5	4	7	2	..	24
Games lost.........	17	20	23	32	17	20	129

In this record it will be seen that Boston and Louisville tie each other in won games, as also in defeats, while St. Louis occupies next position, with the Brooklyns close behind them. But the legal count presents a rather different result, as will be seen by the appended table. The games include all played up to Aug. 31:

	Boston.	Brooklyn.	Chicago.	Louisville.	St. Louis.	Games won.
Boston.............	..	4	7	6	2	19
Brooklyn...........	5	..	4	5	3	17
Chicago............	1	3	..	2	8	14
Louisville.........	4	6	6	..	6	22
St. Louis..........	6	5	4	2	..	17
Games lost.........	16	18	21	15	19	89

By this last table it will be seen that Louisville leads, with Boston second and St. Louis and Brooklyn tieing each other for third place.

Philadelphia, representing its two largest cities. Both clubs had elected not to complete their schedule of games to avoid unprofitable end-of-season western road trips, a clear violation of the League Constitution. Now down to six members, the failure of the Cincinnatis not only made the NL's viability look questionable, but possible associated revenue losses also could produce a serious financial threat, "jeopardizing the whole league," as Pietrusza (1991) put it.[28] Such concerns may have been exacerbated by the ongoing Depression. Additionally, the league had been widely criticized across the professional baseball community for its restrictive and exclusive business model, novel and as yet unproven.[29]

As Hulbert and Young no doubt knew of Keck's financial problems, they may have decided to cut him some slack regarding the dues non-payment. By keeping it secret, the hope would have been that somehow he would find financial backing and keep operating. The fee would eventually be paid and counted as retroactive. But the disbandment dumped it all into the public domain. Hulbert and Young surely knew what actions the Constitution required...and allowed. Article XV stated that it could be "altered or amended," but only at the annual League Directors' meeting in December.

So, what to do? An announcement of strict application of the Constitution meant operating with only five clubs which, as noted above, could threaten the NL's viability. One suspects that option was quickly rejected. But announcing *ad hoc* exceptions and counting the games of both clubs would create other problems. First, the league's claim to be a rules-based organization, bound by its Constitution, would be seriously undermined, making future enforcement difficult. Second, Hulbert's well-known prejudices against eastern cities would appear to be confirmed. The league's many critics could then dismiss its rules-based claims as sheer hypocrisy, as enforcement occurred against the eastern Mutual and Athletic clubs while the midwestern Cincinnatis got a pass. Perhaps more seriously, the NL was now down to only two eastern cities (Boston and Hartford), and others might be deterred from joining, undermining the league's aspirations to be the dominant *national* organization.

SUBTERFUGE

But a third course of action was available: say nothing about the status of the two clubs. Inaction works if the media and the baseball public—ticket-buying fans in particular—proceed under the assumption that the games *might* be counted, which is what happened. The league gets the revenue benefits of the new Cincinnati Club's games, even if a status uncertainty penalty exists as some fans are deterred. Then, when the season ends, with the money safely banked, the Constitution is strictly applied, i.e., league membership is denied to both clubs and their games excluded from the championship reckoning. This would be made easier by the fact that the new club was almost certainly a non-contender.

While attractive to the NL, this approach created risk for the Cincinnatis who would bear the brunt of reduced fan interest, especially given the economic vulnerability of a mid-season entrant. In fact, per the June 19 *Chicago Tribune*: "unless the League will admit the new [Cincinnati] association, they will not go on, they say."[30] Similarly, the *Enquirer* of the same date reported that the new ownership group "will not take the Club up unless they can regain a place in the League."[31] In other words, league membership was a condition of their participation.

Probably for this reason, the NL offered a major quid pro quo. The minutes of the league's December 5, 1877, Directors' Meeting describe "an agreement *in writing, in...July*, 1877 with [the new club]...to secure to the League the carrying out of the League schedule ...of the [old club]" (emphasis added).[32] In exchange, the "League clubs pledged themselves to vote for the admission of the [new club] to full membership" *if* the schedule was completed.[33]

Secrecy was necessary to create the uncertainty required for such a plan to be successful. Public knowledge would, in effect, constitute an announcement that the new club would not be granted league membership until after the season concluded. It would be equivalent to an initial announcement of strict constitutional enforcement, and that none of the new club's games would count. Hulbert, Young, and the owners of the other teams apparently managed to keep their secret, as no reports of the plan in general or the July agreement in particular appeared in the press. Dual standings were widely reported until the season ended, evidence that secrecy had been maintained. And Hulbert, Young, and the other owners were apparently able to stonewall inquiries.

The NL's clandestine plan, of course, yielded monetary benefits from the extra tickets sold to fans who were thinking the games were, or might be, championship games. The cost of unhappy fans apparently was seen as minimal compared to a five-club lineup, the resulting lost revenue, and a possible threat to league viability.

Sports writers howled, but demands for clarification simply could be ignored. While the reporters pointed out the league rules that denied membership to both clubs, it was also apparent that special exceptions could be made by the rule-makers themselves. And the regular reporting of two sets of standings implied that the latter outcome was not improbable, ironically aiding the league's plan despite the newspaper writers' general disapproval of the status uncertainty.

Seymour (1960) recognized the NL's strategy vis-à-vis the 1877 Cincinnatis as "a clever [cunning?] practical solution which upheld League prestige by technically penalizing a violation without interrupting schedules or sacrificing gate receipts."[34] However, he did not mention the league's duplicity or the critical roles played by public uncertainty and secrecy. Ellard's 1908 book *Baseball in Cincinnati: A History*, in addressing the 1877 season, notes merely that "Cincinnati was officially dropped out of the National League...although a scrub team played the schedule through."[35] Similarly, Voigt (1983) mentions only that "for the immoral act of nonpayment of dues, Cincinnati's 1877 record was disallowed."[36]

While the contemporary newspapers did not explicitly identify the NL's gambit, there were some inklings. For example, as early as July 9, the *Daily Eagle* observed that, with the current uncertainty, "if [Cincinnati's games] are not [legal], the public is being led to attend under a species of false pretenses."[37] On July 21, the *Clipper* called out the "Boss of the League" [Hulbert], remarking that "the failure of the League to take action upon the Cincinnati Club's position...is anything but in accordance with their profession of fair-dealing with the baseball public."[38] The September 1 *Clipper* article mentioned above reiterated this point, first noting the sections of the League Constitution that rendered the games of both Cincinnati clubs illegal. It then observed: "All this is well known to the League Board...and allowing the new club to play their games as if they were regular contests in the championship arena does not look like fair-dealing with the public."[39] These statements, perhaps originating with the influential *Clipper* Baseball and Cricket Editor Henry Chadwick, were thinly-veiled accusations.[40]

Be that as it may, the season concluded with Cincinnati's status still unresolved. The league never issued a clarification. Their ploy succeeded.

RESOLUTION

Finally, the matter was resolved at the annual December meetings of the League Board of Directors. The *Clipper* reported that on December 4 the Board awarded the 1877 pennant to Boston based on the "regular League games played by the Boston, Louisville, Hartford [Brooklyn], St. Louis, and Chicago Clubs…All of the games played by…the Cincinnati Club were thrown out of the count."[41] Per the Constitution, the old club's games were excluded for "not having paid the regular entry fee" and the new club was ineligible "having been organized after the opening of the championship season."[42] At the Board of Directors' meeting the next day, the first public mention of the secret July agreement occurred (see above). Noting that the new Cincinnati Club had completed its schedule, per the agreement, the NL upheld its end by unanimously admitting the club for 1878.

But, alas, there was no mention of ticket refunds. ∎

ACKNOWLEDGMENT

I'd like to thank two anonymous reviewers for helpful suggestions.

NOTES

1. Per the official business cycle dating of the National Bureau of Economic Research, accessed March 8, 2023. https://www.nber.org/research/data/us-business-cycle-expansions-and-contractions.
2. For example, see *Spalding's Official Base Ball Guide*, 1878 (Chicago: A.G. Spalding & Bro., 1878), 57; and *Spalding's Official Base Ball Guide*, 1939, ed. by John B. Foster (New York: American Sports Publishing Company, 1939), 63.
3. For example, see 1877 Cincinnati Red Schedule, Baseball-Reference.com, accessed March 8, 2023. https://www.baseball-reference.com/teams/CIN/1877-schedule-scores.shtml.
4. *The Baseball Encyclopedia: The Complete and Official Record of Major League Baseball* (Toronto, Ontario: The Macmillan Company, 1969), 2328.
5. "Local Brevities," *Cincinnati Daily Star*, March 27, 1877, 4.
6. "Who Will Do It Now?" *Cincinnati Enquirer*, March 29, 1877, 4.
7. "The firm of J.L. Keck & Brothers is no more," *Cincinnati Enquirer*, April 8, 1877, 6.
8. "Meeting of the National League Directors Yesterday," *Cincinnati Enquirer*, April 17, 1877, 2.
9. "Mr. Keck Refuses to Send the Cincinnatis on Their Eastern Trip," *Cincinnati Enquirer*, June 17, 1877, 7.
10. "The Cincinnatis Go To Pieces," *Chicago Tribune*, June 19, 1877, 5.
11. "The Cincinnati Red Stockings Stop Down and Out," *Cincinnati Enquirer*, June 19, 1877, 2.
12. *1877 Constitution and Playing Rules of the National League of Professional Base Ball Clubs* (Chicago: A.G. Spalding & Bro., 1877), 5,
13. Source: *1877 Constitution and Playing Rules of the National League of Professional Base Ball Clubs* (Chicago, A.G. Spalding & Bro., 1877) 5, 10.
14. "The Cincinnati Club," *Brooklyn Daily Eagle*, June 25, 1877, 3. League president Hulbert also owned the Chicago Club.
15. Tom Melville, *Early Baseball and the Rise of the National League* (Jefferson NC: McFarland & Company, 2001), 122.
16. "Mr. Keck Refuses to Send the Cincinnatis on Their Eastern Trip."
17. "Base-ball," *Cincinnati Daily Star*, June 23, 1877, 4.
18. "Cincinnati Made Happy," *Chicago Tribune*, July 1, 1877, 7. After Hulbert was called out by several newspapers for his self-serving actions, and at Cincinnati's written request, he penned a response in which he agreed to "willingly" (albeit not "gladly") return Jones (only). See also David Nemec, *The Great Encyclopedia of Nineteenth Century Major League Baseball*, 2nd ed. (Tuscaloosa: The University of Alabama Press, 2006), 130–31.
19. "The Cincinnati Red Stockings Step Down and Out."
20. "The Cincinnatis," *Chicago Tribune*, June 22, 1877, 2.
21. "The Cincinnati Club Record," *New York Clipper*, November 10, 1877, 261.
22. "Base-ball," *Cincinnati Enquirer*, June 24,1877, 6.
23. "Championship Summary," *Courier-Journal* (Louisville), July 9, 1877, 1.
24. "The Championship Record," *New York Clipper*, July 14, 1877, 123.
25. David Pietrusza, *Major Leagues: The Formation, Sometimes Absorption, and Mostly Inevitable Demise of 18 Professional Baseball Organizations, 1871 to Present* (Jefferson, NC: McFarland & Co., 1991), 39.
26. "The Championship," *Chicago Tribune*, July 15, 1877, 7; and "League Race," *Cincinnati Enquirer*, August 6, 1877, 8.
27. "The League Championship," *New York Clipper*, September 1, 1877, 179.
28. Pietrusza.
29. Another few years would pass before the superiority of Hulbert's model of a sports league organization and operation would be accepted.
30. "The Cincinnatis Go To Pieces."
31. "The Cincinnati Red Stockings Step Down and Out."
32. *1878 Constitution and Playing Rules of the National League of Professional Base Ball Clubs* (Chicago: A.G. Spalding & Bro., 1878), 46.
33. *1878 Constitution and Playing Rules of the National League of Professional Base Ball Clubs.*
34. Harold Seymour, *Baseball: The Early Years* (New York: Oxford University Press, 1960), 89.
35. Harry Ellard, *Base Ball in Cincinnati: A History* (Charleston SC: Arcadia Publishing, 1908), 234.
36. David Quentin Voigt, *American Baseball: From the Gentleman's Sport to the Commissioner System*, Vol. 1 (University Park, PA: The Pennsylvania State University Press, 1983), 73.
37. "The League Pennant Contest," *Brooklyn Daily Eagle*, July 9, 1877, 3.
38. "The Championship Record," *New York Clipper*, July 21, 1877, 131.
39. "The League Championship."
40. Chadwick also wrote for the *Brooklyn Daily Eagle*, and may have been directly or indirectly responsible for the above-referenced articles from that paper.
41. "League Association Convention," *New York Clipper*, December 15, 1877, 298.
42. "League Association Convention."

A Stepping Stone to the Majors

The Olympic Base Ball Club of Paterson, 1874–76

John Zinn

As major league baseball grew throughout the late nineteenth century, a limited number of players earned national recognition for their on-the-field prowess. From that small group emerged an even smaller number who also had charisma and became the equivalent of today's rock stars. Especially noteworthy was Paterson's Mike "King" Kelly, considered by some to be baseball's first matinee idol. Thanks to both his performance and his personality, Kelly earned unprecedented amounts of money, not just from baseball—where at one time he was the game's highest-paid player—but also from endorsements and off-the-field activities. In addition to playing baseball, Kelly was an actor, the subject of a hit song and, most importantly for our purposes, the "author" of the first baseball autobiography.[1] Published in 1888, and almost certainly not written by Kelly, the book describes his baseball career beginning with his first attempts to play organized baseball in Paterson, New Jersey. Unfortunately, the book's version of Kelly's early career is incorrect and the inaccuracies have been repeated ever since. Some of this same misinformation has also seeped into the stories of William Purcell, Jim McCormick, and Edward "The Only" Nolan, three contemporary Paterson players who also made it to the major leagues.[2] The goal of this essay is to understand what actually happened in Paterson baseball 1874–76 and to explore its significance. The real story matters because historical accuracy always matters, and more importantly, because what did happen is both interesting and important.

DEBUNKING THE MYTHS OF KELLY'S EARLY CAREER

In his "autobiography," Kelly claimed his baseball career began in 1873, at age 15, when his good friend, Jim McCormick, asked if he wanted to join a new baseball team. Initially, the team was to be called the Haymakers, but with McCormick's support, Kelly convinced the others that Keystones was a better name. Captained by William Purcell, the team featured Nolan as its pitcher until he left for Ohio to join the Columbus Buckeyes in 1876. At that point, according to Kelly,

McCormick became the pitcher and Kelly was the catcher, so the two "got a reputation as the Keystone battery" which "stuck to us for many years after." During the 1876 season, Kelly claimed the Keystones dominated a number of prominent teams, especially the Star Club of Covington, Kentucky, which could not hit McCormick's pitching. However, "the great games" of the 1876 season were played in a "championship" series against the National League Mutuals, with the two teams alternating wins. After that stellar campaign, Kelly began the 1877 season in Port Jervis, New York, and then, following in Nolan's footsteps, joined the Columbus Buckeyes.[3]

One of the few accurate statements in the last paragraph is that Kelly joined the Buckeyes during the 1877 season. Leading off the list of inaccuracies is the Keystone Club name, an error that has been repeated religiously ever since. A close reading of the contemporary Paterson newspapers did not find any mention of a Keystone baseball club in that city through 1876. Beginning in 1874 however, there was a Haymaker Club in Paterson. Of the four future major league players, only Kelly was a member.[4] No information survives of any part Kelly played in naming the team, but if he did, it is far more likely he wanted the team to be called the Haymakers because that was the name of a prominent club in his birthplace, Troy, New York. While the team's name has limited significance, far more important is Kelly's romantic version of a team of teenage novices that more than held its own against some of the leading teams of the day.

As will be seen, the team in question was not the youthful Keystones/Haymakers, but the Olympic Club, a team run by some of Paterson's leading citizens who had both the ability and financial resources necessary to build a competitive team. Not only was Purcell never the captain of the Olympics, he, Kelly, McCormick, and Nolan never played for the Olympics or any other Paterson team at the same time.[5] And while Kelly correctly noted the Olympic Club's 1876 success against the Star Club from Kentucky, McCormick was not part of it because he was still laboring for one of the city's junior clubs. Nor did the two ever become a regular battery for the Keystones, Olympics, or other Paterson team.[6] Also inaccurate is Kelly's claim the team alternated wins with the professional Mutuals. In fact, the Olympics lost both 1876 games with the New York team.[7] Even if these factual errors are of limited importance, the enduring acceptance of Kelly's mythical account obscures the real story of how the management of a fairly typical New Jersey baseball team helped four players get started on their way to the major leagues. Before looking at that story however, it would be helpful to have a sense of how baseball developed in New Jersey in general and Paterson in particular.

THE OLYMPIC BASEBALL CLUB OF PATERSON

When organized baseball expanded in the mid-1850s, New Jersey was one of the first places the game took hold in a significant way. In 1855 the state had at least 14 baseball clubs, more than either New York or Brooklyn (then an independent city), which were the only other places the New York game was played that year. By the end of the 1860 season, 177 clubs had been founded in 21 New Jersey municipalities, second only to New York in both categories.[8] Similar growth might have been expected in Paterson, the state's third-largest city, but with the exception of an 1855 team sponsored by the Young Men's Association, there were few organized clubs until 1860.[9] The Olympic Club, Paterson's premier team, was founded in July 1864 and initially played primarily against other local teams.[10] By 1866, however, the Olympics were competing at a higher level. Particularly noteworthy were three games against the Irvington Club, the same year that upstart team wreaked havoc with the baseball establishment. Although the Olympics lost two of the three games, including an embarrassing 70–6 defeat, they did manage one victory, something some of the best teams in the country struggled to accomplish.[11] Over the next two seasons, the Olympics expanded their horizons even further, touring Connecticut in 1867 and hosting two of the country's top teams, the Atlantics of Brooklyn and the Union Club of Morrisania the following year.[12]

In 1869, however, the Olympic Club's climb up the baseball ladder came to an abrupt halt. The problem, according to the *Paterson Daily Press*, was that baseball (and cricket) had been "carried to excess" in 1868, "causing heavy loss to our industries by the negligence of employees."[13] Organized baseball activity dropped off so dramatically through 1874 that the *Daily Press* at one point asked rhetorically, "What has become of our base ball players?"[14] Though largely inactive, the Olympic Club played an occasional game, such as an 1873 match against a picked nine.[15] In June of 1874, however, it was announced the club would "be resurrected for a brief time," for a game with the Hewitt Club of Ringwood.[16] Playing, "with much of their old time spirit and energy," the Olympics won a decisive 57–18 victory. More importantly, the same article reported the club was to "be revived, provided, they [the players] receive pecuniary support to compensate for the time they lose in practicing."[17] The publicly stated demand for "pecuniary support" was a clear sign a successful rebirth required good management.

THE OLYMPICS REBORN

It took almost a month, but two July meetings firmly established the second incarnation of the Olympics. Some 50 people attended a July 10 meeting, choosing officers and directors with experience, both on and off the field. Especially important from a management perspective was Dr. John Quin, who was elected president. Quin, a local physician, was a prior Olympic Club president and had practical experience running a baseball club.[18] An Irish immigrant with a large medical practice and a reputation for generosity, Quin had been a city alderman and was considered one of Paterson's "most esteemed citizens."[19] With a reported net worth of $25,000 in 1870, the Paterson physician also did not lack for financial resources. The *Daily Press* claimed Quin, "one of the most enthusiastic and most liberal supporters of the club," had convinced several prospective players to join the team who otherwise would have declined.[20] Quin and the other club officers were so successful in rebuilding the Olympic Club that a year later, in 1875, they earned well-deserved praise from both the *New York Sunday Mercury* and the *New York Clipper*.[21] Among those praised was John Westervelt, the club's vice president, who became president himself in 1875.[22] Westervelt seems to have been an effective officer of the Olympic Club, but when he stepped down as Paterson city treasurer in 1879, some $8,000 was missing. After a few days of back and forth, his family and friends made up the difference and it doesn't appear Westervelt was ever charged with a crime.[23]

The Olympic Club was also fortunate to have officers and directors with baseball experience beyond Paterson, especially William St. Lawrence and Milton Sears.[24] St. Lawrence played college baseball while a student at nearby Seton Hall and went on to be a prominent lawyer.[25] Sears, who ran a family retail business, had even broader baseball experience. After playing for the original Olympics, he moved up to the Union Club of Morrisania and later played for two Ohio teams. Sears's exposure to baseball beyond Paterson was a plus for new Olympic players hoping to follow in his footsteps.[26] Another valuable member was Art Fitzgerald, who was considered a "pioneer" in the sign painting business. Although Fitzgerald's specific credentials are unclear, early in their careers both Kelly and McCormick reportedly "never signed a contract until they had consulted Mr. Fitzgerald."[27] Both Fitzgerald and Sears also had prior experience as officers or directors of the Olympic Club.[28]

While each man brought his own unique skills to this endeavor, they shared common traits that were essential to the Olympic Club becoming more than just another local team. Quin, St. Lawrence, Fitzgerald and Sears were successful in their chosen fields. Their basic competence must have been beneficial in operating a successful baseball club. The local prominence of the four men also gave the Olympic Club credibility. There is no better illustration of their standing in Paterson than the fact that each of their deaths, spread over a period of 40 years, was front page news.[29] While the accolades were about far more than their part in the Olympic Club, their contributions greatly increased the club's chances for success both in Paterson and beyond.

Accepting the publicly stated demand for "pecuniary support," the club's leaders wasted little time putting funding in place. Just five days after the initial meeting, the *Daily Press* reported that 40–45 "members" had subscribed over $100. While some of the money went for uniforms and equipment, the club's organizers decided to openly "compensate those of the nine who are workingmen for the time lost from their shops," because this was, "the only way to maintain a good nine."[30] By early August, twenty additional members had been recruited, reportedly "mostly wealthy citizens, who will back up the club financially to any extent."[31] These first financial commitments demonstrated, especially to prospective players, that the club's management was serious. Equally important was management's recognition the club needed ongoing operating income, which it proposed to generate by charging admission to an enclosed grounds.[32]

There was nothing new or revolutionary about this approach, but it was far easier to talk about than to do. One of the major reasons for the failure of the Eureka Club of Newark, one of New Jersey's premier teams of the 1860s, was its inability to successfully execute such a strategy.[33] While the Olympic leadership was unable to create an enclosed facility in 1874, by the following spring the Olympics, along with some other Paterson teams, had formed an association with $2,000 in capital stock and leased land near the Midland Railroad Depot.[34] Finished just in time for a June 17, 1875, game with the Atlantic Club of Brooklyn, the grounds included seats for "ladies and gentlemen," a "neat ticket office," and "convenient dressing rooms."[35] Enclosed by a fence eight to nine feet high, the grounds could reportedly accommodate crowds of up to 10,000, including space for horses and carriages.[36] Admission to Olympic Club games was 25 cents, but was lowered to 10 cents for Paterson junior club matches.[37] Paterson newspapers reported attendance for 18 games in 1875, ranging from 150 to 1,750, an average of almost 600 per game or 10,700 in total. Charging 25 cents for admission, the club generated $2,675 in revenue from these games alone. While attendance figures from this era are far from exact, the estimates indicate the Olympics had a regular revenue stream. Since one-third of the gate money went to the nine players, each Olympic player made about $5.45 per game, more than the daily wage of the most skilled workers in one Paterson silk mill that same year.[38] Through 1876, management continued to upgrade the grounds and explore other potential revenue sources, including converting the field into a skating rink in the winter time.[39]

BUILDING A COMPETITIVE TEAM

An enclosed ground was not in itself enough to attract large, paying crowds. Paterson baseball fans, and hopefully visitors from elsewhere, would only put their quarters down if the Olympics consistently put a good team on the field. Fortunately, the renewed baseball fever in Paterson provided a regular source of new players. In just two years, the number of Paterson baseball clubs grew from about six in 1873 to almost 30 in 1875.[40] This included a group of seven teams which organized a series of 18 games for a trophy donated by Milton Sears of the Olympics.[41] The contending teams included the Haymakers with Mike Kelly, and the Star Club, probably with Jim McCormick.[42] These teams were an informal feeder system for the Olympics, sometimes providing substitutes when the city's top club was short-handed. Kelly and McCormick got started with the Olympics in just that way, filling in for missing Olympic starters in an October 5, 1875, match.[43] One of the missing Olympics that day was Jim Foran, who had himself moved up to the Olympics from another Paterson club.[44] Foran, however, was no baseball neophyte. After playing for the Athletic Club of Philadelphia in 1868, he batted .348 for the 1871 Kekiongas of Fort Wayne in the

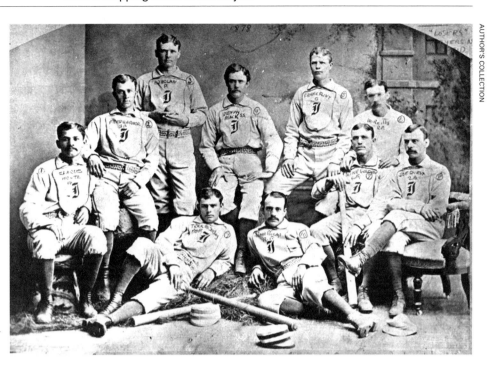

Edward "The Only" Nolan standing third from the left.

National Association's initial season.[45] Foran had since moved to Paterson, giving the Olympics a player with prior professional experience. While the Olympics added a few players from outside of Paterson, such as Foran and 1876 field captain James Lillis of Hudson County and Rutgers College, the vast majority of their players were from the city.[46]

Implicit in management's decision to build an enclosed ground and charge admission was recognition that "the most noted clubs in the country" would only visit Paterson if they received financial compensation. The best source of such money was gate receipts.[47] For example, the Atlantic Club of Brooklyn, the opponent for the June 1875 opening of the grounds, demanded a guarantee of $75 plus 50 percent of the receipts over $75.[48] In 1874, before the club had an enclosed facility, 18 of their 20 games were against New Jersey teams primarily from nearby Newark and Jersey City. Even though the new grounds, or at least the fence, were not available until mid-June of 1875, the Olympics still hosted five games that season against the professional Atlantics, Mutuals, and New Haven clubs. Playing more than twice as many games as in 1874, the club expanded its schedule, increased its revenue and upgraded the level of competition.[49] Although the Olympics lost all five games they played against professional teams, they enjoyed considerable success against New Jersey competition.[50] In fact, the Olympic Club was awarded the state's 1875 amateur championship, only to see it withdrawn in part because of claims they were not really an amateur club.[51] Early in the following season, the Olympic Club was expelled

from the New Jersey State Association of Base Ball Players, but they did not seem to care.[52] The Paterson team had loftier goals in mind.

While the Olympics did not play many more games in 1876, the level of competition did improve. In addition to games with the St. Louis and Mutual teams from the National League, the Olympics also hosted two strong regional teams, the Star Club of Covington, Kentucky and the Buckeyes of Columbus, Ohio. Although they lost all three games to the National League teams, they took two of three from the Kentuckians and won one game from the Buckeyes (with two ties).[53] The Olympics also made their first extended road trip in 1876, a six-game visit to New York State that included matches against teams from Syracuse and Rochester. The upgraded and expanded schedule meant increased revenue, while also assisting with player development. Playing against better competition helps players improve and also brings their names to the attention of higher-level clubs. As we shall see, this was especially true of a September 1876 three game series against the Buckeyes in Paterson.

The players also benefitted from increased media coverage, which was not due solely to an upgraded schedule or better on-the-field performance. Beginning in 1874, club officials began promoting their games in letters to the *New York Clipper*, a prominent sports weekly.[54] As the team improved, management, particularly John Westervelt, continued to inform both the *Clipper* and the *New York Sunday Mercury* of the schedule and game results.[55] In 1875, the team's upcoming games appeared in the *Clipper* five times. One year later this ballooned to 17, almost once per week during the season.

The accomplishments of the Olympic Club's management may be better appreciated in comparison to the experience of another New Jersey team, the Elizabeth Resolutes. Founded in 1864, the Resolutes were New Jersey state champions in 1870 and '72.[56] According to the *Elizabeth Daily Journal*, 1872 was also a "test year" to determine if the city could build and support a championship caliber club.[57] However attendance was so poor at the club's annual meeting in early 1873 that those present voted to disband the team. Although it seemed the Resolutes had no future, a subsequent meeting of 25–50 of the "best base ball men" in Elizabeth, a gathering not unlike the Olympic Club meeting of July 1874, decided otherwise. First, they adopted a new constitution and elected officers and a board of directors. Then, with little planning of any kind, they made the fateful decision to join the National Association and compete against far more talented and better-financed teams.[58] To make matters worse, the Resolutes played their home games outside of Elizabeth and failed to advertise those games.[59] The results were both predictable and disastrous: the club went 2–21 and disbanded before the season was over. The management of the Olympic Club not only chose a more realistic level of competition, but found a better location for their games and advertised regularly.

It is very unlikely that Quin, Westervelt, and company intentionally set out to build a launching pad to the major leagues. It is far more likely they loved baseball, wanted Paterson to have a good team and, at the very least, did not want to lose money in the process. Regardless of their intentions, they created just such a platform. First up, perhaps somewhat surprisingly, was not Kelly or McCormick, but Edward Nolan. Nolan was only 18 when the Olympic Club was reborn in July 1874, but he was no stranger to hard work. At age 13 he worked in a silk mill, probably for less than a dollar a day.[60] It is not known if Nolan played in the June 16, 1874, game with the Hewitt Club, but following the July 15 reorganizational meeting he was listed as the club's left fielder.[61] When the Olympic Club took the field for their next game, however, their pitcher was absent. Nolan stepped in and dominated the opposition, allowing only five runs with 11 of the 27 outs "put out behind the bat."[62] When his pitching success continued, the Olympics were smart enough to use Nolan as their starting pitcher for almost every game over the next two years.

In his first season with the Olympics, Nolan pitched in at least 15 of the club's 20 games, of which the team won 11. It was not always smooth sailing however, either on or off the field. On August 31, the *Daily Press* reported Nolan had left the Olympics to join the Channels, another Paterson team with aspirations of its own. Nolan's motivation was likely financial (this was before the Olympics began sharing gate receipts), since the Channels agreed to pay him $10 per game with the understanding that if the money was, "not forthcoming within ten hours," then, "he throws up his position." Later in the same article, however, the paper somewhat retracted the story. A few days later, the *Press* confirmed Nolan had indeed, "returned

Popular lithograph of Mike Kelly sliding into second.

to the Olympics as pitcher," and shortly after that demonstrated just "how indispensable he is to the success of the club."[63] Even without Nolan, the Channel Club briefly challenged the Olympics for Paterson's top spot, recruiting "a professional pitcher" when they could not get the local phenom.[64] There was talk of the two teams consolidating, and while there does not seem to have been a formal process, several Channel players, including Jim Foran, joined the Olympics for the 1875 season.[65]

While Nolan certainly pitched effectively in 1874, especially for an 18-year-old, playing for the Olympics also allowed him to learn and grow as a pitcher. The best example came in the short-lived Channel rivalry. In the first game of a best-of-three series, the Channels had "studied [Nolan's] pitching so closely, they had no difficulty," pounding him for 19 runs.[66] When the two teams met again on October 2, the Olympics were unwilling to risk a repeat poor performance by Nolan. They started another pitcher instead, but trailed, 10–1, after four innings. Given a second chance, Nolan showed he had learned from the first game. He threw five shutout innings as the Olympics rallied for a 12–10 win.[67] In the deciding game two weeks later, Nolan was again dominant. Not only was his pitching "more than usually effective," he caught "hot liners" in a way "that would have reflected honor on a Japanese juggler."[68] By season's end Nolan had become so popular, young boys in Paterson were putting pedestrians at risk by throwing rocks in imitation of Nolan's "style" of "swift balls," thrown, "with that sudden and peculiar underhand jerk."[69]

Playing for the Olympic Club offered multiple benefits to Nolan, not the least of which was pay well above what he could earn in a Paterson silk mill. Blessed with natural talent and fortunate to be in the right place at the right time, Nolan got the opportunity to display and develop that talent on Paterson's best baseball team. The young pitcher also attracted attention from far outside Paterson. A St. Louis club supposedly offered him $1,000 for the 1875 season, which he reportedly declined.[70] The Olympics could not and would not pay that kind of money, but they did offer Nolan further opportunities to develop before leaving Paterson. In 1875 Nolan pitched in more than twice as many games and against better competition, including three professional clubs. All told, Nolan and his defenders allowed 6.3 total runs per game, down from 9.2 the prior year, despite pitching against better teams. In 14 of those games, he allowed four or fewer runs, holding six opponents to no more than two. By this point the young pitcher had become a fan favorite,

especially with his "admiring lady friends," who gave him "a most resplendent [baseball] suit of blue silk."[71] Still modest, Nolan "kept his coat" on before the game, but when he removed it, he and his female fans were rewarded with "a murmur of surprise and delight" at "his splendid blue silk shirt."[72]

Despite his success, Nolan was hit hard by both the Alpha Club of Newark and the Elizabeth Resolutes, the latter club just two years removed from the National Association.[73] Nor did Nolan do much better on an August road trip to Trenton, where he suffered a 17–3 loss, his worst outing of the year. Leading 3–0 after six innings, the combination of heat and shaky defense caused Nolan to lose "his head" making his pitching "but child's play" to hit.[74] Despite those rough spots, Nolan had a stellar season. It was no surprise when he signed to play for the Columbus Buckeyes in early 1876.[75] After one season in Ohio, Nolan moved to Indianapolis, one level below the National League. There, as Richard Hershberger has documented, he had a memorable season, earning one of baseball's greatest nicknames: "The Only."[76] A year later, Indianapolis, and Nolan with them, was in the National League. Even if Indianapolis had not reached the NL in 1878, there is little doubt that Nolan would have been on another League club, just four years after his Olympic debut.

Logic and Mike Kelly's version of events suggest that after Nolan left Paterson, Jim McCormick stepped in as the Olympics lead pitcher. Logic, however, does not always apply in baseball. According to Kelly, he and McCormick played on the same Paterson team from the beginning of their baseball careers, but there is no documentation to support that claim. Described as, "a new aspirant for baseball honors," McCormick first appeared in Paterson newspaper accounts as a substitute for the Olympics in an October 4, 1875, victory over the Reliance Club of New York.[77] Even with Nolan gone, however, McCormick was not a member of the Olympics in early 1876, pitching instead for the Star Club of Paterson. Other than one other substitute appearance for the Olympics, he stayed with the Star Club through mid-August.[78] McCormick did, however, catch the attention of the local press when he pitched for the Star Club in a 12–7 loss to the Olympics. The *Daily Press* noted that his pitching was "something like Nolan's," and predicted that "practice would give him a very good delivery."[79] Less than a week later, the *Newark Courier* praised McCormick's "puzzling ball" after a dominant performance against the Star Club of Newark.[80]

About that same time, Hugh O'Neil, formerly of the Atlantic Club of Brooklyn and the Olympics' fourth replacement for Nolan, suffered an injury and was unable to pitch.[81] That same day, the *Paterson Daily Guardian* praised McCormick, noting "we would not be surprised if he should at some day prove a second Nolan."[82] Recognizing the solution to their pitching problem was right there in Paterson, the Olympics chose McCormick to pitch in an August 18 game against the Alaska Club of New York, and he never looked back. Pitching with "rare judgement," McCormick allowed only five runs, three in one inning when he briefly "lost his head."[83] The new Olympic pitcher did even better in the next two games, allowing only a total

Paterson, New Jersey, about 1870.

of six runs against the Alaska Club.[84] McCormick pitched in 17 games for the Olympics in 1876, allowing 4.4 runs per game, better even than Nolan in 1875, against arguably better competition.

The new Olympic starter was also fortunate to be given a chance to pitch on a big stage, an opportunity he did not waste. In late September, the Buckeyes, with Nolan, arrived in Paterson for a three-game series. McCormick allowed four runs in the first game, which ended in a tie. In the second game, he shut out the Buckeyes for eight innings, but they rallied to even the score at 4–4 in the ninth. Although Columbus had a runner on third with none out, McCormick showed his mettle and retired the side for a second straight tie. It was small consolation to the Paterson pitcher who, according to the *Daily Guardian*, "weeps and refuses to be comforted."[85] Perhaps the frustration gave McCormick even more motivation in the series finale. He allowed only one run in a 3–1 Olympic victory.[86] Although his stay with the Olympics was relatively brief, McCormick took full advantage of an ideal platform to display his skills. Based on his performance in the three games against Columbus, it was no surprise the club signed him for the 1877 season.[87] Later that same year, McCormick joined Nolan in Indianapolis and moved with the team to the National League in 1878. The significance of the two pitchers' accomplishments was not lost in Paterson, where the *Daily Guardian* proclaimed, "Paterson has furnished two of the best amateur pitchers in the country."[88]

"BLONDIE"

It is probably fitting that William Purcell's Paterson baseball career is the least documented of the four players. Although he had a 12-year major league career,

Purcell has the dubious distinction of being one of the relatively few major league players whose death date and burial site are unknown. While Kelly claimed Purcell was the team captain, he was never captain of the Olympics. He played only eight games for the club. Also, unlike the others, Purcell's name has not been found in box scores for Kelly's Haymakers, McCormick's Star Club, or any other Paterson team. With no advance notice, the future major leaguer played right field for the Olympics in a May 23, 1876, game against a Brooklyn team, batting third and getting two hits.[89] Purcell appeared in seven more Olympics games, highlighted by a June 14 home run off McCormick in a victory over the Star Club.[90] The only other newspaper attention Purcell attracted was criticism for some "decidedly bad" play in the field.[91]

Somewhat surprisingly, when Purcell's name disappeared from the Olympic lineup after a July 4, 1876, game, he did not resurface with another Paterson club. Instead, in early August, Purcell was pitching for the Delaware Club of Port Jervis, New York.[92] Although Purcell returned to Paterson for the winter and briefly played there in early 1877, he went back to Port Jervis and played for the New York team through the middle of June.[93] After pitching effectively against the Cricket Club of Binghamton, he was signed by that team, initially for $30 a month, which was raised to $70 before the season ended.[94] When the Cricket Club disbanded after the 1877 season, the players, including Purcell, were "engaged" to play in Utica the following season.[95] His performance must have been satisfactory since he was then signed by Syracuse when that club joined the National League in 1879. It marked the beginning of a major league career that lasted through 1890.[96] Purcell's tenure with the Olympics was brief, but the visibility of playing for Paterson's top team clearly helped when the Port Jervis team decided to upgrade its roster. Like Nolan and McCormick, Purcell took full advantage of the opportunity.[97]

"KING" KELLY

Mike Kelly's Paterson years are discussed last because, even though he had without question the greatest major league career, he was the last to leave the city. The future Hall of Famer did attract the attention of the press relatively early. The *Daily Press* praised his play at shortstop in a November 1874 Haymaker victory over the Star Club.[98] Kelly must have also caught the attention of the Olympic Club, since at least twice in 1875 he filled in when they were shorthanded. In the second contest in early October, both Paterson papers praised his play at catcher, for doing "remarkably well" in "facing Nolan's pacers" for the first time.[99] In spite of this performance and Kelly's claim that he and McCormick became the team's battery, once Kelly made the Olympic starting lineup in 1876, he played almost exclusively in the outfield.

Kelly's performance in his one season with the Olympic Club was marked by both praise and criticism in the newspapers, suggesting that while he played well, it was also a learning experience. His fielding was called "perfect" in one early season game and when he did get a rare chance to catch in September, he, "played the position like a veteran, his throwing deserving special notice."[100] He went 3 for 8 in two games against the Star Club of Kentucky, got a hit off Nolan in one of the Buckeye games, and gave "a fine display of batting" in executing a fair-foul hit in the final game of the series.[101] The hit off Nolan apparently redeemed Kelly, since Nolan was reportedly determined to hold him hitless. After meeting the challenge, Kelly supposedly "stands several feet higher today than usual."[102] Full box scores survive for 24 of Kelly's 47 games with the 1876 Olympics, in which he batted .279, which hardly seems Hall-of-Fame-worthy at first glance. A closer look, however, reveals a picture of a developing young player. After batting a woeful .218 in the first 13 games, Kelly had a blistering .347 batting average in the last 11 contests.

Further signs of youth and immaturity were negative comments about what sound like attitude issues. In an early season game, the *Daily Press* commented that after hitting safely Kelly was put out at first, "through neglect in not paying attention to the game."[103] Such concerns continued when, supposedly, a game needlessly went into extra innings due to Kelly's

"recklessness" on the bases. Anticipating problems major league managers and umpires would later have with Kelly, the *Daily Guardian* complained, "Captain Lillis had no control over him and he evidently intends to do as he pleases."[104] No wonder the paper later dubbed him, "the irrepressible Kelly."[105] Whether due to concerns about his attitude or simply the informal nature of scouting and player evaluation, Kelly was the only one of the four still in Paterson when the 1877 season began. The Olympic club had a hard time getting organized for the new season, and Kelly began the year playing for the Rutan Club, a relatively new junior team.[106] Named after local funeral director Charles Rutan, according to the *Daily Guardian*, the club's "intention is to bury everything they tackle."[107]

The Olympic Club finally got on the field, and fortunately for Kelly, played three games against the Delaware Club of Port Jervis and Olympic alumnus Bill Purcell.[108] Kelly was signed by the Port Jervis team in late June of 1877, briefly giving the team an all-Paterson battery.[109] Kelly won high and consistent praise for his catching at Port Jervis, marred only by one apparent refusal to chase a passed ball.[110] The Paterson prospect had clearly matured, since the local paper mourned his absence in late August, claiming the club's lack of leadership "contrasted sadly with the Delawares under M. Kelly as captain."[111] The loss was permanent as Kelly headed west to join the Columbus Buckeyes, playing right field and serving as "change [substitute] catcher."[112] Kelly batted just .156 in 23 games in Columbus.[113] That would prove no long-term obstacle, as 1878 found Kelly with Cincinnati on his way to the major leagues and the Hall of Fame.

COMPARABLE TEAMS

Four players from one club reaching the majors is a notable accomplishment. It raises the question of whether the Olympic experience was unique. While no exhaustive study was made by the author, initial research and suggestions from other historians produced four teams from 1869 to 1876 that sent at least four players to the major leagues or the National Association. Of these, the Easton Club from Pennsylvania and the Neshannocks of New Castle, Pennsylvania, differ from the Olympics in that they were not home-grown clubs. The Easton lineup was largely recruited by Jack Smith from, "the ballfields of Philadelphia," and became "arguably the best amateur club in the country," in 1874. Unsurprisingly, the Easton Club was a prime target for professional teams. National Association clubs signed eight of their players.[114] Similarly

Charlie Bennett, Ned Williamson, George Creamer, and Sam Weaver all played for the Neshannocks and in the majors, but only the ill-fated Bennett was from New Castle.[115]

Although highly successful, the Star Club of Boston doesn't seem to have attracted a great deal of contemporary media attention, probably because they were vastly overshadowed by the Red Stocking teams that dominated the National Association. However, five members of the Star Club—Curry Foley, Chub Sullivan, John Morrill, Dennis Sullivan, and Lew Brown—either were born or grew up in Boston and eventually reached the major leagues. The Star club was so talented they won the junior championship of Massachusetts in 1874 without losing a single match.[116] Finally, there is the Alert Club of Rochester, which Priscilla Astifan has written about in her comprehensive history of baseball in that city.[117] Five players from that team—John Glenn, Sam Jackson, Eugene Kimball, John McKelvey, and Ezra Sutton—played in the National Association and/or the National League. Like the Olympics, the Alert Club gave their players the opportunity to play against good competition, especially during extensive 1869 road trips.[118]

In 1875, the same year the Olympic club did or did not win the New Jersey state championship, the *New York Clipper* estimated there were at least 2,000 baseball clubs in the United States.[119] If that estimate is anywhere near accurate, it demonstrates how unusual it was for one club to send four players to the major leagues. While it may be more romantic or heroic to believe what happened in Paterson was a rags-to-riches tale, led by future Hall of Famer Mike Kelly, the truth, as we have seen, is somewhat different. Kelly, McCormick, Purcell, and Nolan had plenty of talent, but their success also depended on a support system provided by another group of men still largely unknown to history. Building a launching pad to the majors was not their intent. They wanted a successful team, understood what went wrong with the original Olympics, and resolved to do better. Unintentionally, these Paterson men anticipated the kinds of things up and coming players, then and now, need to reach the game's highest levels. It may not be the stuff of myth and legend, but it is no less interesting or important. ■

Notes

1. Peter M. Gordon, "King Kelly," SABR BioProject, https://sabr.org/bioproj/person/king-kelly.
2. For the most literal acceptance of Kelly's version of his baseball years in Paterson see Mary Appel's *Slide Kelly Slide: The Wild Life and Times of Mike "King" Kelly Baseball's First Superstar* (Latham, Maryland: Scarecrow Press, 1996), 16–18.
3. Mike Kelly, *Play Ball: Stories of the Diamond Field* (Jefferson, North Carolina: McFarland & Co., 2006, first published 1888), 11–13.
4. *Paterson Daily Press*, September 11, 1874, 3, November 10, 1874, 3.
5. *Paterson Daily Press*, August 22 1874, 3, *Paterson Daily Guardian*, July 13, 1875, August 12, 1876. From 1874 to 1876, the Paterson newspapers list Milton Sears, a man named Wiggins and James Lillis as Olympic captains.
6. *New York Clipper*, July 15, 1876, 123, In the 15 box scores that survive when McCormick pitched for the Olympics, Kelly caught just three games.
7. *Paterson Daily Press*, October 7, 1876, 3, *Paterson Daily Guardian*, October 12, 1876.
8. John G. Zinn, *A Cradle of the National Pastime: New Jersey Baseball, 1855–1880* (Princeton, New Jersey: Morven Museum and Garden, 2019), 28–29.
9. *Newark Daily Advertiser*, August 22, 1855, 2, *New York Sunday Mercury*, May 6, 1860, https://protoball.org/Paterson, NJ.
10. *Paterson Daily Register*, July 15, 1864.
11. *Paterson Daily Press*, July 14, 1866, 3, September 6, 1866, 3, October 6, 1866, 3.
12. *Paterson Daily Press*, September 23, 1867, 2, June 2, 1868, 2, July 28, 1868, 2.
13. *Paterson Daily Press*, July 6, 1869, 2, July 22, 1869, 3.
14. *Paterson Daily Press*, March 29, 1871, 3, August 28, 1872, 3.
15. *Paterson Daily Press*, June 3, 1873, 3.
16. *Paterson Daily Press*, June 11, 1874, 3.
17. *Paterson Daily Press*, June 17, 1874, 3.
18. *Paterson Daily Press*, September 4, 1867, 3, July 11, 1874, 3.
19. *The Paterson Morning Call*, July 14, 1887, 1, *Paterson Daily Register*, April 11, 1862, 2, *Paterson Daily Press*, January 4, 1870, 2.
20. 1870 United States Census, *Paterson Daily Press*, July 16, 1874, 3.
21. *New York Sunday Mercury*, June 27, 1875, *New York Clipper*, July 10, 1875, 117.
22. *Paterson Daily Press*, April 28, 1875, 3.
23. *Paterson Daily Press*, June 5, 1879, 3, June 6, 1879, 3, June 7, 1879, June 9, 1879, June 10, 1879, 3, June 11, 1879, 3.
24. *Paterson Daily Press*, July 11, 1874, 3.
25. *Paterson Evening News*, July 9, 1928, 1, *New York Clipper*, May 21, 1870, 50.
26. *Sporting Life*, April 24, 1909, 1, *Paterson Daily Press*, July 11, 1868, 3, *Morning Call*, April 3, 1909, 1.
27. *Morning Call*, April 22, 1918, 1.
28. *Paterson Daily Press*, October 30, 1866, 3.
29. *Morning Call*, July 14, 1887, 1, April 3, 1909, 1, April 22, 1918, 1, *Paterson Evening News*, July 10, 1928, 1.
30. *Paterson Daily Press*, July 16, 1874, 3.
31. *Paterson Daily Press*, August 5, 1874, 3.
32. *Paterson Daily Press*, July 16, 1874, 3.
33. Zinn, 68, 81, 84.
34. *Paterson Daily Press*, May 26, 1875, 3.
35. *Paterson Daily Guardian*, June 13, 1875.
36. *Paterson Daily Press*, June 18, 1875, 3.
37. *Paterson Daily Press*, June 16, 1875, 3, August 20, 1875, 3.
38. *New York Clipper*, November 27, 1875, 275, Joseph Weeks, *Report on the Statistics of Wages in Manufacturing Industries* (Washington, D.C., Government Printing Office, 1886), 371, The John Dunlop Mill in Paterson reported 1875 daily wages ranging from 25 cents for a cleaner to $5 for a foreman.
39. *Paterson Daily Press*, November 17, 1875, 3, May 6, 1876, 3, August 10, 1876, 3.
40. *Paterson Daily Press*, June 5, 1873, 3, July 16, 1873, 3, July 24, 1873, 3, July 29, 1873, 3, August 11, 1873, 3, *Paterson Daily Guardian*, May 22, 1875, September 28, 1875. On May 22, 1875, the *Daily Guardian* claimed there "about twenty" teams not worthy of media attention in addition to the seven named in September 28, 1875 article.
41. *Paterson Daily Press*, September 13, 1875, 3, *Paterson Daily Guardian*, September 28, 1875.

42. *Paterson Daily Guardian*, September 28, 1875.
43. *Paterson Daily Press*, October 5, 1875, 3.
44. Paterson Daily 44 Press, October 29, 1874, 3.
45. Peter Morris, William J. Ryczek, Jan Finkel, Leonard Levin and Richard Malatzky, *Baseball Founders: The Clubs, Players and Cities of the Northeast That Established the Game* (Jefferson, North Carolina, McFarland & Co., 2013), 238, www.retrosheet.org.
46. *Paterson Daily Guardian*, June 23, 1876, August 12, 1876, *Paterson Daily Press*, June 23, 1876, 3.
47. *Paterson Daily Press*, July 16, 1874, 3.
48. *Paterson Daily Press*, June 16, 1875, 3, June 18, 1875, 3.
49. *New York Clipper*, November 20, 1875, 266.
50. *New York Clipper*, November 20, 1875, 266.
51. *Paterson Daily Press*, November 13, 1875, 3, *New York Clipper*, November 27, 1875, 275, December 11, 1875, 293, the Olympics claimed the players only compensation was a share of the gate receipts.
52. *New York Clipper*, April 22, 1876, 29.
53. *Paterson Daily Press*, May 27, 1876, 3, July 7, 1876, 3, July 8, 1876, 3, July 10, 1876, 3, October 7, 1876, 3, *New York Clipper*, September 20, 1876, 211, October 21, 1876, 235.
54. *New York Clipper*, August 15, 1874, 157.
55. *New York Clipper*, September 18, 1875, 197, *New York Sunday Mercury*, June 27, 1875.
56. Zinn, 93–97.
57. *Elizabeth Daily Journal*, August 8, 1872, 3.
58. *Elizabeth Daily Journal*, January 9, 1873, 3, January 14, 1873, 3.
59. *New York Sunday Mercury*, May 4, 1873, May 11, 1873.
60. 1870 United States Census, Weeks, 371.
61. *Paterson Daily Press*, July 16, 1874, 3.
62. *Paterson Daily Press*, July 17, 1874, 3.
63. *Paterson Daily Press*, August 31, 1874, 3, September 3, 1874, 3, September 4, 1874, 3.
64. *Paterson Daily Press*, September 12, 1874, 3.
65. *Paterson Daily Press*, October 6, 1874, 3, October 7, 1874, 3, October 29, 1874, 3, in addition to Foran, James Mullen, John Mullen, James Lillis, Wiggins and Tredo played at least 10 games for the Olympics in 1875.
66. *Paterson Daily Press*, September 12, 1874, 3.
67. *Paterson Daily Press*, October 3, 1874, 3.
68. *Paterson Daily Press*, October 17, 1874, 3.
69. *Paterson Daily Press*, October 27, 1874, 3.
70. *Paterson Daily Press*, May 25, 1875, 3.
71. *Paterson Daily Guardian*, September 4, 1875.
72. *Paterson Daily Guardian*, September 4, 1875.
73. *Paterson Daily Press*, June 29, 1875, 3, August 10, 1875, 3.
74. *Paterson Daily Press*, August 20, 1875, 3, *Paterson Daily Guardian*, August 18, 1875, *Trenton State Gazette* as quoted in the *Daily Guardian* of August 19, 1875.
75. *New York Clipper*, February 5, 1876, 355.
76. Richard Hershberger, "How Good Was Ed 'The Only' Nolan, *Base Ball 11– New Research on the Early Game*, 2019, 214–15, according to Hershberger's calculations Nolan's 1877 record was 57–29–9.
77. *Paterson Daily Press*, October 5, 1875, 3, *Paterson Daily Guardian*, October 5, 1875.
78. *Paterson Daily Press*, June 17, 1876, *Paterson Daily Guardian*, August 19, 1876.
79. *Paterson Daily Press*, June 15, 1876, 3.
80. *Newark Courier* quoted in the *Paterson Daily Guardian*, June 23, 1876.
81. *Paterson Daily Guardian*, June 23, 1876, *Paterson Daily Press*, June 23, 1876, 3 August 16, 1876, 3.
82. *Paterson Daily Guardian*, August 16, 1876.
83. *Paterson Daily Guardian*, August 19, 1876.
84. *Paterson Daily Guardian*, August 24, 1876, August 26, 1876.
85. *Paterson Daily Guardian*, September 21, 1876.
86. *New York Clipper*, September 30, 1876, 211, *Paterson Daily Guardian*, September 23, 1876.
87. *New York Sunday Mercury*, January 21, 1877.
88. *Paterson Daily Guardian*, September 19, 1876.
89. *Paterson Daily Press*, May 24, 1876, 3.
90. *Paterson Daily Press*, June 15, 1876, 3.
91. *Paterson Daily Guardian*, June 17, 1876, June 21, 1876.
92. *Evening Gazette* (Port Jervis), August 3, 1876, 1.
93. *Paterson Daily Guardian*, May 11, 1877, 3, *Paterson Daily Press*, June 15 1877, 3.
94. *Paterson Daily Press*, June 15, 1877, 3, July 10, 1877, 3.
95. *New York Sunday Mercury*, October 21, 1877.
96. *New York Clipper*, January 11, 1879, 331.
97. *Paterson Daily Guardian*, August 7, 1876.
98. *Paterson Daily Press*, November 10, 1874, 3.
99. *Paterson Daily Press*, July 31, 1875, 3, October 5, 1875, 3, *Paterson Daily Guardian*, October 5, 1875.
100. *Paterson Daily Guardian*, May 20, 1876, September 16, 1876.
101. *Paterson Daily Guardian*, July 7, 1876, July 10, 1876, September 21, 1876, September 23, 1876.
102. *Paterson Daily Guardian*, September 19, 1876, September 21, 1876.
103. *Paterson Daily Press*, May 31, 1876, 3.
104. *Paterson Daily Guardian*, August 12, 1876.
105. *Paterson Daily Guardian*, September 23, 1876.
106. *Paterson Daily Guardian*, May 11, 1877, 3, May 19, 1877, 3, May 24, 1877, 3.
107. *Paterson Daily Guardian*, August 30, 1876.
108. *Paterson Daily Guardian*, May 30, 1877, 3, *New York Clipper*, June 9, 1877, 83.
109. *New York Sunday Mercury*, July 1, 1877.
110. *Evening Gazette*, July 10, 1877, 1, July 14, 1877, 1.
111. *Evening Gazette*, August 21, 1877, 1.
112. *Evening Gazette*, August 7, 1877, 1.
113. *New York Sunday Mercury*, October 14, 1877.
114. Morris, Ryczek, et al, 258–59, email from Richard Hershberger, January 27, 2020, William J. Ryczek, *Blackguards and Red Stockings: A History of Baseball's National Association, 1871–1875* (Wallingford, Connecticut: Colebrook Press, 1992), 179, the eight were George Bradley, Tom Miller, Joe Battin, Denny Mack, Jim Devlin, Chick Fulmer, Bill Parks and John Abadie.
115. *New York Clipper*, March 11, 1876, 394, November 4, 1876, 251.
116. *New York Clipper*, December 19, 1874, 301, *Boston Globe*, May 2, 1887, 8.
117. Priscilla Astifan, *Rochester History*, Volume LXIII, Winter 2001, No 1, 3–6.
118. Priscilla Astifan, *Rochester History*, Volume LXIII, Winter 118 2001, No 1, 5–6.
119. "The Amateur Season of 1875," *New York Clipper*, November 20, 1875, 269.

The Invention of the Baseball Glove

The Case for the Forgotten 1901 Web-Pocketed Glove

John Snell

It is quite a natural thing to ask, "When was the baseball glove invented?" One answer you are likely to discover is that a glove was first used in the game to protect players' hands from injury in 1860.[1] Early gloves were essentially adapted to baseball from other uses. Compared to the baseball glove we know today, they looked more like work gloves— because they were work gloves (Table 1).[2] Should these adapted gloves be called "baseball" gloves? Or did the baseball glove come into existence when new perspectives on the use of the glove led to innovative technological change? (Note: This paper will explore the development of the baseball glove as distinct from the catcher's mitt.)

Let's be clear: the initial protective glove was an important stage of development. The first gloves make all other gloves possible, and the simple protective glove unquestionably improved defensive baseball. But its function was protective, as was the increased padding introduced by Arthur Irwin in 1883. It seems appropriate—and accurate—to distinguish between the appropriated work glove and the gloves that bore innovations designed to facilitate the act of catching the ball, and to apply the term "baseball glove" to the latter.

Viewed in this manner, the first true "baseball glove" occurs some 40 years after protective gloves were first tried. The 1901 "web-pocketed" glove is the first to feature an alteration that transforms the glove into an improved fielding tool. This glove, in concert with other forces of change, brought about the modern game of baseball.

A WORD ABOUT STATISTICS

In an effort to make the case for the 1901 web-pocketed glove as the first baseball glove worthy of the name, I will rely on the major league baseball statistics of the era.[3] Basic statistics of the time include errors per team per game, earned and unearned runs per team per game, runs per game, and league batting averages. As a check on these simple counting statistics, a more

Table 1. A timeline of the development of the baseball glove

1880 to 1900	1901 to 1922	1922 to 1950	1950 to present
Introduction of the glove and additions to padding	*Introduction of webbing and leather tab to form the glove pocket*	*Refinement of the glove pocket*	*Introduction of the hinge and further refinement of the pocket*

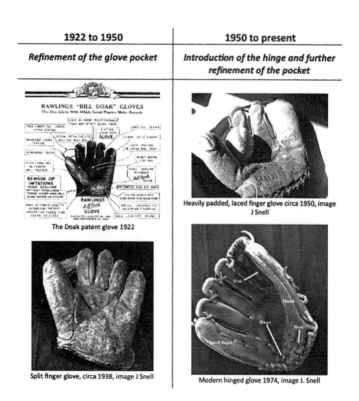

Spalding catalogue 1889 — No. 1-0 Glove.

Spalding catalogue 1901, model X, web pocketed glove.

Arthur Irwin's padded glove, from a Draper& Maynard advertisement circa 1885 — IRWIN GLOVES. DRAPER & MAYNARD

One inch web, circa 1919, image J Snell

RAWLINGS "BILL DOAK" GLOVES — The Doak patent glove 1922

Split finger glove, circa 1938, image J Snell

Heavily padded, laced finger glove circa 1950, image J Snell

Modern hinged glove 1974, image J. Snell

complex metric—one which generates a defensive efficiency measure for purposes of assessing defensive improvement—will be employed.

Errors (*per team per game*)

This is a simple average of the numbers of errors per team per game for each season. It is important to note that when using this statistic as a means of detecting defensive improvement, a year-to-year decrease in the average may not reflect improvement. If the average number of errors per team decreases from one year to the next, and the number of balls in play also decreases, the lower number of errors may simply reflect fewer opportunities. For this paper, errors per team per game are averaged for 1901–19, during which period balls in play did not exhibit a sustained decline. In fact, there was a slight tendency toward increases in the number of balls in play in the period. As a result balls in play may be disregarded as a confounding influence when assessing the error statistics.

Defensive efficiency

Dr. David Gordon expresses this metric as a means to demonstrate improving fielding based on the following formula.[4]

$$DE = 1 - (H + ROE - OPHR)/(AB - OPHR - SO + SH)$$

H = hits, ROE = reached base on an error,
OPHR = out-of-the-park home runs,
AB = at-bats, SO = strikeouts, SH = sacrifice hits.

Defensive efficiency provides a measure of the percentage of balls put into play that the defense then converts into an out. For discussion of data inputs and limitations see Dr. Gordon's paper, "The Rise and Fall of the Deadball Era," in the Fall 2018 issue of the *Baseball Research Journal*.[5]

Unearned runs

Unearned runs are runs that result from, for example, fielding errors or passed balls. This stat expresses the difference between the earned run average per team per game and runs per game.

ARGUMENT

From 1860, gloves in baseball grew in popularity among ballplayers who, while reluctant to be seen as "weak," at least recognized good sense. Between that first glove and 1900, the glove became a common item of equipment with very few bare-handed holdouts remaining as the new century was ushered in. Gloves grew increasingly common, but were largely unchanged pre-1900. From the early- to mid-1880s, the Irwin glove,

originally made and sold by the Draper & Maynard company, became the standard. "Little different from what one might slip over the hand on a cold day, it was literally a glove," writes Charles Alexander in *Our Game*.[6] That all changed in 1901. By then, the game of baseball had reached a form not that different from today's game. The pitching distance had been set in 1893 at 60 feet, 6 inches, a batter could no longer call for a low or high pitch, batters were given three strikes, and pitching motion was largely overhand. The American League became a major league in 1901, doubling the number of major league teams to 16. Teams in both leagues played a 140-game schedule. The game had become, simply better. Gone were the early days of games with six or seven errors, as gloveless players battled uncertain diamonds, often under a cloud of life-threatening intimidation. Gone with those errors were the days when unearned runs were responsible for the majority of scoring. The game had become, simply better. Gone were the early days of games with six or seven errors, as gloveless players battled uncertain diamonds, often under a cloud of life-threatening intimidation. Gone with those errors were the days when unearned runs were responsible for the majority of scoring.

As to the style of play, that was very different from today's game. Baseball managers developed a style of play that came to be known as "inside" or "scientific" baseball, which reached its full development by the end of the first decade of the twentieth century. In his 1913 monograph, "Scientific Baseball," New York Giants manager John McGraw emphasized the importance of employing a contact-hitting approach: "The thing is to hit it, and the science of it all is to put it in a good safe spot, whether it is in the infield or the outfield."[7] Chopping styles of hitting that caused the ball to bounce on the diamond and become difficult to catch, or line drives intended to punch through or over the infielders were encouraged.[8] The idea was to simply put the ball in play and generate runs by advancing runners any way possible, including bunts, the hit and run, and base stealing (including stealing home). Home-run hitting was frowned upon and seen as an ineffective way to generate offense.[9] As McGraw, principal proponent of the scientific approach, wrote: "Send the ball into a certain territory, rather than to try and send it a great distance, and don't forget that flies are fatal to the batter in many instances."[10] Contact hitting put the ball in play effectively in part by exploiting the difficulty experienced by fielders when attempting to corral a bouncing grounder or stop a speeding line drive, equipped with only a meager protective glove.

The shortcomings of the protective glove must have been known to glove makers. In 1901, Spalding introduced the model X and the XB, and the Reach Sporting Goods company the models 00W, 00X. (Quite likely other makers issued similar models, although sufficiently complete documentation could not be found to support other claims.) All of these 1901 models featured the new innovation of leather webbing sewn between the thumb and forefinger to form a shallow pocket. This modification to the glove represented a fundamental change in the way the glove was perceived; it was no longer merely a piece of protective gear but rather a specialized tool for better fielding. Distinguishable from a common work glove or other sporting glove, and modified to improve catching, the 1901 web-pocketed glove may be thought of as the first true, purpose-built baseball glove. (See Table 1.)

While it is true that the webbing on the 1901 glove made for a rather shallow and narrow pocket, particularly by today's standards, the change in the function of the glove was fundamental. Without a pocket of any kind, a glove leaves only the palm and the fingers with which to snare the ball. Introduce a leather pocket and the player gains a flexible catching sling or basket, with considerably more area to catch the ball and exert control. This change explains why the web-pocketed glove—and then the one-inch web glove that followed—quickly became the gloves of choice for players through the first two decades of the new century.

I do not know which glove-making company was first, nor who came up with the idea for the web pocket; the inventor remains unknown. Interestingly, while many ideas intended to improve the glove have patent applications associated with them, I could find none for this early web pocket. Perhaps the idea was suggested by a glove maker who put gloves together on a daily basis, rather than an inventor or corporate executive who would have been more likely to secure their idea by patent? Consider also that to come up with the idea of the pocket takes thinking about the glove as a basket. Women of the era used baskets for many things on a daily basis. Men would have as well, but probably not to the same extent as women. I think it is a safe bet that more than half the glove-making workforce were women, as well. If you consider these points in turn, I believe there is a good chance that a woman invented the baseball glove, or at the very least made the suggestion to make the glove more basket-like by sewing leather webbing between the thumb and first finger.

When this web-pocketed glove appeared in 1901, the number of runs scored (per team, per game) had been in decline since reaching the all-time high in 1894. After 1900, "the scoring decline picked up steam, falling below 4.5 in 1902–03, below 4 in 1904–07 and reaching an all-time low of 3.38 in 1908."[11] Three factors were responsible for declining offensive output from 1901 until its reversal in 1920 with what is known as the hitting revolution. First, rule changes in the first three years of the new century made hitting significantly more difficult. In 1900, the size and shape of home plate was altered.[12] The other significant decree was that foul balls could count as strike one and strike two.[13]

Second was a change in pitching and pitchers, the outcome of the change in pitching distance that occurred in 1893. By 1900, the increased pitching distance had resulted in a new generation of larger, stronger pitchers, who adapted to the change in distance with trick pitches.[14] The increased difficulty of throwing the 60-foot six-inch distance also resulted in teams carrying more pitchers to share the work. Boston manager Frank Selee was the first to implement a four-man rotation for more than 100 games in a season in 1898.[15,16] Throughout the period fewer pitchers were pitching a full game. To the detriment of hitting, pitchers of this new era of baseball were bigger, stronger, and less fatigued.

Better pitching and the rule changes resulted in a dramatic increase in strikeouts: up 55% in the National League in 1901, and up by 50% by 1903 in the American League. Between 1901 and 1908, batting averages declined from .279 to .239.[17] Between the introduction of the web-pocketed glove in 1901 and the low point of the scoring decline in 1908, balls that were put into play were snagged for outs at a rapidly increasing rate: Defensive efficiency (DE) had been steadily improving. While 63% of balls put into play were converted to outs by the defense in 1894, 66% were converted to outs by 1901. After the 1901 introduction of the web-pocketed glove, the DE improves at nearly twice the pace of the previous seven years. By 1908, DE had improved a remarkable 5%, resulting in 71% of balls put in play converted to outs by the defense. Fielding had already improved from 1882 to 1900, with the error rate dropping 84%, possibly attributable to better maintained fields and improved ball manufacturing, but the rate of increase in defensive efficiency post-1901, I attribute to the glove.

Further evidence of defensive improvement may be seen in the error statistics and in declining unearned runs. For example:

- Between 1901 and 1908, errors decline by .69 errors per team, per game from 2.4 to 1.71.[18]

This is the most significant error reduction in so short a period since the league-wide adoption of the protective glove.

- By 1919, nearly one full error per team, per game had been erased and errors per team per game stood at 1.43.[19]

- In 1900, 30% of runs or 1.52 per team per game were unearned.[20]

- By 1919 just 20% of runs or .8 runs per team per game were unearned.[21]

Reductions in errors trim .72 unearned runs per team per game in the 1901 to 1919 period. Runs per team per game declined in the same period by 1.12 runs per game per team. Of this decline in runs, 65% (.72 unearned runs) are directly attributable to error reduction. Some of this improvement may have been the result of growing professionalism among players and improved training. However, in so short a span of time I would argue that the bulk of the decline in errors was the result of the introduction of the web-pocketed glove and its successor, the one-inch web.

By as early as 1908, scientific baseball was locked in a losing battle against the steady and rapid improvement of fielding. The days of hitting the ball at a fielder and forcing an error were gone. Baseball was becoming a game of precision defense like never before. And, while few saw it happening, that precision was a force that would lead to a fundamental change in the way the game was, and is, played right up to the present day.

Luminaries like John McGraw and Connie Mack were deemed legends for refining the scientific approach to baseball. It had once been a winning strategy, and despite its growing inability to produce runs, there seemed no great effort underway to change. By 1918 runs per team per game stood at 3.63, only slightly up from the 1908 low of 3.39 runs per team per game.

The answer to improving run production came not from the adherents of "scientific" baseball, but rather arrived in the outsized form of George Herman "Babe" Ruth. After hitting 29 homers for the Red Sox in 1919—setting the major-league record in his first full season as an outfielder—Ruth was acquired by the New York Yankees in 1920. From that day forward, Ruth's brand of home-run baseball and the success of the Yankees would convince even the toughest adherents of scientific baseball that the answer to declining run production was the long ball.

Not everyone was certain that Ruth's example was the only, or perhaps even the most significant, reason for the sudden change in hitting. Some observers pointed to the clandestine introduction of a livelier ball in the 1920 season as the reason that balls seemed to be jumping from hitters' bats. Journalist F.C. Lane noted in a 1921 article that ball makers denied the existence of a livelier ball and that they had little motive for perpetrating a deception.[22] Lane, an early pioneer of the use of baseball statistics, went on to put the lively ball theory to rest by demonstrating that only home run numbers were affected in this apparent hitting revolution and not other types of hitting to any appreciable degree. "We are irresistibly impelled, therefore, to see in Babe Ruth the true cause for the amazing advance in home runs. He it was who has taught the managers the supreme value of apparently unscientific methods."[23] As it is said, nothing succeeds like success, and Ruth's massive swing was so successful, that after 1920, "...almost any batter that has it in him to wallop the ball is swinging from the handle of the bat with every ounce of strength that nature placed in his wrists and shoulders."[24]

Players, at the behest of their managers, began to eschew contact hitting strategies in favor of taking a powerful swing using the entire length of the bat. Free swinging immediately improved run production. Between the 1919 and 1920 seasons the American League batting average rose by 15 points and hitters added 129 home runs.[25] It took the National League an extra year to see similar increases in run production and hitting averages.[26] Free swinging had caught on as an effective way to score by putting a portion of run production beyond the reach of the defensive player and his much-improved baseball glove: by definition you cannot catch a home run.

Despite their enormous impact on the game, the 1901 glove and the one-inch web variants that follow right up to 1920 are all but forgotten in current versions of baseball history. Not only have the 1901 glove's contributions gone unheralded, its attributes and its firsts have been mistakenly assigned to another glove! In order to restore the reputation of the 1901 web-pocketed glove, it is necessary to say a few things about the glove that has been given false credit: the Doak Glove.

Bill Doak was a pitcher for the St. Louis Cardinals. His design for a glove, as it was ultimately realized by the Rawlings Company in 1922, deepened the glove pocket by building up the heel of the glove with padding and adding a fuller, lace-style connection between the thumb and the index finger. The result was a more secure well for the ball. The Doak glove was so well received by players that it remained in the Rawlings catalogue for 33 years.[27]

If you were to consult currently available sources on the Internet or in libraries you would likely come away with a different impression of the importance of the Doak glove. Many sources consider it to be the first baseball glove of consequence and the progenitor of the modern glove. Many—including the Wikipedia entry for "baseball glove"—state incorrectly that the Doak glove was the first to include a connection between the thumb and forefinger forming the pocket. Here is a sampling of the error in action:

- In his 2008 book, *Baseball: A History of America's Favorite Game*, George Vecsey includes this passage in his list of baseball innovations: "1922: Bill Doak…sewed a leather strip between the thumb and index finger on his glove, thereby creating the earliest pocket."[28]

- *The New Biographical History of Baseball*'s entry for Bill Doak reads, "In 1920, Doak, then a pitcher with the Cardinals, used the first glove with a preformed pocket and reinforced webbing."[29]

- The engaging and informative *Glove Affairs: The Romance, History and Tradition of the Baseball Glove* by Noah Liberman (2003) takes a similar line by presenting a timeline of glove development that jumps from the protective glove to the Doak glove without reference to the 1901 web pocket or the one-inch webs, implying that the Doak glove is the first to incorporate changes to improve fielding.[30]

However the record presented in this paper demonstrates that webs and tab-style webs became available in 1901: fully two decades before Bill Doak's glove. Doak's patent was not insignificant and his innovation stands as an important successor to the 1901 baseball glove and the one-inch web baseball gloves. However, the Doak glove was not the first glove to feature the pocket, nor was it the original source from which the modern glove was developed. Those distinctions, I believe, belong to the 1901 web-pocketed baseball glove.

CONCLUSION

Gloves were used in baseball from about 1860, gaining popularity after Charles Waitt's use in the mid-1870s. These earliest gloves were work gloves adopted by baseball players in an effort to protect their hands from injury. The first glove intended for fielding use was invented in 1901 with the addition of the web pocket— a simple bit of leather sewn between the thumb and forefinger of the glove. The addition of the pocket changed the glove from a protective device to a defensive tool and set the pattern for future changes with the focus on improved catching. This glove change combined with contemporaneous rule changes made hitting more difficult, setting the stage for the fall of "scientific baseball" and the rise of power hitting. In 1920 Babe Ruth conclusively demonstrated that the answer to declining run production lay in hitting beyond the defensive player and his glove. In short order many other hitters adopted free swinging and baseball's love affair with the home run began. A considerable part of the credit for this massive change in baseball is due to the 1901 introduction of the web-pocketed glove—the first true baseball glove. ∎

Notes

1. Peter Morris, *Baseball Fever: Early Baseball in Michigan* (Ann Arbor, MI: University of Michigan Press, 2003).
2. *Spalding's Baseball Guides*, 1889–20 and *Reach Official American League Baseball Guides*, 1890–1920, Smithsonian Library on line https://library.si.edu/digital-library/book/spaldings-base-ball-guide-and-official-league-book, https://library.si.edu/digital-library/book/reach-official-american-league-base-ball-guide. Accessed, September 15, 2022.
3. All statistics are taken from Baseball-Reference.com, https://www.baseball-reference.com. Accessed September to October of 2022. Note that this includes some of the Negro Leagues, whose data were incorporated in 2021.
4. David J. Gordon, "The Rise and Fall of the Deadball Era," *The Baseball Research Journal* 47 (Fall 2018).
   [**Editor's Note**: Bill James developed the Defensive Efficiency Record (DER) using the formula DER = (Total Outs–Strikeouts) / (BIP–HR), which yields substantially the same result.]
5. Gordon, "Rise and Fall of the Deadball Era."
6. Charles C. Alexander, *Our Game: An American Baseball History* (New York: MJF Books, 1991) 47.
7. John McGraw, *Scientific Baseball* (New York: Franklin K. Fox Publishing Co., 1913), 58.
8. Benjamin Rader, *Baseball: A History of America's Game* (Chicago: University of Illinois Press, 1992), 66.
9. Benjamin Rader, *Baseball: A History of America's Game* (Chicago: University of Illinois Press, 1992), 87.
10. McGraw, *Scientific Baseball*, 59.
11. Gordon, "The Rise and Fall of the Deadball Era."
12. Alexander, *Our Game: An American Baseball History*, 73.
13. Rader, *Baseball: A History of America's Game*, 87. The rule was adopted in 1901 in the National League and 1903 in the American League.
14. Gordon, "The Rise and Fall of the Deadball Era."
15. Alexander, *Our Game*, 90.
16. Frank Vaccaro, "The Origins of the Pitching Rotation," *Baseball Research Journal*, Fall 2011, https://sabr.org/journal/article/origins-of-the-pitching-rotation.
17. "Major League Hitting Year-by-Year Averages," Baseball-Reference.com, https://www.baseball-reference.com/leagues/MLB/bat.shtml. Accessed October 20, 2020.
18. "Major League Baseball Fielding Year-by-Year Averages." Baseball-Reference. com, https://www.baseball-reference.com/leagues/MLB/field.shtml. Accessed October 14, 2020.

19. "Major League Baseball Fielding Year-by-Year Averages." Baseball-Reference.com, https://www.baseball-reference.com/leagues/MLB/field.shtml. Accessed October 14, 2020.

20. "Major League Pitching Year-by-Year Averages," and "Major League Baseball Fielding Year-by-Year Averages," Baseball-Reference.com, Accessed October 5, 2020.

21. "Major League Pitching Year-by-Year Averages," and "Major League Baseball Fielding Year-by-Year Averages," Baseball-Reference.com, Accessed October 5, 2020.

22. F. C. Lane, "The Babe Ruth Epidemic in Baseball" Our Game, MLB Blog, June 19, 2017 (originally published in *The Literary Digest*, June 25, 1921). https://ourgame.mlblogs.com/thebabe-ruth-epidemic-in-baseball-e7b158436faf, Accessed October 30, 2022.

23. Lane, "The Babe Ruth Epidemic in Baseball."

24. Lane, "The Babe Ruth Epidemic in Baseball."

25. Rader, *Baseball: A History of America's Game*, 113.

26. Rader, *Baseball: A History of America's Game*, 113.

27. Noah Liberman, "Why did the Baseball Glove Evolve So Slowly?" Our Game, MLB Blog, June 9, 2014, https://ourgame.mlblogs.com/why-did-the-baseball-glove-evolve-so-slowlybff30f33737a. Accessed November 5, 2020.

28. George Vecsey, *Baseball: A History of America's Greatest Game* (New York: Random House, 2008).

29. Donald Dewey and Nicholas Acocella, *The New Biographical History of Baseball* (Chicago: Triumph Books, 2002).

30. Noah Liberman, *Glove Affairs: The Romance, History, and Tradition of the Baseball Glove* (Chicago: Triumph Books, 2003).

The SABR Digital Library

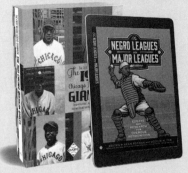

Available wherever books are sold

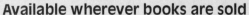

The First Negro League Champion: The 1920 Chicago American Giants

Edited by Frederick C. Bush and Bill Nowlin

Paperback $29.95 244 pages • Ebook $9.99

This book chronicles the team which won the title of champion in the Negro National League's inaugural season. Rube Foster, a Hall of Famer, and his White business partner John Schorling are featured along with biographies of every player on the team include Cristóbal Torriente, a member of both the National Baseball Hall of Fame and the Cuban Baseball Hall of Fame, as well as early Blackball stalwarts Dave "Lefty" Brown, Bingo DeMoss, Judy Gans, Dave Malarcher, Frank Warfield, and Frank Wickware. A comprehensive timeline of the 1920 season and a history of the founding of the Negro National League are included.

We Are, We Can, We Will: The 1992 World Champion Toronto Blue Jays
Edited by Adrian Fung and Bill Nowlin

Forewords by Buck Martinez and Dave Winfield

Paperback US $34.95/Canada $41.95 394 pages • Ebook $9.99

The 1992 Toronto Blue Jays will always be remembered as the first World Series-winning club from Canada. After a near miss in 1991, the 1992 club confidently adopted "We Are, We Can, We Will" as their team motto. This book features biographies of every player who played for the 1992 Toronto Blue Jays including Hall of Famers Dave Winfield, Jack Morris, and Roberto Alomar. Manager Cito Gaston, Hall of Fame general manager Pat Gillick, and radio broadcaster Tom Cheek are also included, as well as a "ballpark biography" of SkyDome. Ten reports describe significant games from the 1992 season illustrating Toronto's championship journey from Opening Day to the last game of the World Series.

From Shibe Park to Connie Mack Stadium: Great Games in Philadelphia's Lost Ballpark
Edited by Gregory H. Wolf
Paperback $39.95 398 pages • Ebook $9.99

This collection evokes memories and the exciting history of the celebrated ballpark through stories of 100 games played there and several feature essays. The games included in this volume reflect every decade in the ballpark's history, from the inaugural game in 1909, to the last in 1970.

Shibe Park was the home of the Philadelphia A's from 1909 until their relocation to Kansas City and the Philadelphia Phillies from 1938 until the ballpark's closure at the end 1970. In 1953 it was renamed Connie Mack Stadium. The ballpark hosted big-league baseball for 62 seasons and more than 6,000 games—over 3,500 games by the A's and 2,500 by the Phillies—and was home to Frank Baker, Del Ennis, Chief Bender, and Robin Roberts.

¡Arriba!: The Heroic Life of Roberto Clemente

edited by Bill Nowlin and Glen Sparks

Paperback $34.95 338 pages • Ebook $9.99

2022 marks the 50th anniversary year of Roberto Clemente's passing. This book celebrates his life and baseball career. Named to 15 All-Star Game squads, Clemente won 12 Gold Gloves, four batting titles, and was the National League's Most Valuable Player in 1966. The first Latino inducted into the National Baseball Hall of Fame, Clemente played 18 seasons for the Pittsburgh Pirates and became the 11th player to reach the 3,000-hit milestone, hitting number 3000 on the season's last day. At the time no one knew he would never play baseball again. Clemente was known for his charitable work. He lost his life on the final day of 1972 while working to provide relief for victims of an earthquake in Nicaragua.

From *The Cool of the Evening*

Paula Kurman

Dear SABR members,

My beloved late husband, Jim Bouton, asked three things of me if I were to outlive him: to make sure his archives were well and safely placed, to donate his 1962 World Series ring to the Hall of Fame, and to write a book about him, based on notes he urged me to keep during the forty-two years we were together.

"Nobody knows me the way you do," he'd say. And "Write that down," he'd say when something funny or meaningful or extraordinary happened to us. "Memory fades. Contemporaneous notes are better."

His archives are now part of the permanent collection at The Library of Congress in Washington DC. In 2022, I donated the World Series ring to the Hall of Fame. That was hard. I'd worn the ring every day for decades. Jim didn't wear rings, "in case a game breaks out and I'm called in to pitch." But the ring is safe now, and in the right place. A rightful place.

And I've just finished writing the book. I've called it *The Cool of the Evening*—a phrase borrowed from Johnny Sain, Jim's favorite pitching coach. It's subtitled "A Love Story."

Writing the book was both painful and wonderful. It brought him back in living color and at the same time highlighted the excruciating loss. I was grateful for the years of notes, kept at his urging. The writing process helped me grieve. The pandemic gave me the solitude I needed to complete the book.

Rosetta Books will be the publisher and the anticipated release is the first quarter of 2024. What follows, therefore, represents the first public viewing of any part of the text. SABR has always been our favorite baseball world organization. It feels natural to me, therefore, that you are the first to see parts of it.

In friendship,
Paula Kurman, Ph.D.
(Mrs. Jim Bouton)

I am among the most fortunate of women. I loved Jim Bouton and was well and truly loved by him for more than four decades. It doesn't get any better than that. I was his lover, his wife, his best friend, his playmate, his business partner, his confidante. We were each other's editors, occasional critics and most appreciative audiences. He was my North Star, and I was his.

* * *

Baseball was Jim's metaphor, all through his life. If things were going well, he'd make great plays in his dreams. His knuckleball would be working, his motion intact. If he were struggling with something in real life, his dreams would reflect his struggle. He'd have trouble making the team, or getting into the rotation, or finding his glove.

These were active dreams, which made them a little risky for me. I was usually okay when he was throwing. Since he wouldn't sleep on his throwing arm, that arm was free to move, unencumbered. More dangerous were the times he was fielding the ball in his sleep. He was a fast, powerful runner and a great fielding pitcher—a good thing unless you happened to be sleeping in his path.

I don't know what other couples discuss in moments of post-coital intimacy. It was during some of ours that I learned how to throw a knuckleball. Jim said it was a better choice than cigarettes.

* * *

So many men asked Jim wistfully over the years, "Don't you miss it? Don't you wish you were back in the Big Leagues?" He didn't. Occasionally he'd re-read some of the stories he'd written in *Ball Four* and enjoy the memories, chuckling to himself. But Jim lived totally in the present. Wallowing in the past was not his thing.

He had no trophy room, no awards displayed, no visible plaques or scrapbooks. Everything was in boxes in the basement. We did have a couple of photographs of him in a Yankees uniform displayed only because

I'd gone to the basement looking for something else. While I was rummaging through the boxes I found a loose pile of photographs I hadn't seen before.

"What's this?" I asked, about a photo of a trio in a group hug, smiling broadly.

"That's me with Mickey and Yogi after a big win."

"Hmm. Probably shouldn't be loose in a box like this."

"Probably not."

And there was another photo of his teammates pouring champagne over his head. I rescued that one, too. Had them both framed and hung them on the wall. That was the extent of the visible reminders of his professional baseball years in our home.

Jim spent no time wishing for the old glory days. But oh, he loved the game itself. Not to watch on TV, or to sit in the stands. We almost never went to professional games. He wanted to *play*, to run in the sunshine, to throw a ball—to take his trusty old glove, suit up, and join a group of guys similarly obsessed. He wanted to work on his motion, get guys out with strategy and a dancing knuckleball. He had no interest in senior leagues, however, or what he called the "beer-belly league" of the Over 40s.

"They can still bat, many of them, but they can't run. Where's the challenge in striking out old men? And I can *walk* to first base before they even start running."

So he'd join local teams of guys in their twenties and thirties—some of them having been up to the Bigs for a cup of coffee, others still dreaming about it. Real hardball played by strong young guys wielding aluminum bats.

"What's it like for a former major leaguer to play amateur baseball?" Jim was frequently asked.

"I wouldn't know. I don't think of myself as a former anything," Jim would say.

When we lived in New Jersey, he'd play for local teams there every year. When we moved to the Berkshires in Massachusetts, he was distracted for a while by the stone work he was doing for our new house. But he couldn't leave baseball for long.

We never got around to finishing the basement, so there was all that unused space down there. Happily, there was enough footage between a makeshift pitcher's mound (a taped-for-traction facsimile outlined on the floor) and a strike zone (outlined in black electrical tape on a wall sixty feet and six inches away).

Lining both sides of the corridor between the "mound" and the target were pieces of sheetrock and bits of lumber from the house construction. This insured that the ball, ricocheting back from the "strike

In the beginning…

zone," would head straight back to Jim, saving it from getting lost in the jumble of cartons and uncategorized junk in the rest of the basement. It wasn't pretty, but it worked.

Jim was working on his pitching skills to be competitive for the historic Saugerties Dutchmen in the Hudson Valley and for a team called Mama's Pizza in the Albany Twilight League—named for the time of day the games were played, not the age of the players. Jim was in his late fifties, then, and in great shape.

Early every morning he would quietly and considerately tiptoe out of the bedroom, then thunder down the stairs to the basement, pick up a hard rubber practice ball and his trusty glove, and step onto the taped-on-the-floor mound for twenty minutes of hard, concentrated throwing. Loud impact sounds would resonate upstairs in our bedroom as the ball hit the concrete wall directly under me. My head still buried in the pillow, I'd laugh to myself. All that care to leave the room quietly, and now Mr. Thunderfootdownthestairs was pounding the hell out of the wall under the bed with his best shots, completely unaware of the sound transmission.

The throwing would go on for twenty minutes, after which he'd thunder back up the stairs, then tiptoe softly back into the bedroom and, seeing that I was awake, pick up his weights for another fifteen minutes of upper body strengthening. No talking. Heavy breathing. Eyes internally focused. I'd get up and head for the shower. While I was toweling off, he'd come into the bathroom, sweating profusely, a look of triumph on his face.

"Babe, I haven't thrown this well in *years*," he'd say, "not even during my comeback! I'm getting my old motion back, getting down real low, my legs are strong…"

This would be accompanied by demonstrations. Fortunately, the bathroom in our new house was large enough to accommodate the activity.

"How wonderful were you this morning?" I'd ask him affectionately.

Would I have been a better wife if I had said to him, *get real, you're not a young man anymore, stop wasting your time?* We were a lot closer to sixty than fifty. If it had been 1896, we'd have been old, maybe already dead. But in 1996 we were healthy, active, working for ourselves, learning new skills.

Besides, I was in no position to discourage him. I took up jazz dancing at forty-seven, began serious ballet training at fifty. I averaged three ballet classes a week until I was sixty-five, when a freak accident and hip surgery forced me to switch to ballroom dancing.

Jim was trying to find his lost motion, that intricate aggregate of muscular contractions, releases and rhythms that propel a knuckleball, spin-less, through the air, deceptively innocent, until at the last moment it flutters and hiccups on a stray air current, unmanning the batter and causing him to swing helplessly at the ball that is no longer there.

No, I never discouraged him. Jim was always in serious training for whatever baseball goal he was working toward. It lit him up, energized him. I loved his focused intensity. No one was more appealing than Jim when he was having a good time. It didn't matter if he didn't reach it, whatever the goal was. We both understood that all the benefits were in the journey.

COLLECTION OF PAULA KURMAN

In typical good humor, Jim jumps from one of the walls he built.

In some games he was astonishingly effective, others not so much. Jim was a thinking pitcher, an intelligent strategist, and a scrappy fielder. Lean and fit, with the instinctive, lifelong understanding of a ball's trajectory that never faded, he'd put 150% of his effort into limiting the damage of a hit ball.

He was also just one of the guys on the bench. No airs, no pulling rank, just camaraderie and a shared love of the game. He just wanted to be one of them. He played competitively into his sixties.

I loved those local games. Every time I watched him lope out to the mound, silently and confidently point his fielders to preferred positions as he took the measure of each batter he faced, I fell in love with him all over again.

* * *

On a trip to Italy in 2004, we went to Florence to see Michelangelo's David. Postcards don't do it justice. In the flesh—or rather, the original marble—it's awe inspiring, overwhelming. Its beauty brought me to tears.

And there was something strangely familiar about it.

"Look, Babe, it's you!" I said, to the amusement of some nearby tourists.

But it was. Not just the lean, masculine beauty of the figure, but that recognizable pose. There was the focused gaze in one direction, the body turned to one side, the throwing hand down and somewhat behind, the stone cradled in the hand, the weight on the back foot, the front foot slightly ahead in the direction of that focused gaze, the left hand loosely holding the slingshot against the left shoulder. Relaxed, but alert and focused.

Replace the stone with a ball and the slingshot with a glove, and there it is. Perfect.

* * *

I remember the game that would be his last in the semi-pro or Twilight League he'd been playing in for years. I had gone with him, as I usually did when the game was being played a fair driving distance from home. He was more tired at the end of a game now, and I was concerned about his ability to drive home safely if the field wasn't local.

He'd begun to develop a pattern of getting off to a rocky start in the first inning, and then hitting his stride in the second inning. I'd hold my breath, wondering if he'd be able to recover. And then I'd see his body find its rhythm, and I'd relax. Somewhat.

On this day, his first inning on the mound was particularly poor, saved in part by some good fielding from his teammates. He got back into the dugout, and I didn't like the way he was sitting. His usual body behavior—catching his breath, toweling off, fussing with equipment, focusing intently on the other team's pitcher—was not in evidence. There was something wrong.

I watched him intently, and when he got up for the second inning, I was sure. He half-walked, half-loped to the mound. There was no energy in it. His chest heaved a few times. Not a good sign. He studied the ball in his hand. I felt so helpless. All I could do was watch.

There was no recovery in that second inning. A couple of men got on base who shouldn't have, and Jim signaled for the manager to come out to the mound. The conversation only took a minute. Jim took himself out of the game and went back to the dugout. As he sat on the bench, he seemed to deflate. My heart broke for him. But there were protocols. I could not run over and put my arms around him. Not until he left that bench. Not till we were out of sight of the other players.

I no longer remember the end of that game, or precisely when Jim felt it was appropriate to leave. I don't know how long I sat and watched him. But when he picked up his equipment bag I went to meet him and we headed towards our car. He put the bag on the back seat and got in on the passenger side. I got in next to him and took his hand, waiting for him to tell me.

"It's over, Babe. It's all over. Not just a bad day. I could feel it in my body. I can't do it anymore."

"I know, sweetheart. I saw it end."

For the rest of that week he worked on building his stone walls. It soothed him—the craftsmanship, the hard physical work, the evidence of an area of remaining mastery. He didn't go down to the basement to throw the ball against the wall. Or do his regular workout with his weights. He was quiet and thoughtful.

The following weekend I was sitting on the porch reading when I heard him leave his office and go down to the basement. A few minutes later he hurried up the stairs calling for me. There was an urgency in his voice.

"Babe? Where are you?"

"Out here on the porch…"

He rushed out, sat next to me, put his arms around me, and started to cry.

"I went down there to put some things away and I saw my glove and ball, just sitting there, waiting for me to play with them—they're like my old friends, they were just sitting there—I know it's silly…"

I hugged him tightly.

"Not silly at all—of course you're upset. Throwing a ball has been a major part of who you are, how you

know yourself—your whole life. To come to the end of that—it would be strange if you *weren't* upset."

We sat for a while and held each other.

"I only feel safe enough to cry when you're with me," he said.

"I'm always with you, Babe."

* * *

August, 2012—Jim has a stroke that damages the language center of his brain. He recovers significantly, but not completely.

March, 2016—After noticeable decline, a differential diagnosis is made. Jim has CAA (cerebral amyloid angiopathy), a rare form of vascular dementia. It's progressive and there is no cure.

* * *

Way back when we were first together, Jim had talked about his friend and editor, Lenny Shecter, who died of cancer in early middle age. Jim admired Lenny's refusal to tell anybody about his illness.

"Why is that a good thing?" I'd asked Jim.

"Because he didn't want anybody feeling sorry for him."

"But he also denied friends and family the chance to be helpful and supportive. And as he changed, the people who loved him were probably confused by what they were observing. I don't get how that's a good thing."

"Well, I always admired him for it."

And that's where we left it. It was a point of disagreement between us, respectfully acknowledged.

But now we needed to think about it again. Unlike Lenny, Jim was a public figure, regularly being interviewed—and he was having word scrambles, pronoun mixups, and mid-sentence blackouts. He had a great deal of trouble understanding compound questions. In the face of puzzling behavior, people get nervous and draw their own conclusions. Did we want reporters to think Jim was drinking? Did we want to cut him off entirely from contact with the media without explanation? How would that be interpreted? Would that just add to the mythology in some quarters that he was high-handed and arrogant?

Navigating the world when you're injured involves managing other people's anxieties. But Jim needed to feel comfortable with how we would decide to move forward from here. How much to say, and to whom. This was his call, not mine.

For the media, we agreed that for now the stroke was enough information. We also decided that I would participate in his interviews, helping only when necessary, and explaining why I was doing so. Jim was relieved by this plan. We worked well together in those situations, and with my presence as a backup he relaxed and did better.

Unpacking compound questions like this from reporters would be my biggest job:

"So, Jim, how did it feel to pitch against _____, a Cy Young award winner, back in 19__, particularly in that tie game in Cleveland, when you were having a shaky start to the season, and so much was at stake, both for the team and for you personally?"

I kid you not; that's how these radio guys talk. They're so afraid you're going to cut them off before they've finished with everything they want to say that it tumbles out like cooked spaghetti. A brain-injured person can't make sense of it.

We'd been hoping for long plateaus and a slow decline. But a few months into 2017 it became apparent that we weren't on a plateau but a steep slope. Going down. Jim's difficulties were now increasingly obvious. We talked about how he was feeling.

He described himself as "resigned," and when I asked him about the things he still enjoyed, he said "Not much. I can't follow things fast enough—I spend most of the time keeping my mouth shut—it's annoying."

A few days later, Jim had one of his really good days. He was more "present," more in focus, more responsive. I took the opportunity to bring up something I'd been thinking about.

"You know, Babe, I think we need to decide something here. People are going to start wondering what's wrong. Why don't we take control of the story right now? Tell it right. And tell it to the right person."

"What are you suggesting?"

"Choose someone we trust in the media, and tell that one person about the cerebral amyloid angiopathy. Accurate and clear facts. And maybe going public will be helpful to other people who are in a similar situation."

"Hmm," he said, and thought for a minute. "Tyler Kepner."

"Exactly," I said. "I had the same thought."

Tyler's wonderful article, would appear in *The New York Times* on Sunday, July 2, 2017.

That same weekend, the Society for American Baseball Research was holding its annual convention in New York. Of all the baseball organizations we'd had contact with over the years, SABR was our favorite. Dedicated to historical research and analysis, its members are passionately turned on by facts and ferreting out new information about America's pastime.

This is a job that requires steel-toed boots, just in case.

"Baseball Nerds," Jim called them. "*My* people."

"Mine, too," I agreed.

John Thorn, our dear friend and Baseball Historian Extraordinaire, was deeply involved with the organization and had already asked Jim to participate in a panel discussion on that Saturday.

"Great," we said in unison.

"John, there'll be an article in the Times the next day about Jim's vascular dementia," I said. "I would have to be with Jim anyway—he has too many word scrambles now to do it alone—but I'd like to use the opportunity to explain CAA...make it our first public disclosure before the article appears. Would that be okay with you?"

John agreed.

I always feel *so* much better with openness. Secrecy is not my thing. Everybody leaks anyway. Thinking you can hide something is delusional; there are so many "tells." We were going to open the windows fully at last, let the fresh air in. And Jim was now fully on board.

There were hundreds of people in attendance. I had forgotten that New Yorkers get their Sunday *Times* on Saturdays, so many of them had already seen Tyler's article and the news would come as no surprise.

Jim was relaxed and happy and in his element. We sat on the dais with other panelists, and John Thorn was his graceful and commanding self as the moderator. He introduced me as the first speaker and I went to the podium. I talked a bit about how Jim and I had met, the differences in our backgrounds, my lack of exposure to sports, and I offhandedly mentioned that

I was a Jewish girl who had grown up in Washington Heights in upper Manhattan.

At which point, Jim, with an exaggeratedly puzzled expression on his face, leaned into his microphone and said in his best Mel Brooks imitation, "You're Jewish?"

There was raucous laughter and huge applause from the crowd. Relief, appreciation, even love, washed over us. He was still Jim, still their mischievous rascal, still hitting just the right note in just the right way. He might scramble and forget words, but there was his trademark sense of humor and his impeccable timing. He wasn't gone. The rest of the discussion went smoothly. We were so used to finishing each other's sentences anyway.

Not long after that significant weekend, we received a "Save the Date" notice from the New York Yankees, inviting Jim back to Old Timers Day coming up in 2018.

Well. How about that.

* * *

As his dementia deepened, Jim's dreams became more vivid. One night, I was awakened from a deep sleep by his erratic movements. He had reached over me and with his left hand was pounding the bed in front of me, frantically searching for something.

"What is it? Babe? What are you doing?" I was barely awake and he was scaring me.

"The ball! The ball! Where is it?" he shouted.

"There's no ball, Babe, no ball.... you're dreaming. Shhh, it's okay, just a dream, there's no ball.... Go back to sleep, sweetheart."

He turned over and settled himself, still not awake.

"I coulda had that ball," he grumbled accusingly.

Even dementia has its funny moments.

* * *

The Yankees followed up their Save the Date notice with an official invitation to Old Timers Day, clearly responding to Tyler Kepner's article in the *Times* and the MLB.com reporting on the SABR conference.

"What do you think, Babe? Do you want to go?" I asked him.

A momentary pause. Then, "Sure. Why not?"

It would be far more complicated than that first time in 1998. Back then, a year after [daughter] Laurie had died, the Yankees responded to a Father's Day letter that [her brother] Michael had written to the newspaper, asking the Yankees to let "bygones be bygones" and invite his father back into the fold to participate in his rightful place as a former Yankee. It had worked.

Jim had been ostracized for years by the baseball establishment for daring to expose the unfair labor practices in the industry in *Ball Four*. When they have to reach into their pockets, baseball executives have memories like elephants and hold grudges like the Hatfields and the McCoys.

In 1998, Jim was deeply grieving, but he was whole. He stepped out onto the field to a standing ovation from a sellout crowd. He even pitched an inning in the Old Timers Game and did well. But twenty years later, in 2018, he was very limited by the dementia. He couldn't follow verbal instructions, couldn't be left alone at any time, and was uneasy in unfamiliar surroundings. How would Jim manage in the locker room or find his way out onto the field when introduced? I certainly couldn't be with him, but he navigated his world now by keeping me in sight. He did this so cleverly that even people who knew us weren't aware of it.

I called the number on the invitation and spoke to the guy coordinating the event to describe the issues. He was very understanding and accommodating. I explained that I couldn't manage the driving and care for Jim at the same time on the trip down and back without Edwin Castro, who aided me with caregiving. And that Jim would have to be accompanied to the locker room, guided through the tunnel to the field and pointed in the right direction when he was introduced. The Yankees agreed to it all, but said that Edwin would have to remain outside the locker room and wouldn't be allowed on the field. That was fine, so long as the men were reconnected as soon as Jim was outside any protected area.

By the beginning of that 2018 baseball season, Jim was quite compromised. He didn't look it from the outside, which was a help. Thinner by far and a little vague at times, but still moving normally, if a little uncertainly. Only those of us who were close to him knew how bad it already was.

I ordered a bunch of tickets for family and friends. Again, the Yankee office graciously accommodated when I asked for our block of seats to be close enough and in direct view of where Jim would be standing on the field. I wanted him to be able to see us waving.

This would be the very first time any of our grandchildren would be seeing their Grandpa in uniform and on the field at Yankee Stadium. None of them had been born yet in 1998. Even if the youngest of them didn't totally get the full impact of this occasion, it was important to the rest of us. We knew it would be the last time, and we wanted all six of them to be there.

The Yankees had planned a weekend of events for the players that included signing autographs for fans at the stadium Saturday afternoon, dinner for the players and their families Saturday night, and the game on Sunday. Would Jim be able to handle three days away from home? A strange hotel room, crowds, the bustle of the city, none of the routines he depended on for security? It was a gamble.

I included tickets for Edwin and his family. Again, the Yankees showed their kindness by offering hotel accommodations for them. Edwin rented a van, big enough for all of us and our luggage, and on that Friday we set off on this adventure together.

Old Timers Day was a familiar concept to Jim and he was with people he trusted completely, so he was cheerful on the drive down, even whistling from time to time. Once in the city heading downtown on Park Avenue, he began to get a little anxious, peering out the window and twisting around in his seat.

"I think we're going in the wrong direction," he said. "Yankee Stadium is back that way," pointing behind us.

"You're right, Babe," I said, "Yankee Stadium is back that way, but first we have to check into the hotel. You'll see. We won't be at the stadium until tomorrow."

But "tomorrow" was one of those concepts he no longer understood. Or any other aspect of time—before, after, later, soon—all just words that mushed together for him.

He got quiet. But I could read his face. He understood that he was missing something here, and so he'd better just say nothing and pay close attention until he could figure it out. It was how he handled his diminished understanding. It was smart. And effective.

That's the hell of dementia. There is reasoning still in place, an intellect still functioning, even memories, but the "potholes" that develop in the brain as the disease progresses take the sense out of it.

He watched my face carefully, as he always did. If I looked relaxed, then he felt safe. He'd ride with it.

The hotel lobby was a chaotic mix of arriving players, their families, and a horde of fans looking for autographs as the players checked in. I was nervous about Jim's ability to handle the sensory overload, but he began to recognize this scene as something he'd lived through many times before. And he recognized some of the players in the crowd. So he was tentative, but not frightened.

The most obvious sign that Jim was uneasy was that he stopped eating. He had nothing at dinner. The following morning I ordered his favorite away-from-home breakfast—bacon, and eggs over easy. He pushed it around on his plate.

On Saturday Jim and I got on the team bus with the other players, heading up to the stadium for a Meet & Greet with ardent Yankee fans.

"You see, Babe, now we're heading in the right direction to Yankee Stadium."

"Will my uniform be there?"

"Yes, but that's for tomorrow. Today you're just going to shake hands with a lot of fans and sign autographs, so you won't need your uniform today."

Jim retreated into silence, trying to process what I'd just told him. But when another player greeted him or reached out to shake hands, he responded in kind, and cheerfully. He still had all the social niceties.

He didn't eat lunch. At the party for the players later that evening, the buffet table was loaded with interesting choices. But although I brought plate after plate to him, he wouldn't touch any of it. This wasn't home. He was alert and guarded, trying to figure things out. It must have been exhausting. At least he was drinking water.

Sunday morning. Jim picked at his breakfast; lost interest quickly.

Afterward, the players were to go onto the team bus and head to the stadium. Another couple of buses were designated for the families and guests of the players, but I would follow in our rented van with the Castros—except for Edwin—so that we could leave for home directly from Yankee Stadium at the end of the day. As was prearranged with the Yankees, Edwin would go on the team bus with Jim.

Jim looked uncertain as he began to understand that I would not be getting on this bus with him. Edwin put his hand companionably on Jim's shoulder and said cheerfully, "We got this," his familiar comment whenever the two of them set off somewhere together. The rest of us watched them get on.

"We'll see you at the stadium!" we said, and moved briskly to the van, which was positioned behind the bus.

It was a bright, sunny day, quite warm. When we got to the stadium, we found our section and settled in. Family and friends began to arrive. I was strung so tightly I practically twanged.

The day's scheduled game and Old Timer introductions were sparsely attended that year. Not at all like the full house of 1998. I'm not sure why. Perhaps the team the Yankees were playing that day was not a favorite competition for the fans. Didn't matter. I had only one focus anyway.

The ceremonies began and I took a deep breath.

COLLECTION OF PAULA KURMAN

When I heard Jim's name announced, I saw him lope out onto the field, guided subtly by Edwin's presence at his side. I was surprised to see that they'd let him go out with Jim. They must have made the decision after evaluating the need themselves. Edwin came off the field as soon as Jim reached the other old-timers and began shaking hands. He was still good with non-verbal cues. I could see that he was comfortable now as the other players reached out to him. They all knew about his illness, of course. Everyone was so kind. I let out the breath I'd been holding.

To my complete astonishment, that outgoing breath morphed into convulsive sobs. I covered my face and tried to stop, but I had no control over it. I was embarrassed.

"Sorry, I'm so sorry," I said, worried about the impact of this breakdown on the grandchildren who lined the row directly in front of me.

"Don't be sorry, Grandma," Georgia said, reaching back and patting my knee with the maturity of a very recent high school graduate. Aspen patted my other knee, and Annabel took my hand and held it quietly until I calmed down. Skyler shot me a concerned glance, as did the two youngest, Alex, then nine, and Jack, seven. But they took it in stride. Nobody needed to have the reason for the breakdown explained.

The ceremonies ended, and the Old Timers who could still lope, loped off the field. The plan was to have Jim change out of his uniform into street clothes and join our group in the stands. In about twenty minutes the two men appeared at the top of the aisle in our section, Jim looking cheerful and tired, Edwin with the grin of a Cheshire Cat. Cellphone pictures of Edwin's presence on the field at Yankee Stadium had already made their way back to his family in Colombia.

There was a lot of hugging all around, and finally Jim settled into a seat with a contented sigh.

"Get this man a hot dog!" I said to no one in particular, my arm around Jim's shoulders—and it was done. Gratefully, I watched him take a bite of food.

At last.

We didn't stay to see the regularly scheduled game. We were exhausted and we still had a three hour drive ahead of us.

It was good to get home. Jim sighed happily as we walked in the door.

"Sanctuary," he said.

We slept soundly.

The next morning, another day of sunshine, we were having breakfast on our screened porch. The hummingbirds were feasting on our dahlias; an occasional breeze flirted with the leaves of the surrounding trees.

Jim was looking thoughtful. His eyes were clear and focused.

"How do you feel, sweetheart?" I asked him.

"I feel fulfilled," he said.

"Really. How do you mean, 'fulfilled'?"

"I feel like I finally belong, I'm part of it, part of them—where I always wanted to be. And you were accepted, too, by the other wives, and by the players. It was different this time. They all wanted to talk to you. The players wanted to know what you thought of things… I felt so proud to be with you…"

He went on like that for several minutes, to my astonishment. He was clear, coherent and deeply moved. And he was accurate. Not only about his memories of the weekend, but his profound understanding of the meaning of events, the changes in people's behavior toward him.

He had always been somewhat cavalier about his ostracism by the baseball establishment. I truly believed that unless someone asked him about it, he never gave it much mind space. And yet… He was clearly moved and gratified by the acceptance he felt that weekend. Whatever the motivation of the Yankees in their gracious hospitality and accommodation to our needs, it doesn't matter. What matters is that they were gracious. The deed itself is what counts. That it brought peace to my beloved at the end of his life is something for which I will always be grateful.

In my mind's eye, I can still see Jim sitting at breakfast on that beautiful bright day, sounding like himself again. I think about that moment often. ∎

Excerpted from *The Cool of the Evening* by Paula Kurman, to be published in the first quarter of 2024 by Rosetta Books.

"My Six Decades with the Yankees"

Tony Morante

This excerpt is from the recent SABR book, *Yankee Stadium 1923–2008: America's First Modern Ballpark*. We are honored to include this reminiscence by longtime Stadium tour director Tony Morante of his time working in baseball.

As a New York Yankees employee from 1958 to 2018, I had the good fortune to witness or partake in the Stadium's illustrious history.

My dad, a Stadium usher, took me to my first game in 1949. The impression of walking out of the passageway in the upper deck behind home plate will last forever. As I was used to the small black and white TV at home, taking in the lush green manicured grass, the azure blue skies dressed in puffy white cumulus clouds, and the aromas from the Stadium vendors, the bombardment of my senses was pure fantasy.

At that time, ushers were allowed to take their youngsters to the game with no expense. The ushers had a shape-up seniority assignment, which took about an hour. While waiting for my dad to be assigned, I went to the right-field seating area. The gates were not open yet, allowing me to scramble for baseballs that landed in that area without much competition. At times, I would come home with two or three baseballs which I shared with my Little League teammates… making me a popular kid!

My visits to the Stadium came to a screeching halt in 1958 when my dad informed me that if I wanted to continue to go to the games, I would now have to earn it as a part-time usher. So he flipped me an usher's mitt (used to clean off the seats), which I reluctantly took, beginning my 60 years of employment in Yankee Stadium while building its reputation as the mecca for outdoor events in our country. And, on December 28, 1958, I witnessed what many still consider the greatest football game ever played as the underdog New York Giants lost to the favored Baltimore Colts but in a very close contest.

In the following year, a new and exclusive section was added to the mezzanine section of the Stadium, extending from the press box in front of the box seats down the third-base line toward the left-field foul pole. This area, known as the Mezzanine Loge, was built at the behest of corporations such as Howard Johnson, Spencer Advertising, Mele Manufacturing, Hansen Real Estate, Bankers Trust Company, and WABC, to name a few. This secluded area is where I worked with my father from the late 1960s to 1973, when the pre-renovation Stadium was in its final year. I assisted the patrons of this section in procuring refreshments.

The 1950s were the greatest decade in the Yankees' history as they went to the World Series fall classic eight times and won six of those World Series. At the heart of the team's success was a strapping blond-haired and blue-eyed phenom from Oklahoma who possessed great power and speed to match—Mickey Mantle. By the end of the decade, Mickey's popularity had significantly grown. But, unfortunately, this became a problem.

As soon as the game ended, fans were permitted to exit by way of the field to the center-field area by the monuments. If the Yankees won, there was a mad rush by some fans to take advantage of this opportunity to approach Mickey Mantle. However, the fans became unruly from time to time, expressing their ardor for their hero, jostling Mickey. So Mickey asked for security to help escort him off the field. Six ushers immediately jumped the low fence at the game's end onto the field to meet The Mick by second base, forming a cordon around him to ensure his safe return to the dugout. The operation, called the "suicide squad," usually went to the younger, faster ushers like me. Remembering when I was called on to guard my idol, Mickey Mantle, was one of my biggest thrills.

I joined the US Navy in 1962 for a four-year stint. While my ship was stationed in Charleston, South Carolina, in 1965, the Vatican announced that Pope Paul VI would come to Yankee Stadium. It was the first time a pope left the Vatican in Italy to visit the Western Hemisphere. Naturally, Yankee Stadium was the venue that he chose. The Stadium beckoned! So I hitchhiked my way up to New York to participate in this joyous celebration, which 90,000 people attended.

Tony Morante visiting "The Babe" in Monument Park prior to the 2008 All-Star Game.

The Yankees stars who contributed to the great success the team enjoyed had passed their prime with a resounding thud as the team hit rock-bottom in 1966. But the memories of those championship seasons came back to life when June 8, 1969, was proclaimed Mickey Mantle Day. Players representing those great years with Mickey participated in paying homage to him. I was assigned to the area by third base in the loge level, where I witnessed the ceremonies.

Announcer Mel Allen, the Voice of the Yankees, introduced Mickey Mantle: "Ladies and gentlemen, a magnificent Yankee, the great number seven, Mickey Mantle." At this point, I stopped working as the sellout crowd gave Mantle a nine-minute standing ovation. By this time, tears streamed down my face. So it was with the men to my right and left. There could not have been a dry eye in the house as we remembered Mickey Mantle's thrills.

In 1973 I took an elective course at Fordham University while pursuing a degree at night involving walking tours of the Bronx. Although I was a ne'er-do-well in my early academic years, the Bronx tours that two historians took us on piqued my interest considerably. I befriended the Bronx historian and instructor, Dr. Gary Hermalyn. Over the next few years, we would have lunch at the Stadium from time to time and we would visit different parts of the ballpark, which led to his proposal for me to conduct a public walking tour. Little did I know at the time that this was a portent of bigger things to come. In due time, I became the Bronx County Historical Society VP. The BCHS was instrumental in helping to prepare the tour's route.

In January of that 1973 there was a changing of the guard. Mr. George M. Steinbrenner, a shipping magnate, became the principal owner and managing partner of the New York Yankees and held the position until his passing in 2010. With a consortium of 13 partners, he purchased the Yankees from CBS in January 1973 for $10 million. During his tenure, he brought seven World Series championships to New York and its fans.

With the passing of five decades of wear and tear, the Stadium was in dire need of refurbishment, which began immediately after the 1973 season ended. The projected cost of the refurbishment was $28 million, but when completed, the price tag had reached over $100 million. New York City Mayor John Lindsay was instrumental in keeping the Yankees franchise in New York. He did not wish to see them emulate the Yankees' former Stadium tenants, the NFL New York Giants, and move to the Meadowlands in New Jersey.

In May of 1973 I experienced a seismic shift in my employment as I shed my usher's uniform for business apparel as I took a position in the club's Group and Season Sales Department.

"Winning, after breathing, is the most important thing in life" was a quote that "The Boss" lived by to the nth degree. This attitude permeated the entire administration. He vowed to bring his mediocre team to a championship in three years, and true to his vow, watched the Yankees climb back to the top of the American League in their newly renovated ballpark in 1976.

Yankees President and General Manager Gabe Paul offered the 6,000 season-ticket holders an opportunity to obtain a seat from their complement of seats from the original Stadium. The Invirex Demolition Co. moved 6,000 seats to the players' parking lot across the street from the Stadium. I oversaw the seats' disbursement, which became a real "event" helping lead to a revival in the field of collectibles and memorabilia.

After 1976 with the advent of free agency and thanks to wise trades by sage GM Gabe Paul, the Yankees won back-to-back World Series championships in 1977 and 1978. Joyous celebrations were rampant in Yankeeland, capped off by ticker-tape parades up Broadway (the Canyon of Heroes) and World Series rings for the players.

Then in 1979, tragedy befell the Yankees. Their captain, catcher Thurman Munson, who was the first Yankee to be named captain since Lou Gehrig in 1939, perished in a plane crash in his new Cessna Citation jet plane while on a test run in Canton, Ohio, on August 2, 1979. Munson played for the Yankees in all his 11 seasons; he never visited the disabled list, and he was voted an All-Star in seven of those years. He won the Rookie of the Year Award in 1970, an MVP Award in 1976, and three Gold Glove Awards. Thurman's devotion to his family led him to seek a pilot's license so he could travel from New York to be with his family on his days off...against the best wishes of Mr. Steinbrenner. When they sat down to discuss Munson's 1979 contract, Mr. Steinbrenner had finally granted permission to Thurman to fly his airplane. After the fatal crash, Mr. Steinbrenner wanted a halt in play to remember the captain but Commissioner Bowie Kuhn issued an order not to miss a scheduled game. Nonetheless, defying the order, Mr. Steinbrenner took the entire Yankee squad to Ohio for the funeral service. He said they planned to be back in time for the game but if not, they would forfeit. I couldn't have been prouder of being a Yankee than at this time!

During the first couple of days of mourning, with emotions pretty much spent, we started to talk about the lighter side of Thurman's gruff exterior. I'll never forget a run-in I had with him in July of 1975, while I worked in the Group and Season Sales Department. We offered a program in which a community or organization that purchased 1,000 tickets to a game would be entitled to certain perks including 20 complimentary seats to the game, four VIP seats by the Yankees dugout, radio and TV promotions, and a ceremony by the Yankees dugout to present a plaque to the Yankee of their choice.

Pepsi-Cola of Bristol, Connecticut, was one such sponsor, purchasing tickets for a twin bill (a term we don't hear too often today) at Shea Stadium, the Yankees' home for the 1974 and 1975 seasons while Yankee Stadium was being refurbished. Two aces, Bill Lee of the Red Sox and Catfish Hunter of the Yankees, tossed up goose eggs through the first eight innings. The Red Sox broke the tie by pushing a run across in the top of the ninth inning. A plaque was to be presented to Munson by the Yankees dugout between games. However, when I went down to the dugout there was no Thurman. I went into the clubhouse by his locker...no Thurm. "Where's Thurm?" I shouted out. "He's in the bathroom" (language was a bit saltier), came the reply. As I entered the bathroom, I shouted, "Thurm, Thurm, it's Tony Morante!" His gruff reply from the stall was, "Whadda you want?" I answered, "We set up a presentation with your friend from Pepsi for a presentation that I told you about." He responded with, "Hell no, I ain't goin'!" Thurm had taken the bitter defeat hard and was in no mood to participate. Yankees sub Fred Stanley helped out by accepting the plaque.

Peace ended the decade of the 1970s as Pope John Paul II visited Yankee Stadium. Shortly after that, the Bronx Historical Society approached me to conduct a walking tour of the Stadium on Veterans Day. Bronx Borough President Stanley Simon led an entourage of 125 people, mostly from his office, to attend. The tour was a game-changer in my life. It led to my work with Yankee Stadium tours.

After touring VIPs at the Stadium for the next five years, we opened the historical tours to schoolchildren in 1985. They caught on immediately. The one-hour tour consisted of the press box, the field, Monument Park, the dugout, and, the clubhouse. The revenue from the Stadium tours benefited the Yankee Foundation, a nonprofit 501(c)(3) arm of the Yankees, which helped to bring educational and recreational programs to inner-city youths. In 1990 we opened the tours to the public. Also, in this year, I was honored to escort Nelson Mandela around Monument Park, which was one of my greatest thrills. In addition, at this time, we instituted the Yankee Caravan, bringing players to schools and hospitals to talk about life.

Around this time, after 14 seasons of mediocre play, the team began to reap the benefits of its farm system and returned to postseason play in 1995, at the precipice of a new dynasty. The Yankees went on to win four World Series in 1996, 1998, 1999, and 2000, and were proclaimed "The Team of the Century." Exciting celebrations followed the World Series victories, including ticker-tape parades from the Battery by floats up Broadway, the Canyon of Heroes, to City Hall for mayoral proclamations, and a great picnic to follow. Shortly after the 1996 World Series, I was called up to Mr. Steinbrenner's office, where I was presented with the 1996 World Series Championship ring in my name! What a great feeling it was for me!

Mickey Mantle, his wife Merlyn, and son Mickey Jr. attend the first Mickey Mantle Day at the old Yankee Stadium, September 18, 1965.

In 1998 Mr. Steinbrenner permitted me to open a Yankee Stadium Tours Department. Tours began to grow rapidly at the start of the new century. A big push came in 2003 when the great Japanese ballplayer Hideki Matsui came to the Yankees. Since baseball was introduced to Japan in 1872, the game had become the national pastime in Japan. Matsui's arrival brought a tremendous infusion of Japanese tourists to Yankee Stadium during the period through 2009, when he left the Yankees. I myself conducted countless tours for enthusiastic Japanese tourists and the Japanese media. Hysterically, many tourists who had seen me on TV in Japan (something unbeknownst to me) asked me to take a picture with them. When I questioned the Japanese interpreter, "Why all the fuss?" the reply was that the tourists recognized me from TV back home. I was honored! This period in time had a great influence on the globalization of our game.

In addition to the tours, we designed presentations on leadership in collaboration with middle-school teachers. Also, the Stadium Tours department presented a 45-minute PowerPoint educational program to the students on the Suite Level of the original Stadium. I also visited the middle schools with the program. In 2008, our last season in the Stadium, we opened special tours in conjunction with the Wounded Warrior Foundation and the Special Operations Warrior Foundation, including introductions to the ballplayers during batting practice. Over 150,000 people attended the Stadium Tours in our final season. Then, in 2009, the Yankees christened the new Yankee Stadium by winning the World Series, the same way that they christened the original stadium in 1923, replete with ceremonies and a ticker-tape parade up Broadway.

In July 2010, two Yankee icons passed away within three days of each other, Bob Sheppard, the Yankees public-address announcer for 57 years (1951–2007), and George Steinbrenner.

The erudite and dulcet tones of Shep's voice were given the sobriquet "The Voice of God" by Reggie Jackson. And Derek Jeter insisted on being introduced as he stepped into the batter's box by Shep's recording, "Now batting, number 2, Derek Jeeetah" until he retired.

Shep and I had a lot of fun in the press room before lunch or dinner. He had his own private table for four in the press room's corner where only invited guests were allowed to sit in his company. I was one of the guests from time to time. Being that he was a St. John's University professor and I, a Fordham University graduate, there was always live banter between us on who had the greatest sports teams. We enjoyed the laughter!

My relationship with "The Boss," Mr. Steinbrenner, was also unique. After giving me the opportunity to open the Yankee Stadium Tours Department, he said, "Tony, you don't have to report to anybody, just let me know how you're doing." So, year after year, as the tours were steadily improving, I sent favorable reports on their growth. The letters of acknowledgment that he sent to me are treasured.

Although Mr. Steinbrenner showed a lot of bluster, he was a humble man. One of his many quotes that stuck with me was, "If you do a good deed for someone and more than two people know about it, you and that person, then you are doing it for the wrong reason." Once, while leading a Stadium tour, I stopped the group by an exhibit of The Boss in the Yankees Museum and told of his benevolent side that maybe most did not see. Someone in the crowd shouted out how much gratitude he had for Mr. Steinbrenner after he helped his family out of dire straits. To my dismay, The Boss's daughter Jennifer was on the tour and reprimanded me as we left the museum for showing off the benevolence of her father.

In 2014 the National Assessment for Educational Progress stated that only 18 percent of our eighth-grade students were proficient in social studies. It was alarming to realize that 82 percent of our youngsters were at risk. So I designed a program that would help those struggling students understand American history through the eyes of baseball. In retirement, and not wanting to abandon the program, I wrote the book *BASEBALL The New York Game—How the National Pastime Paralleled U.S. History*, which was published in 2021.

Circuses, rodeos, Negro baseball, Women's Professional Baseball Exhibitions, three Papal masses, Jehovah's Witnesses assemblies, college and professional football, soccer, boxing, circuses, rodeos, and other interdenominational faith healings, besides 26 World Series championships, all passed through this structure that for 84 years[1] was one of our country's crown jewels, Yankee Stadium.

Thank you, my family, friends, and colleagues for helping me to wrap my life around our national pastime. You helped me achieve the distinction of being inducted into the 2022 Class of the New York State Baseball Hall of Fame. ■

Note

1. Although the Stadium was technically used for 84 seasons (1923–73, 1976–2008), it is generally talked about in terms of its 85-year lifespan (1923–2008).

"We Were the Only Girls to Play at Yankee Stadium"

Tim Wiles

This excerpt is from the recent SABR book, *Yankee Stadium 1923–2008: America's First Modern Ballpark*, and also appears at www.grassrootsbaseball.org.

Between 1923 and 2008, Yankee Stadium hosted 6,746 American League and related professional baseball games, including 161 postseason games and four All-Star Games. More than 200 Negro League games have also taken place there. On August 11, 1950, the ballpark hosted its first and only game between two teams of female professional baseball players, when the Chicago Colleens and the Springfield Sallies of the All-American Girls Professional Baseball League (AAGPBL) played a three-inning exhibition before that day's contest between the Yankees and the Philadelphia Athletics.[1]

The New York Times called the game "a spirited exhibition," noting that the "Colleens, managed by Dave Bancroft, famed Giant shortstop of thirty years ago, won by a score of 1–0."[2] The *New York Herald Tribune* saw the game differently, noting that the Colleens won, 3–0. "Umpires were provided by the Yankees: Ralph Houk at home plate. Gene Woodling at first, Ed Lopat at second and Allie Reynolds at third."[3]

At present, we do not know who got on base, scored, or drove in runs in this historic game, as no box score, scorecard, or narrative game account has yet been found. We do know the name of the first woman to throw a pitch at Yankee Stadium, though: "No other woman had ever pitched off that mound before me," said Gloria 'Tippy' Schweigert, the 16-year-old who started that day for the Colleens.[4] This source credits her with throwing a no-hitter in the start, though no game account confirms that.[5]

In November 2022, this author spoke to all three of the surviving players who took the field that day: Joanne McComb, Mary Moore, and Toni Palermo. All expressed difficulty recalling much beyond the honor of playing in the House That Ruth Built.

"I played first base, I know that," recalled McComb. "I was more impressed with the surroundings. The game itself, to me, was just another game."[6]

Mary Moore played second base and recalled hitting a ball into the infield and running toward first base, where she took a spill on wet grounds after veering off to the right, muddying her bright white uniform. She can't recall if she was safe or out, but "I would think that I would remember if I was safe."[7]

Toni Palermo played shortstop, recalling that Phil Rizzuto loaned her his glove—and she used it in the game. She also could not recall game details, but noted, "I just know that I really enjoyed it, that I had his glove and I felt like a star out there. I was a confident player. I wanted every ball hit to me, no matter what the situation, and with his glove, I felt even more powerful."[8] Palermo also recalled Casey Stengel working with her on double plays before the game, teaching her to time the approaching ball, get it on the hop she wanted, and to just kick the corner of the bag. "And it made a difference," she recalled.[9] None of the three could confirm the game score.

Beyond the lack of a box score, another intriguing loss for history is the fact that, according to Merrie Fidler, the Yankees organization wrote an enthusiastic letter to the AAGPBL after the game, which included the sentence "The game was carried in its entirety on television and there has been a great deal of interesting comment around the city since."[10] This footage has not survived.

Playing in Yankee Stadium was a source of pride for many of the players that day, as they often gave that as their favorite memory when asked on questionnaires, by reporters, and at panel discussions.

"Imagine, if you will, back then, being a girl and playing professional baseball on the field at Yankee Stadium. Think what it must feel like to us, walking and running around the outfield, standing in the same batter's box where the likes of Babe Ruth, Phil Rizzuto, and Joe DiMaggio had stood. It was truly amazing and exciting for us," recalled pitcher Pat Brown in her autobiography *A League of My Own*.[11]

The Yankees and A's players were friendly with the female players, and there was much interaction on the field and in the dugouts. Said Jane Moffet, "I...found myself in the dugout with several of the Yankees ball players, I was with Yogi, Whitey Ford, Casey Stengel, and others. Casey and Yogi were very friendly and stayed with us in the dugout talking baseball. I went out and warmed up the pitcher, and we played our three-inning game. Then we stayed for the game. I have been a devoted Yankee fan ever since. All in the life of a rookie."[12]

Joanne McComb recalled Johnny Mize: "He was a character. He sat on the bench with us during the game, and offered to trade us chewing tobacco for bubble gum."[13]

McComb listed the game as her favorite baseball memory and recalled, "The Yankee players acted as

An advertisement in the New York Daily News on August 11, 1950, touts the "All America Girls" (sic) appearance at Yankee Stadium.

our bat boys in the dugout with us."[14] Mary Lou Kolanko mentioned that "I warmed up playing catch with Phil Rizzuto."[15]

Barbara "Bobbie" Liebrich, who along with Pat Barringer was one of the two player-manager-chaperones on the touring teams, remembered that "[a]fter the game I and the other manager (Barringer) were on Paul and Dizzy Dean's TV show."[16] Liebrich and Barringer were also the keepers of the excellent set of three tour scrapbooks and a photo album documenting the annual tours, which is housed at the National Baseball Hall of Fame Library in Cooperstown.

"I'm just sorry I broke my ankle, because after that, the teams went up and played at Yankee Stadium, and I missed that game," lamented Shirley Burkovich.[17]

"I remember the game at Yankee Stadium," said Jacqueline "Jackie" Mattson. "What a thrilling experience it was to meet Yogi Berra. His offer to let me use his bat was hilarious. What a club it was! It had a thick handle and was very heavy at the end. I was 5'5" tall and weighed one hundred pounds. If I had swung Yogi's bat, it would have spun me in a circle, once or twice around. Needless to say, I used my own evenly balanced bat with its nice thin handle."[18]

"We were the only girls to play at Yankee Stadium," Mattson said. "That was an experience in itself. The stadium was the hugest thing that you'd ever seen."[19]

Pat Brown, who was in the A's dugout, said: "We were all talking to the (A's) players who had come into our dugout, and, at the same time, were cheering for our team playing out on the field. Suddenly everyone became very, very quiet, and we all looked toward the entry to the dugout. A tall thin man with white hair and a nice smile had just entered the dugout. We all knew who he was, and we respectfully waited for him to speak. It was Connie Mack, the manager of the Athletics, a man who was indeed a legend in baseball."[20]

"Everybody was in awe," she said.[21] "It turned out that this was to be his last year managing. In 1956, when I read in the paper that he had died, I remembered him as that very special person who took the time to come into the dugout and say hello to some women professional players. Some things you can never forget."[22]

"What a thrill! We even met Mr. Connie Mack, wearing his customary vested suit and his straw hat," recalled Pat Courtney.[23] "I was so impressed with Connie Mack—his demeanor, and always so well dressed," remembered Joanne McComb.[24]

"We did play in Yankee Stadium which was a *great* thrill," recalled player Mary Moore in a 2004 interview with AAGPBL historian Merrie Fidler. "Walking onto that field was like in a movie. It just was so beautiful—manicured. It was—I mean words just can't describe it, actually. We played very good ball at the time and you could just hear the crowd 'oooh' and 'aaah' and it was just awesome. It's really—you can't even describe it. You know, when we were touring around the country, we played at some nice places and then some of them they were almost like cow pastures."[25]

The game in Yankee Stadium came roughly midway during the 1950 traveling exhibition schedule conducted by the two teams. From 1948 to 1950, the Colleens and Sallies toured through much of North America in order to promote the league, generate revenue, and recruit new players.[26] The Colleens and Sallies were also considered farm teams, not just scouting the available talent at their many stops, but also refining the skills of those players already on their rosters, in preparation for call-ups to the established, fixed location teams in Midwestern cities like Rockford, South Bend, Peoria, and Kalamazoo.

"We had good, good crowds because half the proceeds would go to some local charity," noted Mary Moore. "Murray Howe, our public relations guy, he was always ahead of us and he had press coverage and we had to take turns giving interviews on radio in each town that we went into. So we did have good advance publicity."[27]

The Liebrich-Barringer scrapbook collection reveals fundraisers to raise money for swimming pool construction; the Fresh Air Fund; a high-school band that needed funds to pay expenses to Chicago to play at the Lions International convention; a scholarship fund for a young pianist to the New England Conservatory; polio benefits; police and fire departments; Boys Club Building Fund; Optimist Club's Boys Work program; funds for needy families; Community Chest funds; and a city playground fund.[28] Admission was usually $1 for adults and 50 cents for children. A few locations had discounted bleacher seats, and at least one Southern venue, Duncan Park in Spartanburg, South Carolina, offered "Colored Bleachers" for 50 cents.[29]

Between June 3 and September 4, the players traveled by bus through Illinois, Ohio, West Virginia, and points southward, including Roanoke, Asheville, Macon, Knoxville, and Hazard, Kentucky. Then it was over to Hagerstown, Maryland, and then up through New Jersey, New York, Pennsylvania, then back south for games in Washington (where they played two games at Griffith Stadium), Virginia, Maryland, and Delaware. Then it was New York again, Massachusetts, Connecticut, Maine, New Hampshire, Vermont, and games in Sherbrooke and Montreal, Quebec. They finished up by working their way west across New York and Ohio.[30] The teams scheduled 95 games in that stretch, playing 83, with 12 rainouts.[31]

The players were mostly in their late teens or early 20s, and only one, Canadian center fielder Joan Schatz, was married at the time.[32] The bus rides were long, often conducted overnight, with players assembling on the bus after their postgame showers. "The bus driver, Walt, loved to sing along with those songs, he had a beautiful voice, we traveled at night, and Wimp (Baumgartner) would stand up in front of the bus with him, and we'd sing songs all night. We had good singers on those teams!" recounted Isabel Maria Lucila Alvarez de Leon y Cerdan, also known as Lefty Alvarez. "The days were ours to do with whatever we wanted. We had to do laundry, and catch up on our sleep, and do letter-writing. But in a couple of places, like New York, we went to Radio City Music Hall and Coney Island. It was a beautiful experience to get to do that and travel all over. We played through all the South, the East, the New England states and Canada, so there are places I would have never gotten to see, to do all this *and get paid for it* was really nice."[33]

Speaking of the 1949 tour, Jane Moffett reminisced: "We traveled 26,000 miles that first summer in a bus. We played every day and prayed for rain because that was the only way we got time off. We could play a game and the next stop could be 200 miles away. A lot of police departments, fire departments and organizations would sponsor us as a fundraiser and we got called frequently to be on radio shows."[34] Anna Mae O'Dowd added, "There was a lot of singing and a lot of jokes on the bus. It was fun. Of course, you got very tired too. I remember that well."[35]

Mary Moore, who led the Sallies in games played (77), hits (75), total bases (96), home runs (3), runs scored (65), and RBIs (48) in 1950, recalled, "We toured 21 states and Canada that first year. On the farm team level, we got $25 a week and $21 for meals that wasn't taxable, plus all of our travel and housing expenses taken care of."[36]

Many of these young women had never been away from home, and the opportunity to see the country, and Canada, was educational. Massachusetts native Pat Brown was surely not the only player whose eyes were opened to segregation: "I learned a lot that summer of 1950 while traveling through the segregated South. I had never seen such signs before as 'Colored Only,' or 'White Only.' Even some of the posters announcing our games advertised separate seating for 'Colored.' I was only a teenager, but after what I had seen, nobody had to tell me that segregation was wrong; I just knew it. Those images and other situations stayed with me, and I became a firm believer in civil rights and equality. Even today, I cannot erase those images from my mind."[37]

A week before the Yankee Stadium game, the AAGPBL made national news when former Yankee star Wally Pipp called 26-year-old Rockford Peaches first baseman Dottie Kamenshek, a perennial all-star who was hitting .343 at the time, the "fanciest-fielding first baseman I've ever seen, man or woman."[38] Shortly thereafter, Kamenshek and AAGPBL President Fred Leo were contacted by officials with the Fort Lauderdale team and the Florida International League, offering to buy her out. Both Kamenshek and Leo turned down the offers. Kamenshek thought the offer was not sincere, and Leo said, "Rockford couldn't afford to lose her. I also told them we felt that women should play baseball among themselves and that they could not help but appear inferior in athletic competition with men."[39]

When asked about Pipp's comments, Bancroft replied that "Kamenshek was 'an extraordinary player,' but that he leaned against any woman being able to play in the major leagues. But he also added, 'Remember, it was only a short time ago that most major league players, managers, and sportswriters rejected the idea of Negroes ever playing the big top. Time marches on.'"[40]

Of managing the women's teams, Bancroft told writer Will Wedge, "It's fun here, mixed with the usual headaches of a skipper, and it pays better than the minors. And it sure comes under the head of new experiences, and even at 57, and as gray-haired as I am, I can be attracted by novelty.

"But don't get me wrong. This girls baseball is more than a novelty, because it is good brisk baseball, and we give the customers a fast show, the games running only about an hour and a half. And I'm telling you that the adeptness of 99% of these dolls simply amazes me and their sport has caught on well in the Midwest....These girls just can't get enough baseball. They want to bat for an hour before the game, but after twenty minutes on the mound, I've had more than enough exercise."[41]

Historian Merrie Fidler has also discovered that the AAGPBL planned, but apparently never held, another game in Yankee Stadium in the 1950 season. According to an article she found in a Scranton newspaper, "The (Kenosha) Comets and (Racine) Belles are scheduled in a nine-inning exhibition as a preliminary to the regular American League scheduled contest between Chicago and the Yankees....Considerable interest has been evidenced throughout the East in the game played by the AAGPBL after barnstorming tours by farm clubs last year. The two teams will fly by a chartered airliner to New York, and will return by air in time to resume their scheduled games at Fort Wayne and South Bend."[42]

In myriad interviews conducted over the last 30 years, since the film *A League of Their Own* was released, a trope emerges that these young women used their high salaries and newfound freedom to blaze new trails for their gender, which often involved higher education—at that time not at all common for young women. Pat Brown's autobiography repeats that pattern.

In a related article, Brown sums up, as no other player has done, the value of playing in the AAGPBL. This is the list of "Lessons from Pat Brown's Baseball Life" that she wrote about: "Toughness, assertiveness, teamwork, belief in self, independence, broader perspective, acting under pressure, and courage."[43] One quality she did not list was confidence. But she addressed it elsewhere: "I myself was only 17, 18 when I went out there to play. I was very shy, quiet through high school. The league changed me. It gave me confidence, it built me up. I finally realized that I wasn't a freak because I was athletic. Before I started playing, people said to me, 'It's wrong that you want to play baseball. It's okay when you're a little kid, when you're a tomboy.' Once I became a professional baseball player, I felt vindicated."[44]

Joanne McComb in her days with the All-American Girls.

Pat Brown went on to earn not just her master's in library science, but also her law degree and a master's in divinity.[45]

The entire tour was a rare opportunity for young women to expand their horizons through travel, athletic achievement, and making good money while enlightening crowds and opening eyes all across North America. We'll give the last word to Mary Moore: "Playing and getting to see the country like that and getting paid for it was more than you could ever dream of—I mean it was a dream come true—what else? You loved to play ball and you're seeing the country and you're traveling and everything and you couldn't ask for anything more."[46]

Women did have one more chance to play at Yankee Stadium, in a Negro American League doubleheader on July 11, 1954, between the Kansas City Monarchs and the Indianapolis Clowns. A newspaper article in advance of the game said, "The girls take a back seat to no one on the field either. They both really play baseball and Miss Toni Stone of the Monarchs, and Miss Connie Morgan of the Clowns have displayed plenty of ability."[47] While advance publicity had both women slated to play second base, the lack of a box score makes it currently impossible to know if either actually played. ■

Author's Note

The author is grateful for research help from Merrie Fidler, official historian of the AAGPBL Players Association; Brian Richards, senior museum curator of the New York Yankees; Cassidy Lent and Rachel Wells of the National Baseball Hall of Fame library; former players Joanne McComb, Mary Moore, and Toni Palermo; Adam Berenbak of the National Archives; and historians Carol Sheldon and Ryan Woodward.

Notes

1. John Drebinger, "Yanks Bench DiMaggio, Stagger to 7–6 Victory Over Athletics," *The New York Times*, August 12, 1950.
2. Drebinger.
3. Untitled *New York Herald Tribune* article dated August 12, 1950, retrieved from Liebrich-Barringer AAGPBL Tour Scrapbooks (MSS 10, 1-D-2), National Baseball Hall of Fame Library, Cooperstown, New York, September 30, 2022.
4. W.C. Madden, *The Women of the All-American Girls Professional Baseball League: A Biographical Dictionary* (Jefferson, North Carolina: McFarland & Company, 1997), 220.
5. Madden, 220.
6. Joanne McComb, telephone interview, November 22, 2022.
7. Mary Moore, telephone interview, November 6, 2022.
8. Toni Palermo, telephone interview, November 6, 2022.
9. Palermo interview.
10. Merrie A. Fidler. *The Origins and History of the All-American Girls Professional Baseball League* (Jefferson, North Carolina: McFarland & Company, 2006), 110.
11. Patricia I. Brown, *A League of My Own: Memoir of a Pitcher for the All-American Girls Professional Baseball League* (Jefferson, North Carolina: McFarland & Company, 2003), 66.
12. Kat D. Williams, *Isabel "Lefty" Alvarez: The Improbable Life of a Cuban American Baseball Star* (Lincoln: University of Nebraska Press, 2020), 59.
13. McComb interview.
14. Joanne McComb. Player questionnaire in the research files of the National Baseball Hall of Fame, 1997.
15. Joanne McComb, *Touching Bases*, the newsletter of the AAGPBL Players Association, January 2005.
16. Mary Lou Kolanko, *Touching Bases*.
17. Madden, 148.
18. Brown, 173.
19. Andy Horschak, "Brewers, ex-Comet Preserve the Legacy of the AAGPBL," undated clipping, likely from the *Kenosha News*, retrieved from Liebrich-Barringer AAGPBL Tour Scrapbooks.
20. Brown, 67.
21. Dennis Daniels, "Move over Cobb, Ruth & Williams!" *Boston Herald*, October 12, 1988: 31.
22. Brown, 67.
23. Brown, 162.
24. McComb interview.
25. Mary Moore, interview with AAGPBL historian Merrie Fidler, conducted by phone in March 2004. Interview transcript provided by Merrie Fidler.
26. https://www.aagpbl.org/history/league-history. Retrieved October 21, 2022.
27. Moore interview.
28. Numerous articles from the AAGPBL Tour Scrapbooks.
29. Numerous newspaper game advertisements from the AAGPBL Tour Scrapbooks.
30. Tour schedule and results from the AAGPBL Tour Scrapbooks.
31. Typescript of schedule and results, AAGPBL Tour Scrapbooks.
32. Mary Hayes, "Yank Stadium to Queen City: Diamond Damsels Hit With Patrons," *News* (city unidentified) from AAGPBL Tour Scrapbooks.
33. Jim Sargent, *We Were the All-American Girls* (Jefferson, North Carolina: McFarland, 2013), 281.
34. Jessica Driscoll. "Former Pitman Resident Honored as Baseball First," *Gloucester County Times* (Woodbury, New Jersey), July 5, 2010.
35. Katie Sartoris. "Annie O'Dowd Recalls Time Spent in All-American Girls Professional Baseball League," *Villages Daily Sun* (The Villages, Florida), May 31, 2013.
36. Pat Andrews. "Female Star Returns Downriver: LP Grad Depicted in 'A League of Their Own,'" *Heritage Newspapers/News-Herald* (Taylor, Michigan), October 25, 1995: 4-C.
37. Brown, 70–72.
38. Fidler, 223.
39. Ed Sainsbury (United Press), "Florida Nine Tries to Sign Woman Player," unknown newspaper, August 3, 1950, AAGPBL Tour Scrapbooks.
40. Will Wedge, "Setting the Pace," *The New York Sun*, August 5, 1948, AAGPBL Tour Scrapbooks.
41. Wedge.
42. "Girl Ball Teams in Stadium Game: Jean Marlowe to Play in New York July 17," *Scranton* (Pennsylvania) *Times Tribune*, May 31, 1950: 41.
43. Patricia I. Brown and Elizabeth M. McKenzie, "First Person … A Law Librarian at Cooperstown," *Law Library Journal*, Volume 93:1. Winter, 2001.
44. Liz Galst, "The Way It Was: A Real Professional Ballplayer Looks at League," *Boston Phoenix*, July 3, 1992: Arts Section 7.
45. Carol Sheldon, "Patricia Brown," *Boston Herald*. Player profile provided at AAGPBL website. https://www.aagpbl.org/profiles/patricia-brown-pat/219. Retrieved November 22, 2022.
46. Mary Moore interview.
47. "Clowns-KC Monarchs at Stadium Sunday: Bitter Rivalry for NAL Girl Players in Focus," *New York Amsterdam News*, July 10, 1954: 23.

The Henry Chadwick Award was established by SABR to honor baseball's great researchers—historians, statisticians, analysts, and archivists—for their invaluable contributions to making baseball the game that links America's present with its past.

Apart from honoring individuals for the length and breadth of their contributions to the study and enjoyment of baseball, the Chadwick Award will educate the baseball community about sometimes little known but vastly important contributions from the game's past and thus encourage the next generation of researchers.

The contributions of nominees must have had public impact. This may be demonstrated by publication of research in any of a variety of formats: books, magazine articles, and websites. The compilation of a significant database or archive that has facilitated the published research of others will also be considered in the realm of public impact.

STEVE GIETSCHIER by Lyle Spatz

These are the qualifications for the Henry Chadwick Award: "The contributions of nominees must have had public impact. This may be demonstrated by publication of research in any of a variety of formats: books, magazine articles, websites, etc. The compilation of a significant database or archive that has facilitated the published research of others will also be considered in the realm of public impact."

Perhaps more than for any of the previous winners of this award, that description fits Steve Gietschier.

Steven Philip Gietschier was born in Brooklyn in 1948, but his family moved to Hicksville, Long Island, soon after. Though Dodgers fandom was in his genes, the team was gone as Steve was developing his lifelong love of baseball. When the Mets came on the scene in 1962, he quickly became their devoted fan, and though he has lived in and around St. Louis for 37 years, he remains a Mets fan to this day.

After receiving his undergraduate degree in 1970 from Georgetown University's School of Foreign Service, Steve attended Ohio State University where he earned a Masters Degree (1971) and PhD (1977) in History. He worked at the Ohio Historical Society while pursuing his graduate degrees and then, in 1978, moved on to the South Carolina Department of Archives and History.

He was still there when an ad in the October/November 1985 newsletter of the Society of American Archivists captured his attention. *The Sporting News* was looking for an archivist, preferably one familiar with sports and sports history. Steve, an archivist and an avid sports fan, envisioned his dream job. He applied for the position and, after a series of interviews, was hired. He began working at *TSN* in September 1986. From day one, he discovered their holdings were vast, valuable, and completely disorganized.

Hired to organize *TSN*'s varied collection of books, historical materials, and photographs, he transformed their archives into the renowned *Sporting News* Research Center, providing reference and research services to writers, editors, and members of the public. Steve spent 22 years at *The Sporting News*. His job title changed several times—Director of Historical Records, 1986–2000; Senior Managing Editor, Research, 2000–07; Managing Editor, Research, 2007–08; and Archives Manager, 2008—but he always strived to serve both internal customers (*TSN* writers and editors) and external customers, including lots of SABR members.

When *TSN* redesigned the *Baseball Guide* in 1992, Steve took over writing the "Year in Review" essay, which he continued to write until the *Guide*'s final edition in 2006. Steve is rightly proud that he continued the tradition of an annual guide and an annual year-in-review essay, originated by Henry Chadwick himself, in 1860. On a personal note, starting in 2004, he used his position as the editor of the late and sorely missed *Sporting News Record Book* to publish the records-changes found by SABR researchers.

When *The Sporting News* relocated to Charlotte, North Carolina, in 2008, Steve stayed behind. He served as the University Curator and as a Professor of History from 2009 to 2020 at Lindenwood University, in St. Charles, Missouri. Since 2021, he has served as an Archival consultant for Sporting News Enterprises UK.

Steve has written or edited numerous articles on baseball history and has taught college-level courses on baseball and other American sports. His latest book, *Baseball: The Turbulent Midcentury Years*, will be published by the University of Nebraska Press in 2023. The book picks up where the second volume of the two-volume history of baseball by Harold Seymour and Dorothy Seymour Mills left off. How fitting for one of this year's honorees, already linked to Henry Chadwick, to be linked to two of the award's first honorees.

Steve and Donna Gietschier live in Florissant, Missouri. They are fortunate to have their two daughters, Katie Meyers and Sarah Hartman—as well as four grandsons: Andy and Patrick Meyers, and Joey and Max Hartman—living nearby. ∎

MARK RUCKER by John Thorn

From daguerreotypes to stereo views to modern wire photos, from printed illustrations on posters, cards, and prints to sheet music, Mark Rucker has researched baseball's pictorial record as no one else ever has done. Indeed, before his efforts, those who wished to publish baseball images in their books, films, scholarly articles, or museum exhibitions had little choice beyond the repositories of the National Baseball Hall of Fame or *The Sporting News*. Media outlets wishing more than team-issued headshots had to rely upon their own spelunking at general photo archives like Bettmann, Culver, or Brown Brothers.

It is not too much to say that in baseball Mark Rucker founded the field of pictorial research, which later became a SABR committee. Legions of devotees followed, and new fields of collecting emerged. As he was the first in the field, he is the first pictorial researcher to win a Henry Chadwick Award.

SABR has played an important role in his career, Mark offered. "It gave me a context for the early baseball objects I was [already] hunting for—and finding. My new friends gave me a sympathetic ear concerning buried and arcane topics. I took a nineteenth-century dive that was completely unexpected. SABR opened doors for me. I was able to go where few had gone before, and a SABR credential was recognized wherever I needed to go for research. All the way to Cuba." There he amassed the material for the book Smoke, which he created with Peter Bjarkman, another Chadwick Award winner.

"Maybe most importantly," Mark continued, "SABR saved me from the snakepit of baseball collectors.... They were interested in history 10% and in money 90%. In response, a group of equally competitive, but reliable and ethical collectors emerged, for whom collecting was historical preservation. This, with the fortunate timing of the Reagan recession, made things easy, if you worked like a dog. Material was pouring out of attics and basements as at no time before."

Rucker amassed an archive and began licensing images to *The New York Times*, *Sports Illustrated*, *Vanity Fair*, and numerous other publications. He also supplied images and research services for many HBO programs and was chief visual consultant to Ken Burns's documentary film, *Baseball*. He has collaborated on books with Larry Ritter, David Nemec, Peter Bjarkman and—for a book on Ted Williams—Richard Ben Cramer, Daniel Okrent, and John Thorn.

With Thorn, he cofounded SABR's Nineteenth Century Committee four decades ago. But his greatest contribution to pictorial research has come recently, with his donation of The Rucker Archive of about 80,000 baseball images in 2019. SABR announced its plans for digitization and cataloging in January 2023. (See: https://sabr.org/latest/coming-soon-to-sabr-org-rucker-archive-historical-baseball-photographs.)

Mark was a painter whose strong visual orientation made him unique as an archivist and as a collector. "As a combination curator and hoarder, I would look for and store as much baseball imagery as I could find—of all kinds—but only if there was eye appeal. That is what kept me entertained."

The pictorial editions of *The National Pastime* provided Rucker and Thorn—and SABR—a new way to do baseball research.

"How many places did we go? We got into the storerooms and secret compartments in historical societies, libraries, and museums. We made public the thefts from the New York Public Library, documented as we composed our Spalding Collection proof sheets from box after box [without inventory or identifications]. We met unbelievable characters in searching out imagery for those publications. We met collectors who cared about history.

"Until the *TNP* pictorials SABR was a visually dead organization. Those three pubs opened a window for the membership—and I leapt through. I was able to cultivate a network of picture people in SABR throughout the continent, developing an ever-growing list of resources."

As the first Chadwick Award winner in the area of pictorial research, Mark was asked, what remains to be accomplished, for you or for others in this field?

"I think I was the first pictorial researcher to receive the Bob Davids Award a few years back. I remember being razzed by a few members who did not appreciate my selection. I then realized that SABR is a statistical [and textual] organization at its core…. Most members looked on photos and illustrations as decoration. So the change—the recognition—is refreshing, and I am enjoying it.

"What I would like to see is for SABR to blossom visually by creatively using the image bank I provided. I would like to see SABR set a designer/marketer loose on the collection. I never did have the time or the financial backing to take it to its potential, but SABR could."

Yes, SABR could.

The interview concluded with what might have been, for any collector, a softball of a query: Do you have a favorite baseball image? After weighing other candidates, Rucker concluded that this was the one: the Cincinnati Red Stockings at the grounds of the Forest City of Cleveland, October 1870 (see below).

Welcome to SABR's research honor roll, Mark. ■

SABR / THE RUCKER ARCHIVE

ROBERT WHITING by Todd Peterson

Robert "Bob" Whiting was born in 1942 in Long Branch, New Jersey, and grew up in rural Eureka, California, in the 1950s listening to recreated MLB broadcasts on the radio. Whiting originally fell in love with the 1955 Brooklyn Dodgers featuring Duke Snider, Roy Campanella, Gil Hodges, and Jackie Robinson—the team that finally made next year, this year, by downing the Yankees in the World Series. After the move to the West

Coast, he became a fan of the San Francisco Giants of Willie Mays, Willie McCovey, and Juan Marichal.

Whiting first arrived in Japan in 1962 as a US Air Force Intelligence officer, and began studying politics and culture at Tokyo's Sophia University after his discharge. Whiting later recalled, "In the beginning, the

only thing I could understand was baseball on TV because half the terms were English derivatives—safu, outo, sutoraikku and boru…Every night there was a nationwide telecast of the Yomirui Giants games, which featured the legendary Sadaharu Oh and Shigeo Nagashima." The young scholar became a fan of ironman Yutaka Enatsu, the Japanese Sandy Koufax, who recorded 401 strikeouts for the Hanshin Tigers in 1968.

Bob graduated from Sophia in 1969, taking a job editing educational materials for the Encyclopedia Britannica of Japan. Often the company's only foreign employee, Whiting came to the realization that practices such as daily meetings, unpaid overtime, and "karoshi" (death from overwork) were commonplace not only in Japanese corporations, but in their educational system and baseball as well. ("Practice until you die" was the mantra of early baseball powerhouse Waseda University.)

Whiting moved to New York's Upper West Side in 1973, regaling anyone who would listen with tales of how the values of Japanese society and culture—total dedication, year-round training, teamwork, self-sacrifice, and xenophobia—were ingrained in their baseball traditions. His friends encouraged him to write a book about the differences between the Japanese and American approaches to baseball. One year and 100,000 words later, *The Chrysanthemum and the Bat* was published. Whiting's debut was excerpted in *Sports Illustrated*, and was selected as the best sports book of 1977 by *TIME*, with the translation becoming a Japanese best-seller.

In 1989, Whiting's second book, *You Gotta Have Wa*, was a rumination on Japanese society as viewed through the prism of baseball. Wa was named a Book of the Month Club selection and sold over 300,000 copies worldwide, making several honors lists along the way. *The San Francisco Chronicle* deemed it "one of the best-written sports books ever," and it became required reading in many American colleges, as well as the US State Department. In 1991, *Hon No Hanasahi* magazine rated Whiting's masterpiece as one of the best nonfiction works in Japan's history; and in 2020 it was chosen by SABR as one of the fifty top baseball books from the previous fifty years.

Whiting went on to produce several other best-selling baseball volumes including former Expos' player Warren Cromartie's autobiography, *Slugging It Out in Japan* (1991); *The Meaning of Ichiro* (2004), a treatise about Japanese players in American baseball; and a biography of former National League Rookie of the Year, Hideo Nomo, *The Book of Nomo* (2011).

The expat has written for over forty years for such Japanese press platforms as *Tokyo Daily Sports*, *The Weekly Sankei*, *Number*, and *Shukan Asahi*, and the major daily *Yukan Fuj*. In 2005 he was honored with a Lifetime Achievement Award by the Foreign Sportswriters Association of Japan. Whiting's work also popped up in numerous American publications including *Sport*, *Smithsonian*, *The New York Times*, *Newsweek*, and *US News & World Report*.

After Cromartie criticized the Yomiuri Giants' front office during a 1987 interview with Whiting, the writer was banned from the Tokyo Dome for two years. He was banished again in 1990 for his article showing that the Giants were inflating attendance figures. Whiting counted the Tokyo Dome's seats, added the average standing room numbers, and proved that there were usually about 10,000 fewer fans than the regularly announced full house of 56,000. This ban lasted until 2004 when Whiting covered the MLB opener between the Yankees and Devil Rays.

Whiting pivoted away from baseball in 1999 with the publication of *Tokyo Underworld*, a best-selling account of Japanese organized crime and the corrupt side of Japanese-American political relations. He has also authored several other books, mostly collections of his columns and articles, as well as a manga series about an American ballplayer in Japan, and a history of the Tokyo Olympics of 1964 and 2020. His writings have sold a total of over one million and a half copies worldwide.

Bob has also appeared in numerous documentaries and television shows, including the top-rated Japanese *News Station*, as well as CNN's *Larry King Live*, the PBS *MacNeil/Lehrer News Hour*, *Nightline*, ESPN's *SportsCenter*, and HBO's *Real Sports*. His memoir, *Tokyo Junkie*, appeared in 2021, and *Tokyo Outsiders*, a sequel to *Tokyo Underworld* about foreign criminals in Japan, is due out in the US in 2024. Whiting is currently working on a book with Nissan auto executive Greg Kelly who was imprisoned in Japan for over three years due to alleged malfeasance. Not one to keep idle, Bob recently started a Substack site "Robert Whiting's Japan," featuring his recent oeuvre.

Robert Whiting claimed he wrote *The Chrysanthemum and the Bat*, on a bet. A half century later, the wager is still paying dividends as he has become one of the world's premier baseball writers, repeatedly demonstrating how the game has influenced and shaped the global culture. Whiting currently resides in Tokyo with his wife of forty years, Machiko Kondo, a former United Nations High Commissioner for Refugees agency officer. ∎

Contributors

BENJAMIN ALTER published an article in the Fall 2022 *Baseball Research Journal*. Last summer, he co-delivered a paper at SABR's annual Jerry Malloy Negro League Conference. Prior to retiring in 2021, he was a principal with an environmental consulting firm, authored a textbook on environmental consulting, and was an adjunct professor at the City University of New York (CUNY). When not pursuing his passion for baseball, Mr. Alter pursues his many other passions, including music, fitness, history, and geology.

KEVIN W. BARWIN is a retired Northwest Regional Audit Supervisor with the Commonwealth of Pennsylvania with a BA degree from the University of Pittsburgh and a MBA degree from Clarion University. He has contributed to the SABR Biography Project and has written several baseball related articles contained in his book *The Paperboy From the Paper City*. Kevin can be reached at kbdb5417@yahoo.com. He resides among his library of over a thousand baseball books in Erie, Pennsylvania.

GARY BELLEVILLE is a retired Information Technology professional living in Victoria, British Columbia. He has written articles for SABR's *Baseball Research Journal*, Games Project, and Baseball Biography Project, in addition to contributing to several SABR books. Gary grew up in Ottawa, Ontario, and graduated from the University of Waterloo with a Bachelor of Mathematics (Computer Science) degree.

STEPHEN D BOREN, MD graduated from the University of Illinois College of Medicine and completed his emergency medicine residency at Milwaukee County Hospital. He has been a member of SABR since January 1, 1979. He has published a number of articles in SABR publications and Baseball Digest. While originally from Chicago, he and his wife, Louise, and his watchdog golden retriever, Charlie, now live in Aiken, South Carolina.

JOHN Z. CLAY is research assistant at the University of Texas at Austin. He is a member of the System Integration and Design Informatics Laboratory, where he conducts research on human creativity, mindfulness, engineering systems thinking and generative design. Mr. Clay has a passion for baseball analytics and encourages interested parties to contact him via email at john.za.clay@gmail.com.

WOODY ECKARD, PhD is Professor of Economics Emeritus at the University of Colorado-Denver Business School. His academic publishing record includes several papers on sports economics. More recently he has published in SABR's *Baseball Research Journal*, *The National Pastime*, and *Nineteenth Century Notes*. He and his wife Jacky live in Evergreen, Colorado, with their two dogs Petey and Violet. He is a Rockies fan, both the baseball team and the mountains, and a SABR member for over 20 years.

DAVID J. GORDON, MD, PhD is a retired cardiovascular clinical trialist, formerly with the National Institutes of Health. Since his retirement he has written two books, *Baseball Generations* and *The American Cardiovascular Pandemic: A 100 year History*, and has contributed several articles to the *Baseball Research Journal*.

PAULA KURMAN was a child actress, and as an adult was Professor of interpersonal communication at Hunter College, a private consultant to industry, a keynote speaker, an essayist, and a seminar leader. Dr. Kurman's new book, a memoir called *The Cool of the Evening: A Love Story*, will be out in the first quarter of 2024, published by Rosetta Books, and will appear in hardcover, audio, and digital formats.

HERM KRABBENHOFT, a SABR member since 1981, is hoping to see his first in-person major-league triple play this season.

MUYUAN LI works at Blizzard Entertainment where she manages several data teams. She is an avid fan of both real and fantasy baseball and frequently drives down the road to watch Shohei Ohtani make history and drop bombs. She holds a B.B.A. in Applied Information Management Systems from Loyola Marymount University. If you have feedback or would like to request replication data please email her at muli@blizzard.com.

TONY MORANTE, a SABR member since 1995, started working at Yankee Stadium in 1958 as an usher and instituted the Yankee Stadium Tour program in 1985, bringing Yankees history to life for school children, visitors, and employee orientations until his retirement in 2018. Morante served in the United States Navy and is a graduate of Fordham University. Since retiring from work at the Stadium, Morante has presented his work on baseball history in Cooperstown and for various SABR chapters, and in 2021 published a book presenting US history through the lens of baseball entitled *Baseball: The New York Game*.

Visual artist and educator **TODD PETERSON** lives in Overland Park, Kansas. He is the author of *Early Black Baseball in Minnesota* and the editor of *The Negro Leagues Were Major Leagues*. Peterson is also a co-chair of SABR's Negro Leagues Research Committee.

GREG PLITHIDES recently joined SABR as a new member in summer 2022. An engineer by training, he has a particular love for fantasy baseball and a natural proclivity for Sabermetrics. He holds a B.S. in Mechanical Engineering from Columbia University.

MAX PLITHIDES is a PhD candidate at the University of California, Los Angeles, and an Adjunct Professor in the Department of Political Science and International Relations at Loyola Marymount University.

WILLIAM SHKURTI ("Bill") is retired after serving twenty years as the Chief Financial Officer for The Ohio State University. He holds a BA in Economics and a Masters in Public Policy from that institution. He has written several books and articles about Ohio history. He is a Vietnam veteran and a lifelong (and long-suffering) Cleveland Guardians fan.

JAMES A. "SNUFFY" SMITH, JR., who passed away in 2010, is deservedly included as a co-author of the article "Instant Relief" in this issue. He was a pioneer in researching triple plays in the major leagues. Before his passing, Smith had authored or co-authored some 80 articles on triple plays, and he had documented the complete details for 40 IRTPs included here. This article is a logical extension and expansion of an earlier article—"Instant Relief: One Pitch, Three Outs, Game Over"— co-authored by Smith and published in *Baseball America* (August 18, 1997, page 59). Jim presented at the SABR national conventions in Pittsburgh in 1995 and Kansas City in 1996. He won the McFarland-SABR Baseball Research Award in 1996 for the "Baseball Quarterly Review Triple Play Project." Smith was a frequent contributor to SABR's Baseball Records Committee Newsletter. His last contribution, "Team Totals for Triple Plays: For and Against," appeared in the February and April issues in 2010.

JOHN SNELL, BA, MNRM, is a retired Environmental Specialist, formerly with the Canadian National Parks Service. Since retiring, he spends his time writing, building furniture and following baseball and basketball. He lives in Calgary, Alberta, Canada, with his lovely wife Selene.

LYLE SPATZ has been a SABR member for 51 years. He chaired the Baseball Records Committee from 1991 to 2016.

JOHN THORN is the official historian of Major League Baseball and the author of many books and essays.

STEW THORNLEY has been a SABR member since 1979 and helped to found the Halsey Hall Chapter (Where the Action Is!) in 1985. He has received the SABR-Macmillan Baseball Research Award in 1988, the *USA Today* Baseball Weekly Award (for the best convention research presentation) in 1998, and the Bob Davids Award in 2016.

TIM WILES was director of research at the Baseball Hall of Fame library from 1995–2014. He is the author of two baseball books and many articles, often focusing on women in baseball. He is currently the director of the Guilderland (NY) Public Library, and contributes to www.grassrootsbaseball.org on women in baseball.

JOHN ZINN is a baseball historian with special interest in the Brooklyn Dodgers and New Jersey baseball history. He is the author of three books about the Brooklyn Dodgers and is a two-time winner of the Ron Gabriel award for research on the Dodgers. John was also the recipient of the 2020 Russell Gabay Award by SABR's Elysian Fields Chapter. A longtime SABR member, he also writes a baseball history blog entitled A Manly Pastime. John is the scorekeeper for the Flemington Neshanock vintage baseball team. He holds BA and MBA degrees from Rutgers University and is a Vietnam veteran.

Join us in Chicago for SABR's 51st Annual Convention!

SABR 51 will take place July 5-9, 2023 at the beautiful and historic Palmer House Hilton in Downtown Chicago. Our host hotel sits in the heart of the Chicago Loop, conveniently located within walking distance from the famous lakefront, Chicago River, Michigan Avenue, and Grant Park.

Our All-Star lineup of featured speakers and exciting events includes:

• White Sox play-by-play and Fox Sports national broadcaster Jason Benetti will deliver an address during the convention's Awards Luncheon.
• Legendary team owner, promoter, and publicist Mike Veeck will be featured in "Fun is Good: A Veeck Family Legacy," a conversation highlighting his family's storied impact on baseball and its deep Chicago ties.
• Longtime MLB executive and SABR Director Dan Evans and filmmaker Matt Flesch will host a Q&A and film screening of Last Comiskey, a new documentary on the Chicago White Sox' final season at Comiskey Park in 1990.
• A panel on the All-American Girls Professional Baseball League will include former player and women's baseball ambassador Maybelle Blair, with Dr. Kat Williams of the International Women's Baseball Center, and Kristie Erickson of The History Museum in South Bend.
• Beloved ballpark organist Nancy Faust will provide entertainment during the SABR 51 Welcome Reception on Wednesday, July 5.
• Chicago White Sox vs. St. Louis Cardinals game on Friday, July 7

Of course, there is a lot more on the way — innovative panel discussions, ground-breaking research presentations, and more opportunities to make and renew cherished baseball friendships.

Register today at sabr.org/convention or call 602-496-1460